T0304812

Churchill's D-Day

Churchill's D-Day

The Inside Story

RICHARD DANNATT and ALLEN PACKWOOD

HODDER &
STOUGHTON

First published in Great Britain in 2024 by Hodder & Stoughton Limited
An Hachette UK company

3

Copyright © Richard Dannatt and Allen Packwood 2024

The right of Richard Dannatt and Allen Packwood to be identified
as the Authors of the Work has been asserted by them in accordance
with the Copyright, Designs and Patents Act 1988.

Published in association with Churchill Heritage Ltd.

A CIP catalogue record for this title is available from the British Library

Hardback ISBN 9781399727839
Trade Paperback ISBN 9781399727846
ebook ISBN 9781399727860

Typeset in Bembo MT by Hewer Text UK Ltd, Edinburgh
Printed and bound in Great Britain by Clays Ltd, Elcograf S.p.A.

Hodder & Stoughton policy is to use papers that are natural, renewable
and recyclable products and made from wood grown in sustainable forests.
The logging and manufacturing processes are expected to conform
to the environmental regulations of the country of origin.

Hodder & Stoughton Limited
Carmelite House
50 Victoria Embankment
London EC4Y 0DZ

www.hodder.co.uk

To all those under Allied Command who
lost their lives in the Normandy campaign

Contents

Preface

Winston Churchill is remembered as the Prime Minister who led Britain to victory during the Second World War. Yet his reputation rests on the events of 1940, rather than those of 1944. It is his oratory during the Battle of Britain and the Blitz that continues to be quoted: his promise of 'blood, toil, tears and sweat', his determination to wage war until victory and his defiant assertion that Britain would 'never surrender'. In the public sphere, he is rarely mentioned in connection with D-Day. When he is, the narrative is often negative, suggesting that Churchill deliberately delayed and obstructed attempts to stage the cross-Channel assault at an earlier date, thereby unnecessarily prolonging the war and the suffering of countless millions in Europe.

As the British leader, Churchill was involved in the planning and implementation of Operation Overlord (the invasion of France) from its outset. This book seeks to analyse and explain his role.

It is a complicated history that can only be understood in the context of British defeat and weakness in the first years of the Second World War. It involves weaving together different strands: of shifting political alliances, conflicting military strategies, evolving tactical needs and huge logistical challenges. Events will take us to Downing Street, Parliament, the White House and the Kremlin; to North Africa, Greece, Italy and France. We will meet an extremely varied cast of characters, some of them already well known to history: national leaders such as President Roosevelt, Marshal Stalin and General de Gaulle; military commanders like Generals Alexander, Brooke, Eisenhower, Marshall, Montgomery and Patton or Admirals Cunningham, Mountbatten and Ramsay. But we will also introduce others who are not household names, a cross-section of some of the diverse range of men and women who made D-Day possible by doing their jobs, at times in the face of great danger, often in secrecy and under great stress. They include service men and women such as Company Sergeant Major Stan Hollis of the 6th Battalion Green Howards, John Anthony Hugill – known as Tony – of 30 Assault Unit, Wren officer Christian Oldham (later Christian Lamb), Canadian bomber pilot Roland MacKenzie and American paratrooper T. L. Rodgers; organisers and administrators like the young Joan Bright (later Joan Astley), who worked in the middle of the Whitehall information web, General Frederick Morgan, the man charged with developing the D-Day plan, and Commander John Hughes-Hallett, who helped prepare the naval assault force; deception experts such as Colonel John Bevan and the novelist Dennis Wheatley; scientists and innovators like Geoffrey Pyke and Major General Percy Hobart. The list goes on. The outcome of 6 June 1944 depended on the contribution of so many.

At the heart of our narrative sits the British Prime Minister. Sixty-nine years old in June 1944, Winston Leonard Spencer-Churchill was already a man with a long and complex history. A powerful orator, professional writer and amateur painter, he had enjoyed a roller-coaster of a political career. First elected to Parliament in 1900, he had served in many of the major offices of state. Highly conscious of his lineage as a descendant and biographer of the great eighteenth-century British general John Churchill, first Duke of Marlborough, he had served in the army and had previously exercised ministerial responsibility for all three armed services. Unafraid to court controversy, he had changed political parties twice (moving from Conservative to Liberal in 1904 and back again twenty years later in 1924) and had established a reputation as a vocal defender of the British Empire and a bellicose opponent of both communism and fascism. For the decade prior to the Second World War, he had been out of office and for much of the 1930s was viewed by many as a maverick, an opportunist or a relic of a previous age. But his fiery oratory, consistent opposition to the appeasement of Hitler and calls for British rearmament had seen him return to prominence and secure the premiership. Writing this book has reminded us again and again that the success of D-Day was not in any way a foregone conclusion. Many at the time doubted it would work – and there are many reasons why it might have ended in disaster. By reproducing carefully chosen contemporary documents we have tried to illuminate the way decisions were made – and sought to convey the risks attending each one. As well as providing further insight on some of the military questions faced by Churchill we hope that our selection of telegrams, letters and other material from the time will further illuminate key personalities and debates.

D-Day, 6 June 1944, was undoubtedly a turning point in history. Winston Churchill's influence on events has increasingly been questioned, but what is undeniable is that he was a force to be reckoned with, and one who was not going to be silent at such a moment of extreme national (and international) jeopardy.

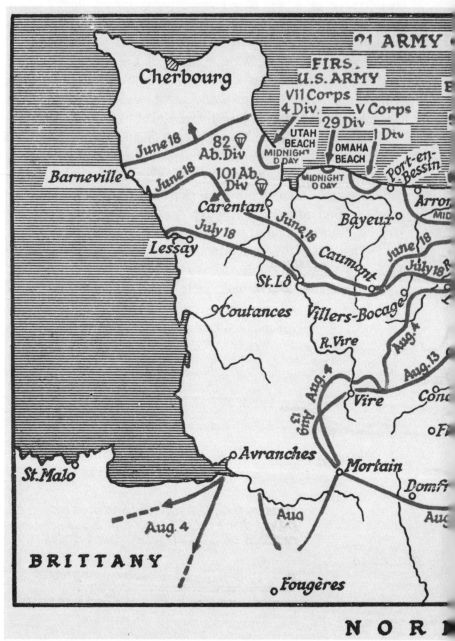

Map of Normandy as published by W. S. Churchill,
The Second World War, volume VI, p. 29.

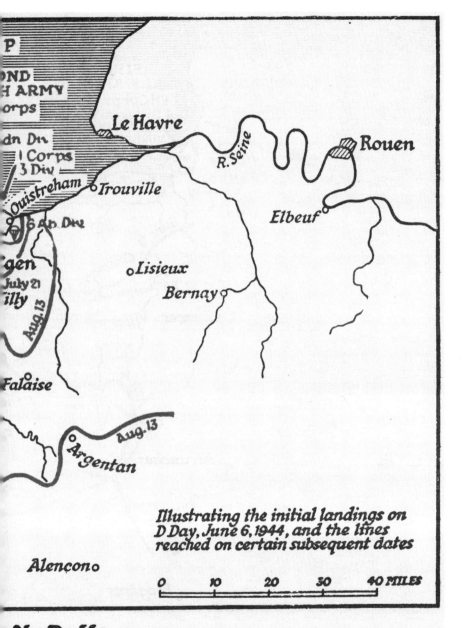

P

OND
H ARMY
orps

dn Dn
I Corps
3 Div

Ouistreham
Trouville

6 Ab. Div

gen
July 21
illy
Aug. 13

Falaise

Aug. 13
Argentan

Le Havre

R. Seine

Rouen

Elbeuf

Lisieux

Bernay

*Illustrating the initial landings on
D Day, June 6, 1944, and the lines
reached on certain subsequent dates*

Alençon

0   10   20   30   40 MILES

N D Y

PART ONE
Planning

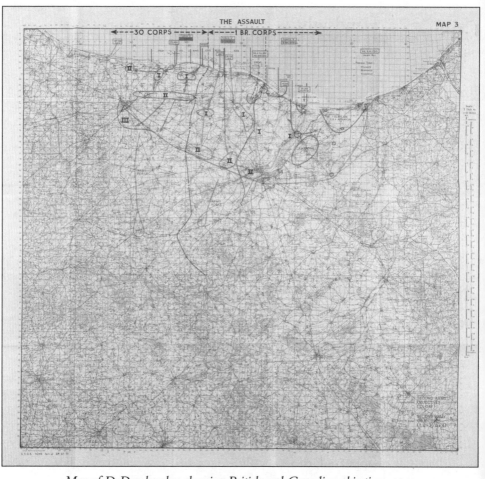

Map of D-Day beaches showing British and Canadian objectives, 1944

Hindsight Is a Wonderful Thing

'Are you going to lay there and get killed, or
get up and do something about it?'

I N THE EARLY morning of Tuesday 6 June 1944, as Britain
slept, Company Sergeant Major Stan Hollis of 6th Battalion
Green Howards clambered down the scrambling nets on the side
of the cargo ship *Empire Lance* and into the landing craft taking
him the final sea-sickening miles to Gold beach. As Hollis's craft
lurched towards shore, he saw a German position in the middle of
the sector towards which he and his men were heading. Seizing a
Lewis gun from another soldier, Stan gave the pillbox two maga-
zines of automatic fire. No fire was returned. A few minutes later,
having sprinted up the beach, Hollis discovered his 'pillbox' was
only the tram shelter for the local light railway. (The 'Hollis Hut'
is now in the proud possession of his regiment.)

The much-awaited Allied 'second front' in the West, code-
named Operation Overlord, had begun to take shape. As the cover
of night disappeared, the early summer sun illuminated the greatest armada of ships ever assembled. The first landings began at
06.30. Overnight, paratroopers from the British 6th Airborne
Division had secured the eastern flank of the landing zone while
the US 82nd and 101st Airborne Divisions had seized the western
flank to reduce the risk of German counter-attacks. Ironically, the
unseasonal bad weather, which had already forced a twenty-four-
hour postponement of the amphibious assault, had persuaded the

German High Command that the weather was too bad for the Allies to launch their assault that day. Field Marshal Rommel, in command of Army Group B in the Normandy sector, had returned to Germany to celebrate his wife's birthday, while senior officers from the Seventh Army were gathering in Rennes for a study day to review their anti-invasion plans.

As the day commenced, HMS *Belfast* (now maintained in the Thames by the United Kingdom's Imperial War Museum) began its bombardment of the German defences above Gold beach onto which Stan Hollis's Green Howard soldiers were storming ashore. Further west, the assault by the US 4th Infantry Division had secured Utah beach at a cost of only 197 casualties, but the fighting on Omaha beach still hung in the balance. The untested US 29th Infantry Division assaulted the western half of the eight-kilometre beach while the battle-hardened 1st Infantry Division was allocated the eastern sector. The beach was over-looked by rising bluffs defended by the experienced German 352nd Infantry Division recently reassigned to Normandy from the Russian front. The intensity of the fighting is captured in the opening sequences of Steven Spielberg's film *Saving Private Ryan*. The spectre of disaster hovered as casualties mounted. An unidentified US lieutenant is credited with cajoling reluctant infantrymen: 'Are you going to lay there and get killed, or get up and do something about it?' The fighting on Omaha beach came closest to realising the Allied leadership's nightmare of the failure of Overlord. There was no plan B, only evacuation.

The British people awoke to the news of the landings on their radios. Prime Minister Winston Churchill entered the Chamber of the House of Commons at three minutes to twelve and was quickly called to the despatch box. According to the MP Harold Nicolson he looked as 'white as a sheet' and Nicolson feared that he was 'about to announce some terrible disaster'. The excited chatter of the waiting MPs was replaced with an expectant hush. Churchill had two pieces of news to impart. He started, not with the Normandy landings, but with an account of the liberation of Rome on the previous Sunday, heaping praise on the British general Harold Alexander, the Italian theatre commander, whose name was greeted with a tremendous cheer by the assembled politicians. The Prime Minister then proceeded to detail the recent phases of the Italian campaign, from the Anzio landings of 22 January through to the Allied entry into the eternal city (coincidentally, the fourth anniversary of Churchill's famous 'Never Surrender' speech).

No doubt there was an element of theatre in his delaying mention of Normandy. Churchill was a consummate parliamentary performer. He knew that his audience was hanging on his every word, waiting anxiously for the first report of the landings. But by delaying, he was also emphasising the equal weight he attached to events in Italy, where the Allied armies were under British command. He saw this 'memorable and glorious event' – the capture of Rome – as having vindicated his continuing support for operations in the Mediterranean. Operations that he was keen to stress were ongoing, reporting that 'The Allied forces, with the Americans in the van, are driving ahead, Northwards, in relentless pursuit of the enemy.' Churchill remained keen to maintain combined British–American operations in the Italian peninsula but feared that the Americans would now give primacy to France and Overlord.

Having made his point, he came to the day's main announcement about the Normandy landings. His remarks were short, simple and factual. Obviously, there was much he could not say. The situation was still evolving. The fog of war hung over events, and, mindful of security, he did not want to prejudice the landings by giving helpful information to the enemy. Even so, it is worth printing his remarks here in full:

> I have also to announce to the House that during the night and the early hours of this morning the first of the series of landings in force upon the European Continent has taken place. In this case the liberating assault fell upon the coast of France. An immense armada of upwards of 4,000 ships, together with several thousand smaller craft, crossed the Channel. Massed airborne landings have

been successfully effected behind the enemy lines and landings on the beaches are proceeding at various points at the present time. The fire of the shore batteries has been largely quelled. The obstacles that were constructed in the sea have not proved so difficult as was apprehended. The Anglo-American Allies are sustained by about 11,000 first line aircraft, which can be drawn upon as may be needed for the purposes of the battle. I cannot, of course, commit myself to any particular details. Reports are coming in in rapid succession. So far the commanders who are engaged report that everything is proceeding according to plan. And what a plan! This vast operation is undoubtedly the most complicated and difficult that has ever occurred. It involves tides, wind, waves, visibility, both from the air and the sea standpoint, and the combined employment of land, air and sea forces in the highest degree of intimacy and in contact with conditions which could not and cannot be fully foreseen.

There are already hopes that actual tactical surprise has been attained, and we hope to furnish the enemy with a succession of surprises during the course of the fighting. The battle that has now begun will grow constantly in scale and in intensity for many weeks to come and I shall not attempt to speculate upon its course. This I may say, however. Complete unity prevails throughout the Allied Armies. There is a brotherhood in arms between us and our friends of the United States. There is complete confidence in the supreme commander, General Eisenhower, and his lieutenants, and also in the commander of the Expeditionary Force, General Montgomery. The ardour and spirit of the troops, as I saw myself, embarking in these last few days was splendid to witness. Nothing that equipment, science or forethought could do has been neglected, and the whole process of opening this great new front will be pursued with the utmost resolution both by the commanders and by the United States and British Governments whom they serve.

These were words that were carefully chosen to emphasise the complexity of the operation: the use of deception measures to contain the element of surprise and convince the enemy that this might be the first of several assaults; the unity of the American and British commanders; and the morale and training of the troops. Churchill was right that all were essential for a successful operation on this scale.

His speech may seem rather short and muted, especially when compared with his famous oratory from 1940. There is no great peroration, no references to 'finest hour', no promises of 'blood, toil, tears and sweat', no exhortations to 'never surrender'. Churchill spoke only for a few minutes before promising to return to the House, perhaps before it adjourned later that day, to give an update. This was an interim statement, made at a moment when the outcome of the battle was still unknown.

Given the unique circumstances, the Prime Minister's remarks were received by the House without debate or criticism. Now was not the time for speeches or disunity, though two long-standing Churchill critics did make comments. The veteran communist politician Willie Gallacher expressed 'my own feeling, and I am sure the feeling of every Member of the House, that our hearts and thoughts are with these lads who have gone across to the Continent and with their mothers here at home'. The socialist MP Aneurin Bevan asked whether the Prime Minister would be framing a message from the House to the people of France. Both may seem innocuous interventions, but they surely served to remind Churchill of the huge responsibility he was bearing for the lives of both British soldiers and French civilians. Two groups that were suffering casualties at that time.

Churchill's statement stands in marked contrast to the way in which he would later describe this same moment, the launching of the assault, in his wartime memoirs. Revisiting the events of D-Day in 1950–51, he would write: 'The immense cross-Channel enterprise for the liberation of France had begun. All the ships were at sea. We had the mastery of the oceans and of the air. The Hitler tyranny was doomed.' That quote, taken from the penultimate paragraph of *Closing the Ring*, itself the penultimate book in his epic six-volume history of *The Second World War*, could not be more confident, concluding, 'Nor, though the road might be long and hard, could we doubt that decisive victory would be gained.'

But it is a quote that sums up the problem we have when talking about Operation Overlord; namely, the luxury of knowing that it worked. With hindsight it is easy for us to sit here and say that it is clear this was the right strategy, one that brought the war to an end in a fast and decisive manner, and that ultimately secured the freedom of Western Europe from both fascism and perhaps communism. In spite of what he wrote later, it was not so easy, simple and predictable for Churchill, or for the American President, Franklin Roosevelt, and the other British and American political and military leaders in 1944.

By the time the relevant volume of his war memoirs was published in 1952, Churchill was back in 10 Downing Street as a peacetime Prime Minister, and General Eisenhower, the Supreme Commander for the D-Day operation, was about to become President of the United States. The reputation of both men had been assured by victory and their story had become synonymous with the triumph of the West; a story that now deliberately downplayed the role of their former Soviet allies – turned Cold War enemies – and that already viewed the events of 1944 through a different lens; one that was coloured by nostalgia, influenced by new post-war realities and composed with the benefit of hindsight. D-Day was already becoming the stuff of myth. It is a trend that would only accelerate, fuelled by Hollywood movies such as *D-Day: The Sixth of June* (1956) and *The Longest Day* (1962).

Strip away those layers of hindsight, look afresh at the events as they appeared to Churchill and his contemporaries at the time, and a less confident, more confusing story emerges.

By June 1944 Churchill had been Prime Minister for just over four years. With his bulldog scowl, spotted bow-tie, two-fingered 'V for Victory' salute and ever-present cigar, he had become one of the most famous and instantly recognisable figures of his age. In some respects, his prime ministerial office was not unlike a modern Tudor court, where his own eccentric band of special advisers rubbed shoulders with family members, civil servants, politicians and military commanders. By creating for himself the new position of Minister of Defence and combining it with the office of Prime Minister, he had made sure that the political and military leadership reported directly to him, with Winston chairing the War Cabinet, the Defence Committee and meeting regularly with the Chiefs of Staff (the military heads of the army, navy and air force). Never one to lack self-belief, he was confident in his own abilities as a strategist and, as we shall see, had brought strong views to all phases of the debates about the nature and timing of D-Day.

But to what extent was that strategy influenced by the ghosts of his past? It is common for the dining halls of Oxford and Cambridge colleges to be covered with the portraits of their former distinguished fellows and alumni. In contrast, the dining hall of Churchill College, Cambridge, built as the British national and Commonwealth memorial to Sir Winston, holds just one picture. It is of a younger Churchill, thinner, more angular, and still sporting the remnants of his youthful red hair. Depicted against a sombre black background, with bags beneath his eyes, this is a dark, stark portrait. It captures Churchill in 1916 at the age of forty-one. The original was painted by William Orpen and still belongs to the Churchill family. The version that hangs in Churchill College is a specially commissioned copy by the artist John Leigh-Pemberton. It was recommended by Churchill's widow, Clementine, as one of the truest depictions of her husband and it captures him not during his 'finest hour' but rather at his lowest ebb, after losing office over the Dardanelles Crisis.

Churchill had started the First World War as the First Lord of the Admiralty, the civilian minister in charge of the largest navy in the world. The fleet had been modernised and mobilised, and his stock was high. But hopes of a decisive naval battle between the British Grand Fleet and the German High Seas Fleet had failed to materialise. Faced with the stalemate of trench warfare on the Western Front in France and Belgium, the navy was relegated to the less glorious role of protecting British trade routes and blockading Germany. Casting around for ways of relieving pressure on the Allied armies, Churchill focused on opening up a new front against

Turkey, Germany's weaker ally. He quickly became the leading advocate in Cabinet of a plan to use ships to force the Dardanelles Straits, the narrow waters guarded by the Gallipoli Peninsula that led into the Sea of Marmara. The aim was to force a passage through the Straits, besiege Constantinople [now Istanbul] and knock Turkey out of the war, while in the process providing new supply routes to Britain's ally, Russia. The problem was that the Straits were heavily protected by forts and mines. When the naval expeditionary force under Admiral Carden and then Admiral de Robeck failed to clear a way through, losing three battleships, the War Cabinet took the fateful decision to use troops to seize the Gallipoli Peninsula. British, French, Australian and New Zealand forces were landed in April 1915, but faced with heavy Turkish resistance from entrenched positions in the mountainous terrain overlooking the landing grounds, they were unable to break out of the beachheads and were evacuated in January 1916. The casualties were considerable, about a quarter of a million Allied dead or wounded. Among those who survived were some who would go on to play a prominent role in the Second World War, such as young Captain William Slim, later commander of British forces in Burma (now Myanmar), and Clement Attlee, who would become leader of the Labour Party, wartime Deputy Prime Minister and post-war Prime Minister.

The immediate aftermath of the initial failed naval operation saw a complete breakdown between Churchill and his First Sea Lord (senior naval commander) Admiral Lord 'Jacky' Fisher. When Fisher left his post in protest in May 1915, Prime Minister Asquith took the opportunity to restructure his government, bringing in Conservatives who had not forgiven Churchill for his defection to the Liberal Party in 1904 (he would not re-join the Tories until 1924). Their price was Churchill's removal. Winston found himself demoted to the lesser position of Chancellor of the Duchy of Lancaster, facing hostile criticism from the press and public and unable to defend himself while military operations were ongoing.

The Orpen portrait captures Churchill at this moment of crisis.

Winston Churchill by Sir William Orpen, 1915

It looked to many as though his hitherto promising career was over. His father Lord Randolph Churchill had enjoyed a meteoric political rise but had thrown everything away with an ill-judged political resignation at the age of just thirty-seven. History seemed to be repeating itself. Clementine thought her husband would die of grief. Ultimately, Winston would claw his way back to the political front rank, but it would take time. Resigning from the government, he chose to restore his personal honour by serving for six months in the trenches of the Western Front, commanding a battalion of Royal Scots Fusiliers. There was then an anxious wait for the report of the Dardanelles Commission of Inquiry, which largely exonerated him from blame, before he could write his own comprehensive justification for his actions as part of his multi-volume history of the First World War, entitled *The World Crisis*, published in the 1920s. But even then, the stigma of failure at the Dardanelles continued to hang over him, becoming a staple of critical cartoons and hostile heckles.

Books have been written on the reasons for the Allied failure at the Dardanelles, and debate still rages. It is often said that it was this failure that made Churchill extremely cautious about D-Day. The film *Churchill*, starring Brian Cox in the title role and released in 2017, opens with the British Prime Minister walking on a beach in 1944 and recoiling as, in his mind's eye, the waters run red with the blood of British troops. The suggestion in the movie is that, unlike Eisenhower and the military commanders of the day, he had seen this before at Gallipoli and was therefore determined to do all he could to prevent it happening again. It is a script that depicts him trying to obstruct the landings with only days to go. The question of Churchill's opposition to D-Day and the extent to which he actively interfered to prevent or delay the operation is a theme to which we will return.

What lessons did Churchill take from the Dardanelles campaign? It certainly made him aware of the political risks associated with advocating major operations. He felt he had been made a scapegoat and unfairly brought down, given his inability to influence events on the ground. Without complete control, 'Men are ill-advised to try such ventures. The lesson had sunk into my nature.'

He was also clearly aware of the difficulty inherent in such large amphibious operations, trying to coordinate naval, ground and air forces belonging to independent countries all under their own commanders. The importance of establishing clear command structures with good communications based on the very best intelligence is obvious in his reflection that 'Without the title deeds of positive achievement no one had the power to give clear brutal orders which would command unquestioning respect. Power was widely disseminated among the many important personages who in this period formed the governing instrument. Knowledge was very unequally shared.' But this did not stop him continuing to think about the challenges of seizing an enemy-held shoreline or of promoting other similar operations.

When writing about the origins of Overlord in his Second World War memoirs, Churchill chose to highlight a paper on Naval War Policy that he had created for the attention of Prime Minister Lloyd George almost twenty-seven years before D-Day on 7 July 1917. Then, his aim had been to show how the Royal Navy could retake the offensive in the First World War. One of his main suggestions had been the seizing of the Heligoland Islands of Sylt and/or Borkum, located just off the German coast, for use as a forward base for an attack against the enemy.

The operation he described in his paper certainly had some similarities with the later 1944 cross-Channel assault. It required mastery of the seas, would be preceded by a heavy bombardment (albeit primarily naval in an age before air warfare) and would culminate in:

The landing under cover of the guns of the Fleet, aided by gas and smoke, of the troops upon the island, from torpedo-proof transports by means of bullet-proof lighters. Approximately 100 should be provided for landing a division. In addition a number (say) 50, tank landing lighters would be provided, each carrying a tank or tanks, fitted for wire-cutting in its bow, which, by means of a drawbridge or shelving bow, would land under its own power, to prevent the infantry from being held up by wire when attacking the gorges of the forts and batteries. This is a new feature, and removes one of the very great previous difficulties, namely the rapid landing of field artillery to cut wire.

Winston also anticipated the need to establish an aerial base, 'sufficiently powerful to hold its own air' and the 'establishment of oilers and storeships in the anchorage' for the landing of the necessary stores. This paper illustrates his grasp of the challenges to be faced and proves that, less than two years after the Dardanelles campaign, he was already prepared to champion other similar attacks from the sea. He appreciated that the wars of the future would involve combined operations, but he was also aware of the difficulties, particularly if conducted at scale. As it turned out, his interwar career would take him in different directions, and it fell upon others to try and develop the equipment and tactics for combined operations in an atmosphere of austerity, retrenchment and disarmament.

More broadly, the war of 1914–18 certainly had a profound impact on Churchill's life and on his thinking. Friends had been lost, his career had almost been destroyed and his world view challenged. The British Empire had been severely weakened and the fabric of ordinary British life ripped apart, with war memorials appearing in almost every village. As wartime Prime Minister from 1940, he could not contemplate the cost of another bloody stalemate in Europe, writing:

> the fearful price we had had to pay in human life and blood for the great offensives of the First World War was graven in my mind. Memories of the Somme and Passchendaele and many lesser frontal attacks upon the Germans were not to be blotted out by time or reflection.

But there is another interrelated criticism of Churchill. Namely that he did not want to fight in France in 1942 or 1943 because he was prioritising the defence of the British Empire. Much has been written about his imperialism. He was certainly a lifelong supporter of the British Empire and, in November 1942, would famously assert that he had not become the King's first minister (e.g. Prime Minister) to preside over its liquidation. His was a world view built on a belief in the superiority of the Western democracies and the white European races. Yet Britain was also dependent on its Empire for men and materials; a global power with colonies, linked dominions and mandates. No British Prime Minister would have been willing or able to walk away from those responsibilities in 1940 and that meant keeping forces in Africa, the Mediterranean and the Pacific as well as maintaining supply lines to Britain across the seas and oceans. Britain had no choice but to fight in several theatres, and this book will look at the decisions that were taken with regard to priorities versus resources and their impact on the timing and nature of D-Day.

Churchill was certainly not alone in wrestling with these problems, and another recurring question within this book is the extent to which he could or did act independently. He was undoubtedly a powerful Prime Minister, but he was running a coalition government within a parliamentary system and presiding over an enormous civil bureaucracy and military services that had their own long-standing structures and systems. General John Kennedy, who became Assistant Chief of the Imperial General Staff, described it as 'essentially a government of committees . . . Winston is of course the dominating personality . . . Yet Winston's views do not often prevail if they are contrary to the general trend of opinion among the service staffs.' From 1941 onwards, he was also a partner with the United States and the Soviet Union in an international alliance against fascism; an alliance that was increasingly being led from Washington DC and Moscow. There was no doubt that France and north-western Europe were most easily liberated from the offshore base provided by the United Kingdom, but it was equally evident that Britain could not undertake that liberation on its own.

Churchill was certainly sensitive to criticisms about his

reluctance to open a Second Front in Western Europe and very keen to rebut them, writing in Volume II of his war memoirs that

> In view of the many accounts which are extant and multiplying of my supposed aversion from any kind of large-scale opposed-landing, such as took place in Normandy in 1944, it may be convenient if I make it clear that from the very beginning I provided a great deal of the impulse and authority for creating the immense apparatus and armada for the landing of armour on beaches, without which it is now universally recognised that all such major operations would have been impossible.

This book will look in detail at exactly what that role comprised, but to fully understand what was at stake for Churchill and the British Chiefs of Staff in 1944, it is necessary to go back in time to the desperate first years of the Second World War and follow the long evolution of Overlord; to explain the broader Allied strategy from which it emerged and show how it was the culmination of years of planning, preparation and effort (of blood, toil, tears and sweat).

10, Downing Street,
Whitehall.

I spoke the other day of the colossal

military disaster which occurred when the French High

Command ~~neglected~~ failed to withdraw the Northern armies from

Belgium at the moment when they knew that the French

Front was decisively broken at Sedan and on the Meuse.

This delay entailed the loss of ~~at least fifteen~~ French

Divisions and threw out of action for the critical period

the whole British Expeditionary Force. Our Army ~~indeed~~

no doubt ~~escaped~~, but with the loss of all ~~its~~ cannon, vehicles

and/equipment. This inevitably took some weeks to repair,

and in those weeks the ~~great~~ battle of France has been

lost. When we consider the heroic resistance made by the

French Army at ~~enormous~~ odds in this battle, and the

~~enormous~~ losses inflicted upon the enemy, and the exhaustion

of the enemy, it may well be thought that these twenty-five

Divisions of the best troops might have turned the scale.

However General Weygand had to fight without them. Only

~~the~~ two British Divisions or their equivalent were

Draft for Churchill's broadcast, 18 June 1940

2

Dealing with Defeat

'He spoke in English, and evidently under stress. "We
have been defeated." As I did not immediately respond he
said again: "We are beaten; we have lost the battle."'

I T I S O N E of those extraordinary coincidences in history that
the date of 8 May during the Second World War loomed large.
It was on 8 May 1940 that Winston Churchill delivered one of his
most important but less remembered speeches in the House of
Commons. The mood in the British Parliament was fractious.
Opposition to Prime Minister Neville Chamberlain's government
was mounting and the debate on the disastrous Norwegian
campaign had become a vote of confidence in Chamberlain's
leadership – here was the moment that would set Churchill on the
path to 10 Downing Street. It was also on 8 May in 1945 that the
war in Europe finally ended. What happened in those intervening
five years has become the stuff of legend. Legends require heroes
– Winston Churchill became that hero. But his rise was not
inevitable.

His appointment with destiny rested on securing the keys to 10
Downing Street. At the beginning of May 1940 Winston Churchill
was First Lord of the Admiralty, the civilian minister in charge of
the navy in Neville Chamberlain's Conservative government. His
vocal opposition to Hitler had seen him brought back into the
Cabinet on the outbreak of war after ten years in the political
wilderness. As criticism of Chamberlain's war leadership mounted,

Churchill was increasingly seen as one of the contenders to replace him, but it was far from a *fait accompli*.

The entry from the diary of Leo Aubrey Kennedy, diplomatic correspondent of *The Times*, for 4 May provides a rather unflattering snapshot of Churchill on the eve of his premiership:

> After this Norway breakdown there is of course a lot of criticism of Gov[ernmen]t & general despondence. M.P.'s are all especially discontented. There is a drive against Chamberlain. I can't quite see who can advantageously take his place. Curiously enough what is really needed is that <u>Winston</u> should be made to take a rest. He is overdoing himself and taking the strain by stoking himself unduly with champagne, liqueurs etc.; Dines out and dines well almost every night. Sleeps after luncheon, then to the House O' Commons, then a good and long dinner, and doesn't resume work at the Admiralty till after 10 pm, and goes on till 1 or 2 am. He has got into the habit of calling conferences and subordinates after 1 am, which naturally upsets some of the Admirals who are men of sound habits. So there is a general atmosphere of strain at the Admiralty which is all wrong. Yet Winston is such a popular hero and so much the war-leader that he cannot be dropped. But he ought somehow to be rested!

Churchill had two major problems to overcome. First, he was still seen by many, especially within his own Conservative Party and the British establishment, as an unstable maverick and opportunist. Second, he was a leading member of Neville Chamberlain's Cabinet and heavily implicated in the military failure that now threatened to bring down the Prime Minister and his government. The 'Norway breakdown' referred to by Kennedy was the Narvik campaign, a hastily and poorly planned British intervention in Scandinavia in April 1940.

Rearming very late in the 1930s after the failure of the policy of appeasement, Britain and France began the war in 1939 with the same broad strategy with which the Great War had ended – to blockade Germany in a long war and starve her of resources, leading to eventual surrender. The battlefield lessons of the Hundred

Days campaign in 1918 were largely forgotten by both the British government and her army, although they were studied carefully by Germany, where the high command knew that they could never win a protracted war. It led them to develop their *blitzkrieg* capability, mobile armour supported by airpower, which had defeated Poland between 1 September and 6 October 1939. Notwithstanding that illustration of modern warfare, the British Expeditionary Force that deployed to France in the autumn of 1939 joined the French Army under the operational belief that the power of the defensive, delivered by the extensive fortifications and firepower of the Maginot Line in north-eastern France, would contain Germany, while the strategy of blockade would deliver ultimate success.

Consistent with this misplaced strategy, plans began to be formulated in London for the mining of neutral Norway's territorial waters to prevent the export of iron ore from Gällivare in Sweden to Germany through Norwegian ports. There was a well-founded belief that if the supply of Swedish iron ore to Germany could be interdicted, German industry would come to a stop in a very short time, possibly measurable in just weeks. Winston Churchill, as the new First Lord of the Admiralty, saw the blocking of this iron ore supply as a strong move to take the war to Germany, rather than relying on the passive defensive posture of the armies in France. As in the First World War, he was always looking for ways to take the offensive to the enemy. At Chamberlain's request, he had taken over the chairmanship of the Military Coordination Committee from Lord Chatfield, but his strong personality and constant interventions had failed to bring harmony at the top. According to Ian Jacob, a member of the secretariat charged with administering the meetings, 'Churchill was so much larger in every way than his colleagues on this committee that it ran like a coach with one wheel twice the size of the other three, and achieved very little with much friction.'

Churchill's voice was only one among many in the higher direction of the war, and – as yet – perhaps the loudest but not the most powerful. His attempts to impose his views on the Cabinet, the army, the Royal Air Force and the military commanders, without the authority or machinery to control the operation, contributed to the ensuing failure.

Norway 1940: The Epitome of a Muddle

The Norway campaign from 8 April to 10 June 1940 was characterised, disastrously, by muddled thinking and poor planning at the strategic, operational and tactical levels of war. Its failure was a deep embarrassment for Britain and her Allies, a catastrophe for the Norwegians and another military success for Nazi Germany

At the top of the strategic chain of command was the Supreme War Council, set up under the terms of the Anglo-French Alliance. Below that was the War Cabinet of nine members, which included the three single service ministers. From October 1939 there was also the Military Coordination Committee charged with ensuring coordination between the three armed services. Unfortunately, its chairman – initially Lord Chatfield, then Churchill – was given no executive powers. The fourth level of decision-making was the Chiefs of Staff Committee, chaired by the Chief of Staff who had been longest in post. At the start of the war, this was Air Chief Marshal Sir Cyril Newall, the Chief of the Air Staff, the service least involved with the Norway campaign. To illustrate the problem, in April 1940, the first month of the Norwegian campaign, this cumbersome structure resulted in no fewer than ninety-four meetings: the War Cabinet met thirty-one times, the Military Coordination Committee twenty-one times and the Chiefs of Staff Committee forty-two times – the Chiefs of Staff, or a deputy, attending all ninety-four meetings. Were they capable of rational or clear-headed thought? Against this must be contrasted the dictatorial command arrangements in Germany that saw Adolf Hitler's hands on all the principal levers of power and decision-making. When democracies face dictatorships, time is not on the side of consensus. Neville Chamberlain was not a Winston Churchill.

If the British machinery for directing the war at the strategic level was inefficient, the arrangements at the operational, or campaign, level were equally deficient. There was no overall joint commander for the operation nor an integrated staff. Each element of the proposed plan was to be commanded by a senior officer from their respective service. The landing force was to be commanded by Major General Pierse Mackesy and the naval units by Admiral of the Fleet, William Boyle, the Earl of Cork and Orrery, two ranks senior but not in overall command. This unsatisfactory situation was compounded by the eventual inclusion of troops from France and Poland and the need to coordinate with the Norwegians themselves. Another measure of the dysfunctionality of the command arrangements was that the two senior officers met for the first time on the quarterdeck of the Admiral's flagship in the Norwegian port of Harstad, only after the operation had already begun. It was reported that both men, having saluted respectfully, then fitted their monocles to look at each other. It was only at this point that Cork, who had received no written orders but had been briefed personally by Churchill on the short car journey from the Admiralty to the House of Commons, discovered that Mackesy had been ordered not to make an opposed landing. Cork had been briefed in a diametrically different way.

Space does not allow for detailed discussion of the orders, counter-orders, plans made and discarded that characterised the planning and preparation for the British involvement in Norway. Sadly, as deficient as were the command-and-control arrangements was the intelligence surrounding potential German operations in Scandinavia. On 8 April 1940, as the Royal Navy began to lay mines in Norwegian waters off the northern port of Narvik, the Germany military prepared to launch Operation Weserübung – their attack on Denmark and Norway. This took the British completely by surprise. On 9 April, German paratroopers dropped on Danish soil and the Kriegsmarine landed soldiers in Copenhagen. Denmark surrendered very quickly. Simultaneously, German paratroopers captured the airfields at Oslo and Stavanger. Unfortunately, the Royal Navy interpreted this German naval activity as a precursor to their navy breaking out into the North Sea and threatening both the security of the United Kingdom and that of the sea lanes of communication to the United States. The British troops, embarked for securing Narvik and showing solidarity with the Norwegians, were hastily disembarked as the fleet set to sea to contain the Kriegsmarine. They were left on the dockside in a confusion of manpower and logistic stores. Too late, it was realised that the German operation was focused on controlling Norway itself.

In haste, troops were re-embarked, with one of the brigades being landed in a different port from its commander. From that moment on, the Allied troops were always at a disadvantage – often without air and artillery support, certainly outnumbered and struggling to agree common cause with their Norwegian hosts and common colleagues. Narvik, the focus of the iron ore export trade, was initially held but then abandoned by the British and her Allies when the overall Norway campaign proved unsustainable and defeat in France became inevitable. Norway was then condemned to a five-year occupation by Nazi Germany. It was little wonder then that Churchill sought a more centralised command structure on becoming Prime Minister.

British attempts to forestall a feared German advance by occupying Norway quickly ended in defeat, bringing about the very Nazi occupation that they had hoped to prevent. The Germans simply outmanoeuvred the British. Ironically, while Adolf Hitler celebrated this victory, the failure of the Norway campaign propelled Winston Churchill into 10 Downing Street, though it could have brought him down.

To many at the time, this failed amphibious operation was only too reminiscent of another Winston-led project. History seemed to be repeating itself and Churchill continued to be haunted by the ghosts of Gallipoli. General Ironside, the Chief of the Imperial General Staff, felt that in Norway we 'have muddled things in every way. Always too late. Changing plans and nobody directing.' Had nothing been learnt?

Both Ironside and General Ismay, Churchill's military adviser and Chief of Staff, were clear that amphibious operations of this type were incredibly difficult. Ismay would later reflect on this operation that

> Amphibious operations are a very specialised form of warfare . . . They require highly trained personnel, a great variety of technical equipment, a detailed knowledge of the points at which the landings are to take place, accurate information about the enemy's strength and dispositions, and perhaps above all, meticulous planning and preparation.

He clearly felt Narvik had failed because none of those elements were in place. To this day the Joint Services Command and Staff College use the failures at Gallipoli in 1915/16 and in Norway in 1940 as object lessons on how not to construct and conduct an amphibious operation against a peer enemy. The book *Anatomy of a Campaign: The British Fiasco in Norway* by John Kiszely, himself a former Director of the Higher Command and Staff Course at the Army Staff College, Camberley, is an enduring indictment of the British failure. Like Gallipoli, the Norwegian campaign was born of Churchill's best intentions. In both cases, he had wanted to progress rapidly the conduct of the wars against Germany – in 1915 to find an alternative to the trench deadlock on the Western Front and in early 1940 to tighten the economic pressure on Germany by interdicting the supply of Swedish iron ore to Germany, on which her industry so heavily depended. However attractive both aspirations were in grand strategic terms and however bravely British troops fought at the tactical level on the ground in both campaigns, the absence of sound preparation and planning at the operational – or campaign – level doomed both ventures to failure.

Despite the strategic muddle and the operational-level confusion, the British soldier on the ground, the sailor at sea and the airman aloft did all that their country could have demanded. A snapshot illustrates the consequences of the muddle and confusion. Stan Hollis's regiment, the Green Howards, sent its 1st Battalion to fight in Norway. After six months on the Maginot Line in France, it was suddenly recalled to England on 17 April, then transported to Scotland and found itself, with no winter warfare equipment or training, despatched on four Royal Navy ships to Norway on 26 April. Disembarking at Åndalsnes, well south of Narvik, fierce battles were fought by the battalion, sometimes in three or four feet of snow, stemming the German advance down the Gubransdalen valley towards the town of Otta, where casualties were heavy among officers and men. Amid further confusion about the operational plan, the battalion was re-embarked at Åndalsnes on 2 May, arriving in Scapa Flow the next morning. We talk about a week being a long time in politics, but what about a week in the life of a British infantryman? The final evacuation of some 29,000 British servicemen was complete by 10 June when the situation in Norway, exacerbated by events in France, was deemed hopeless and the survival of the British Army, for another day, became paramount. King Haakon VII of Norway would ultimately become Colonel in Chief of the Green Howards, in honour of the 1st Battalion's heroic defence of Otta (an honour continued through King Olav V to King Harold V, until the Green Howards were amalgamated with other regiments in 2006), but all this lay far in the future for Stan Hollis in 1940.

In the immediate term, the ensuing parliamentary debate on the failures of the campaign quickly became a test of Chamberlain's government. Churchill was now walking a deadly tightrope. He had to wind up the debate for the government. He needed to defend the action while also preserving his reputation as a potential prime minister in waiting. On 15 November 1915 the failure at Gallipoli had cost him his job as First Lord of the Admiralty. Now, almost a quarter of a century later, he found himself defending the same post and a similar action as he endeavoured to explain the failure in Norway to a fractious House of Commons. Fellow MP Harold Nicolson felt he managed to achieve this 'almost impossible task . . . with absolute loyalty and apparent sincerity while demonstrating by the brilliance of his personality that he has really nothing to do with this confused and timid gang'.

He was helped by the fact that those leading the charge against Chamberlain, men like Admiral Sir Roger Keyes and Leo Amery, had no interest in bringing Churchill down. The various opposition groupings were only united in their desire for a more vigorous and efficient prosecution of the war. Churchill's long vocal campaign against the appeasement of Hitler meant that he was considered so much the war leader that he could not be dropped. But that did not mean that he would automatically become Prime Minister. The debate became a vote of confidence in Chamberlain. The embattled Prime Minister appealed to his friends to support him but when the government majority was slashed from 213 to just 81, it was clear that his government would have to be reconstructed.

It was external factors that facilitated Churchill's survival and transformed his prospects. Neville Chamberlain may have weathered the storm of criticism over his failed appeasement policies, but the early months of the war had demonstrated that he was no war leader, nor indeed did he have either the ability or appetite to be so. There was a growing, if grudging, acceptance by many in the Conservative Party that change was needed and that a national cross-party government should be formed. The new Prime Minister would need to be a Conservative, as they remained the largest party in the House (an election while fighting in Europe being out of the question). The Labour Party was indicating that it would not serve under Chamberlain. Lord Halifax, the Foreign Secretary, was the preferred choice of many in the establishment, including the King and Chamberlain, but he was in the House of Lords. The power was in the Commons. More a man of diplomacy than war, Halifax had the sense to see that he would struggle to control MPs in their current belligerent mood. The crucial meeting to determine the succession happened on the late afternoon of 9 May (though Churchill later placed it on the 10th). Chamberlain, Churchill and Halifax gathered in private conclave in 10 Downing Street. The Chief Whip, David Margesson, was in attendance but no minutes were taken. When Chamberlain raised the question of who might succeed him, there was an awkward silence. Then Halifax ruled himself out. Winston 'did not demur'.

The stars were already coalescing around Churchill. And now fate intervened. Early in the morning of 10 May, the Germans launched *Fall Gelb* (Case Yellow) – their attack on Holland, Belgium, Luxembourg and France. Even now Chamberlain hesitated, suggesting it might be wrong to go at a moment of such crisis, but the Labour Party confirmed that they would not enter a coalition with him at the helm, and he finally accepted the inevitable and resigned.

Why Did Things Go So Wrong for the British Army in France in May–June 1940?

The British Expeditionary Force had deployed to France on the outbreak of war in September 1939 and had spent that winter developing the Gort Line [named after General Lord Gort, their Commander-in-Chief] – an extension of the French Maginot Line. This was the French response to the First World War: a heavily fortified line of static defence, to protect the fatal avenue – as historian, Richard Holmes, called it – between Germany and France, and down which the Germans had successfully advanced in 1870 and, nearly to success, in 1914. The French response was reflected in concrete and fixed gun emplacements – they shall not pass – albeit tempered by the realisation that battle tanks had a role in counter-manoeuvre. The Gort Line, constructed by sweating British engineers and infantrymen during the so-called Phoney War of the winter of 1939–40, was the British Expeditionary Force's contribution to the renewed *entente cordiale*.

The Germans and the British had learnt different lessons from the battles on the Western Front in 1918: the German Spring Offensive in March and the Allied Hundred Days campaign that began in August. The Germans had demonstrated that specially trained troops, breaking through an enemy frontline, could cause panic in the rear and lead to a defeatist mindset, and that in any future war such a situation should be exploited by armoured troops, not marching infantry, who would quickly become exhausted. They studied the British use of tanks – tanks closely supported by infantry, artillery and air power – and reflected on the lessons from the Hundred Days campaign drawn after the war by J. F. C. Fuller and Basil Liddell Hart. These British military theorists expounded the virtues of an armoured thrust leading to an expanding torrent of threat into an enemy's rear areas. In Britain, these novel ideas were toyed with through half-hearted experiments involving the deployment of an armoured force in the late 1920s and early 1930s, but they were rejected. Financial constraints, the distractions of Empire and Irish Home Rule, an innate conservatism in the military establishment, and a conviction that the First World War had been, or must be, the war to end all wars, meant that the BEF that deployed in 1939 to France was a mechanised army in lorries, but one that would face a German Army in tanks, closely supported by air power. The German commanders Heinz Guderian and Erich von Manstein had learnt and applied the writings of Fuller and Liddell Hart, but the British had not.

There were a few exceptions. Later, we will meet Major General Percy Hobart. He was one of the few who anticipated the scale and speed of mechanised warfare. He would also play a key role in applying heavy armour on D-Day. Liddell Hart will also make another appearance, though for a rather different reason.

It was against this background that Winston Churchill found himself at his moment of destiny. With Britain in deep crisis, Churchill quickly created a very strong centralised administration run out of his Downing Street Private Office. By making himself not just Prime Minister, but also Minister of Defence (a new role that he created), he made sure that he had control over both policy and strategy. His was a national coalition government bringing together members of the main political parties: the Conservatives and the Labour Party as well as the Liberal Party, the National Liberals and National Labour. There was an informal understanding that this super-coalition would remain in being for the duration of the wartime emergency (in practice until the end of the war in Europe), but Churchill could not assume that this would automatically remain the case. The member parties could opt to leave and a successful vote of no-confidence in the government by parliamentary backbenchers might lead to his removal at any point – as had happened to his predecessor, Neville Chamberlain. This meant that Churchill was not entirely free to choose his own government ministers, as he had to make sure that his coalition partners, particularly the Labour and Liberal Parties, were rewarded with some of the key offices of state.

He chose to govern primarily through a small inner War Cabinet. Its composition changed between 1940 and 1945 but it initially consisted of just five ministers: Churchill, Chamberlain, his erstwhile rival the Foreign Secretary Lord Halifax, and the Labour leaders Clement Attlee and Arthur Greenwood. Halifax was sent to America as Ambassador and replaced by Anthony Eden as Foreign Secretary in December 1940. Clement Attlee became Deputy Prime Minister in 1942. Others came and went. Churchill deliberately kept the three service ministers, the First Lord of the Admiralty (the navy), the Secretary of State for War (the army) and Secretary of State for Air (the air force) out of the War Cabinet, summoning them only when needed – as was the case with all other government ministers. This allowed him to exercise more direct control over the military by having the Chiefs of Staff report to him directly as Minister of Defence. The Chiefs were the military heads of the three services, the senior British commanders, comprising the First Sea Lord (navy), the Chief of the Imperial General Staff (army) and the Chief of the Air Staff (air force). Churchill chaired the Defence Committee, which decided on important operations, and his Military Chief of Staff, General 'Pug' Ismay, represented him at the regular Chiefs of Staff meetings. As Prime Minister he created a powerful War Cabinet Secretariat, including the Cabinet Secretary, the Downing Street Private Secretaries (male career civil servants) and a military secretariat under Ismay. To this he added his own team of personal secretaries (nearly all female), an assortment of special assistants and advisers, his own map room and a statistical unit to help research, analyse and interpret information. He also sought direct access to the Joint Planning Staff.

This system was immediately tested. The criticisms of the Norwegian campaign quickly paled into insignificance as the disastrous battles in Holland, Belgium and France unfolded. Numerically superior but operationally outclassed, the Dutch, Belgian, British and French armies were split by the audacious German thrust through the Ardennes, across the Meuse and towards the Channel. It all happened within a matter of days.

In the early hours of 15 May, Churchill's slumber was broken by a desperate telephone call from the French Prime Minister, Paul Reynaud: 'He spoke in English, and evidently under stress. "We have been defeated." As I did not immediately respond he said again: "We are beaten; we have lost the battle."'

This was far more serious than Norway. British war planning had been built on the foundations of Anglo-French cooperation. The two countries had formed a Supreme War Council bringing together their respective leaders to coordinate strategy. In the event of any major German offensive in north-western Europe, it was expected that the British Expeditionary Force would fight under the command of the larger French Army. The Royal Air Force would help secure the skies above France while the Royal Navy would keep the Channel open and blockade German ports.

The implications of the fall of France were catastrophic. Defeat on the continent meant the loss of Britain's major ally and brought German forces to within easy striking distance of the UK's shores. What signal would this send to other countries? Would President Roosevelt and the United States view the war in Europe as lost? Might Spain take advantage of British weakness to seize Gibraltar? Would Mussolini bring fascist Italy into the conflict and attack British interests in Malta, Egypt or the Middle East? What about the French Fleet? If allowed to fall into enemy hands and combined with German and Italian naval forces, it would threaten British supremacy in the Mediterranean and Atlantic. Could Japan enter the conflict and move against the British Empire in the East? Such were the questions flashing through Churchill's mind. As he later wrote:

> The reader of these pages in future years should realise how dense and baffling is the veil of the Unknown. Now in the full light of the after-time it is easy to see where we were ignorant or too much alarmed, where we were careless or clumsy. Twice in two months we had been taken completely by surprise . . . What else had they got ready – prepared and organised to the last inch?

Yet, in spite of this, he initially refused to accept Reynaud's pessimism. At this stage Churchill still felt the French defeat was largely psychological. After tense debates in the British War Cabinet, he supported sending further British fighter aircraft for the defence of France. But the reality hit home when he visited Paris the following day and observed the deteriorating situation for himself. The Germans were now expected to arrive in the French capital within hours, where both the French ministry for Foreign Affairs and the British Embassy were burning their archives. 'Utter dejection was written on every face.' Determined to support his beloved French ally to the last, Churchill asked the fundamental question of Marshal Maurice Gamelin, the French Commander-in-Chief: '*Ou est la Masse de Manoeuvre?*' Where were the French operational reserves? '*Aucune.*' There are none, was the stunning reply. Churchill must have known at that moment the battle for France was lost. He told Lady Campbell, the wife of the British Ambassador, 'This place will shortly become a charnel house.'

The Dutch quickly surrendered; after more of a fight, so too did the Belgians, leaving the First French Army and the British Expeditionary Force with the unenviable choice between encirclement and annihilation, or evacuation to Britain. Fortunately for the future prosecution of the war, Lord Gort recommended the latter. The so-called miracle of Dunkirk ensued, and the majority of the British Army found its way back home, courtesy of the Royal Navy and the fleet of little ships, albeit without almost all its equipment. For Stan Hollis, the retreat to Dunkirk was a bewildering disaster. As his commanding officer's despatch motorbike rider, leading counter-attacks along with his comrades in the 6th Green Howards, he was among the last to defend the Dunkirk beachhead and be evacuated, with Stan on a stretcher, having been recommended for a Military Medal and wounded during the withdrawal.

But Churchill had not yet given up on France. Edward Spears, a close friend of the British Prime Minister, now freshly installed as Churchill's personal representative to Prime Minister Reynaud, witnessed Winston's arrival in Paris on Friday 31 May 1940 and recalled him being as 'fresh as a daisy, obviously in grand form . . . Danger, the evocation of battle, invariably acted as a tonic and stimulant to Winston Churchill.' His energy contrasted with the defeatism of the French leadership. No doubt he liked to be at the heart of the action, but it also fell upon him to project an image of confidence. Against the backdrop of the unfolding crisis on the beaches of Dunkirk, he emphasised in his clumsy French that the Franco-British soldiers would leave the beaches '*bras dessus, bras dessous*' (arm in arm).

In the end, more than 338,000 men (of whom some 140,000 were French and Belgian) were successfully taken across the Channel. This was far higher than initial estimates, but Churchill was still careful in his report to the Commons of 4 June 1940 'not to assign to this deliverance the attributes of a victory. Wars are not won by evacuations.' Responding to criticism by the soldiers on the beaches about the absence of the Royal Air Force and the perception that they were left exposed to attacks by the Luftwaffe, he argued that the British fighter planes had provided a largely effective cordon. A similar argument could be made in favour of the Royal Navy, which had organised, supplemented and defended the smaller merchant ships used to undertake the operation. The advice that Churchill was getting from his Chiefs of Staff was that Britain could still resist invasion and re-equip its army if it could hold the skies and seas surrounding the country. The power to do both would also be vital to any successful return to France. And it is interesting to note that the hurried naval planning and implementation for Dunkirk (code-named Operation Dynamo) was carried out by Vice Admiral Bertram Ramsay, who would ultimately do the same for Operation Neptune (the naval aspect of Overlord) in 1944. Some of the seeds for D-Day were already being planted in defeat. With the benefit of hindsight, perhaps Winston was right to state that 'there was a victory, inside this deliverance, which should be noted'.

At the time, victory was less apparent, and his speech that day is now best remembered for its lines about defending our island: 'whatever the cost may be' by fighting on the beaches and the landing grounds and in the fields, streets and hills. But he did not just mean in Britain, defiantly declaring that 'we shall fight in France'. Even now, he hoped to salvage something from the wreckage of the original Allied strategy. Rescued French forces were quickly repatriated. The 51st Highland Division continued to fight in France before ultimately being forced to surrender. And the 52nd Lowland Division, together with the 1st Canadian Division, were quickly despatched as a second British Expeditionary Force, only to be evacuated just days later. Under huge pressure from the French to send more fighter aircraft, Churchill's natural instinct was to do just that. His political and military colleagues rightly persuaded him to hold them back.

And yet Churchill still refused to abandon France. As the end game approached and German forces moved towards Paris, he made repeated attempts to try and rally the French government, which was now retreating southwards. He urged the French to continue the war from their north African empire and to fight a guerrilla campaign in France. He advocated continued resistance by the Allies in Brittany. Despite the clear dangers in flying so close to the frontline, he met with Reynaud at Briare on 11 June and at Tours just two days later on the 13th. The accounts of their final meeting could not be more poignant. The British delegation landed on an airport runway pock-marked with bomb craters, with no one there to greet them. They had to borrow a car and persuade a café to open in order to get a meal. When they finally obtained a meeting with the French Prime Minister, an exhausted and depressed Reynaud saw 'no light at the end of the tunnel' and asked to be allowed to make a separate peace with Germany. Churchill, while refusing to agree to this, recognised that there was little that he could do to prevent it. He begged Reynaud to make one more appeal to President Roosevelt for an American intervention before pursuing such a course. Then he ended on a characteristically defiant note, confirming that 'his confidence that Hitlerism would be smashed and that Nazidom could not and would not over-rule Europe remained absolutely unshaken'.

It would take time. In the interim, some of the Frenchmen he met at those fateful meetings would face German retribution. Georges Mandel, Reynaud's Minister of the Interior and an outspoken critic of Nazism, would be executed, while Paul Reynaud would be imprisoned. Yet it was also at this time that Churchill first noticed General Charles de Gaulle, then a junior French Under Secretary of State for War, and clearly in favour of continuing the conflict. Churchill may or may not have referred to him as a man of destiny, but he clearly identified him as someone the British could work with. Spears smuggled him out of France in an aeroplane just before the armistice and de Gaulle famously addressed the French nation via the radio services of the BBC on 18 June. He spoke just after Churchill had made his 'Finest Hour' broadcast, urging French soldiers and workers to join him in Britain to continue the struggle against Germany and declaring that the flame of French resistance will not be extinguished. The Free French movement was born.

It was the message of continued resistance that Churchill wanted to promote. He wanted to find creative ways of keeping France in the fight even after the fall of France. He had even been prepared to endorse a scheme, promoted by Jean Monnet (a future founding father of European unity, then working in London on coordinating Franco-British war supplies), de Gaulle and others, for full Franco-British union. It allowed Jock Colville, one of Churchill's Private Secretaries, to joke in his diary that the French *fleur-de-lys* might be about to be restored to the British Royal Standard.

The pooling of national sovereignty would certainly have been a powerful symbolic gesture. It would also have allowed the transfer of French arms, troops and gold to British soil, while potentially keeping French North Africa and the French Fleet in the conflict on the Allied side. Sadly, it was not to be. The offer was made but only reached France after the collapse of Reynaud's government. The new regime under Marshal Pétain, Laval and Admiral Darlan was set upon the armistice and obtaining what independence they could still get from Hitler. They were in no mood for unity with Britain. This would have repercussions. Hitler would occupy Paris and northern France. Meanwhile, the Vichy republic would be set up in the south, nominally independent but in reality dependent for its existence on Germany. Britain would be forced to view Vichy France as a potentially hostile power and to look across the Atlantic for a new alliance with the United States. If there was a glimmer of hope it lay to the West where the fall of France acted a real spur to American rearmament. President Roosevelt had cause to be anxious. If Britain fell too, then Germany would have clear access across the Atlantic.

It is against this bleak backdrop that Churchill made his 'Finest Hour' broadcast on 18 June 1940. Referring to the offer 'to conclude a union of common citizenship' with France, he pledged that

However matters may go in France or with the French Government, or other French Governments, we in this Island and in the British Empire will never lose our sense of comradeship with the French people. If we are now called upon to endure what they have been suffering, we shall emulate their courage, and if final victory rewards our toils they shall share the gains, aye, and freedom shall be restored to all.

Broadcasting over the BBC at 21.00 hours, Churchill had no choice but to respond to the unfolding crisis. He had prepared carefully. The heavily annotated draft notes for his speech show him wrestling with the implications of these momentous events and struggling to find the right response. They are literally a first draft of history. Dictated to his duty secretary, they were first set down in normal typescript for the Prime Minister to correct. Once the text had been approved, it was then taken away and retyped at a size that fitted comfortably into his jacket pocket and in the blank verse format that he used to aid his delivery.

His peroration was one that still echoes down the ages, helping to secure his place in history. Having noted that, 'What General Weygand calls "the battle of France" is over. The battle of Britain is about to begin,' Churchill built up to a dramatic finale, laden with deliberate echoes of Shakespeare's Henry V, declaring:

Let us therefore brace ourselves to
our duty, and so bear ourselves that
    if the British Empire and
        Commonwealth lasts for a
            thousand years, men will still
        say,
'This was their Finest Hour.'[*]

Yet to his Private Secretary Jock Colville listening to his boss on the wireless, this was far from a triumph. 'It was too long and he [Churchill] sounded tired . . . He smoked a cigar the whole time he was broadcasting.' It was little wonder if Churchill was tired. Few leaders in modern times can have

[*]The layout of this extract reflects how Winston liked to set out the text of his speeches, in a blank verse format, like poetry.

endured the sustained pressure that he had experienced during the previous six weeks.

Churchill was a Francophile. His American mother had been brought up largely in Paris, at the court of Emperor Napoleon III. An admirer of French history and culture, he had fought alongside French troops in the First World War and worked with their leading politicians in war and peace. His love of French food and wine is well documented. The south of France is where he had always gone to write, to paint, to gamble and to recharge his batteries. He had failed to foresee the speed and totality of the French collapse and he had worked tirelessly to try and prevent it. The diary of his daughter Mary, then just seventeen, provides an insight into the prevailing mood of depression that the French armistice engendered within his personal family circle. Her entry for Monday 17 June reads:

> Today came the announcement that following Reynaud's resignation and Pétain's assumption of the leadership France asks for peace terms.
>
> *Oh chère France* – I can never love you one jot less – but why have you failed in this. We have been expecting this – & yet now it <u>has</u> come – we all feel shocked – bereaved of a great & brilliant ally. Now we are alone . . .

Churchill had embraced de Gaulle and his Free French movement and pledged himself to a policy of restoring what he called the 'genius of France'. Britain may not have left the continent willingly, but in the short term she was in no position to contemplate a return in strength. Now came some very hard decisions. Churchill's promise of comradeship was to be immediately tested by events.

Within days, those elements of the French Fleet that refused to surrender to the Royal Navy were engaged by the British and several French ships were sunk. It was done on Churchill's orders, in spite of the reservations expressed by many of his senior naval advisers. At Mers-el-Kébir in French Algeria, almost one thousand three hundred French sailors lost their lives at the hands of their former British allies. Churchill was moved to tears when announcing the action in the House of Commons, but most MPs cheered. The action sent a clear message to the United States. Britain was not going to go the way of France. But relations with de Gaulle and the Free French were undoubtedly damaged. At a Downing Street lunch, de Gaulle implied that rather than rallying the French behind the British, this action might tempt them to turn their guns against their former allies. His words incurred the wrath of his hostess, the Prime Minister's loyal wife Clementine, a fluent French speaker, but relations with France were now complicated.

By the end of 1940, Britain had been forced out of continental Europe. Churchill's immediate priority was national survival. In the coming weeks, the young men of the Royal Air Force and the just-in-time supply of Hurricanes and Spitfires would thwart Hitler's ambition to invade the English coast. Had Lord Halifax, not Winston, succeeded Chamberlain as Prime Minister then the outcome might have been very different. Halifax favoured some form of negotiation to prevent further bloodshed and his ultimately unsuccessful bid to advocate this course of action while serving as Churchill's Foreign Secretary provides the inspiration and starting point for the Hollywood movie *Darkest Hour* (2017). It was an argument that Churchill won on the grounds that any German invasion could still be resisted.

Ironically, Britain was protected from enemy invasion by the very same obstacles that prevented an early British return to the continent. It was just as difficult for Hitler to launch a successful amphibious invasion of Britain as it was for Churchill to cross back to France. There was an uneasy stalemate as the two opposing armies fortified the beaches on either side of the Channel. But this did not mean that Churchill had given up on cross-Channel operations. He knew that the defeats in Norway and France had left Britain too weak for a return in force, especially while the Luftwaffe were still bombing British cities and factories. His room for manoeuvre was severely limited; his political position might not have survived another major defeat. But that did not mean he countenanced doing nothing.

In a minute to General Ismay, issued on 4 June 1940, the very day of his 'fight on the beaches' speech, Churchill wrote:

> The completely defensive habit of mind which has ruined the French must not be allowed to ruin all our initiative. It is of the highest consequence to keep the largest number of German forces all along the coasts of the countries they have conquered, and we should immediately set to work to organise raiding forces on these coasts where the populations are friendly . . . How wonderful it would be if the Germans could be made to wonder where they were going to be struck next, instead of forcing us to try to wall in the Island and roof it over!

Resistance in France was to be encouraged. The order went out to set Europe ablaze. A new Special Operations Executive (SOE) was set up to coordinate operations behind enemy lines. Commando operations were gradually scaled up; starting with small single-boat attacks led by men like Captain March-Phillips and graduating to larger raids, such as Operation Chariot, which boldly knocked out the Normandy dry docks at St Nazaire.

It was into this male-dominated world that a young woman was suddenly plunged, finding herself at 'the vanguard of a revolution'. Aged just twenty-nine, Joan Bright was efficient and adventurous, glamourous and respectable, sociable and trustworthy. One of five daughters in 'an average family with a less than average income', her upbringing may have lacked money, but it was rich in experience. She was born in Argentina to British parents and spent her early years in Spain before returning to England. Actively encouraged by her family to find her own way in life, she trained as a secretary and never looked back: 'With a shorthand pad and typewriter I could be a valuable and mobile interpreter of others' thoughts, a human machine with the power to give and receive confidence.'

In the early 1930s she worked at the British Legation in Mexico City. On her return she turned down roles working for the British Conservative politician, Duff Cooper, and the German Deputy Führer Rudolf Hess. What she accepted instead was a top-secret job working for a new clandestine unit within the British Secret Intelligence Service. Section D of MI(R) was charged with planning subversion and sabotage behind enemy lines. She joined in the spring of 1939, doing her bit for the British war effort before war had even been declared.

From offices in London's Caxton Street, she helped organise the first guerrilla operations in Norway, in support of the Narvik campaign. Section D did not last. It was quickly subsumed within Churchill's new Special Operations Executive, with some of its functions passing to Combined Operations, but Joan observed the small beginnings of the fightback that would lead to Normandy in 1944. Her skills had not gone unnoticed. She was moved to the Joint Planning Secretariat at the heart of the British war machine and was soon working and living in the eye of the storm. When the Luftwaffe unleashed their bombs in the Blitz, a concerted bombing campaign to cow London and other British cities, she lived through it all. Her flat was destroyed, colleagues were killed – but Joan kept calm and carried on.

Churchill's response was to promise the people that he would 'give it 'em [the Germans] back'. One strong strand of that pledge was to step up operations against enemy targets in France. These were to be planned and executed by his new Combined Operations Command, its leaders chosen for their willingness to take the fight to the enemy. He turned first to Admiral Sir Roger Keyes, a veteran of naval raids during the First World War, and then to Lord Louis Mountbatten, a personal favourite with Royal connections. By the time of his appointment in 1942, Mountbatten's exploits onboard HMS *Kelly* had already been turned into a wartime propaganda movie, *In Which We Serve*, by Noel Coward. Larger than life on the big screen, Mountbatten was depicted as the sort of dashing commander that would always take the fight to the enemy, described by the historian Correlli Barnett as 'the Sam

Goldwyn of Combined Operations'. This was exactly the image Churchill wanted his commanders to embody.

The Combined Operations Command emerged from the failures of Gallipoli and Narvik. It was a deliberate attempt to coordinate amphibious operations and end inter-service muddle and rivalry. Mountbatten was promoted to Vice Admiral but was also given the honorary army and air force ranks of Lieutenant General and Air Marshal to reflect the unique tri-service nature of his new command. He became a member of the Chiefs of Staff Committee, gaining a place at the top table and direct access to the Prime Minister. It was clear to Mountbatten that his brief was to facilitate the return to France. But it was also clear that it was going to take time to build up the necessary resources, experience and expertise. To do so, he set about building a team. The forty-year-old Captain John Hughes-Hallett was an early and eager recruit. He had been running a Combined Training Centre in Scotland and quickly established himself as Mountbatten's key naval adviser. But Mountbatten, like Churchill, was also prepared to include more eccentric figures who would challenge the political orthodoxy and military status quo.

They certainly did not come any more unorthodox than Geoffrey Pyke, a hyperactive ideas man and former radical educationalist who cared nothing for his own personal appearance or for obeying orders. Introduced to Mountbatten by Leo Amery, he became Director of Programmes at Combined Operations and proceeded to bombard his chief with long papers suggesting new equipment and stratagems. Mountbatten called these 'Pykeisms', and they were often prefaced by their eccentric author with aphorisms; quotes like, 'The inconceivables of only two years ago are today's realities.'

Pyke's response to defeat in Norway was to suggest new ways of continuing the fight. He too advocated for a behind-the-lines guerrilla campaign, but one that harnessed new technology; advocating hit-and-run actions by specially trained troops on fast mobile snowploughs, which he now began to design. When challenged about how such equipment could be kept from the Germans, his response was to argue that it should be hidden in plain sight: making the snowploughs look German and adorning them with such notices as '*Verboten*' or 'Special-Death-Ray Department', which would stop investigations by inquisitive enemy soldiers. It was not to be his only wild idea. The complex preparations for D-Day would require contributions from both experienced service professionals and maverick thinkers.

Yet, as Combined Operations began to contemplate a return to France, the war was already moving to other theatres. The road to D-Day would be a long one that would detour through Washington DC and North Africa. Narvik and Dunkirk had been visceral reminders of the difficulties of amphibious operations and the limitations of British military power.

The pressures on the Prime Minister were immense and his room for manoeuvre limited; even with all the new structures and centralisation, Churchill had to prioritise and delegate. He chose to concentrate on military strategy, security and foreign policy, allowing other ministers considerable independence on domestic affairs and the economy (both at home and around the Empire). He had to work closely with the Dominion Governments, on whom he was dependent for troops and resources, and he regularly allowed their leaders or senior visiting representatives to attend War Cabinet meetings. The war was being run through a huge number of ministries, departments and committees, some public, some secret, and however hands-on Churchill may have wanted to be, he could only do so much.

For Churchill, after his inspiring speeches to rally and buttress the morale and will of the British people, came the realisation that wars were not won by evacuations but by success on the battle-field. He was personally committed to a policy of waging war until final victory, and victory meant the defeat of the Germans in Europe. But that prospect still seemed a very long way off, if ever possible, in the autumn of 1940.

THE WHITE HOUSE
WASHINGTON

April 3
11 pm

Dear Winston

What Harry ~ Gen. Marshall will
tell you all about has my heart &
mind in it. Your people & mine
demand the reestablishment of a front
to draw off pressure on the Russians,
& these peoples are wise enough
to see that the Russians are today
killing more Germans & destroying
more equipment than you & I
put together. Even if full

success is not attained, the
big objection will be.
So to it! Syria & Egypt
will be made more secure, even if
the Germans find out about
our plans.
Best of luck — make Harry
go to bed early & tell him
obey Dr. Fulton USN. whom
I am sending with him as
super nurse with full
authority

As ever
FDR

Letter from Roosevelt to Churchill, 3 April 1942

3

Arguments with Allies

'No lover ever studied every whim of his mistress
as I did those of President Roosevelt.'

'NEVER IN THE field of human conflict was so much owed
by so many to so few.'

With those immortal words, Winston Churchill summed up
the achievement of the young fighter pilots during the Battle of
Britain.

With them, came the awful realisation that Great Britain and
her Empire were alone and on the frontline. The Royal Air Force
had secured the skies, the Royal Navy controlled the domestic
waters around the British Isles, but the army at home was still
licking its wounds after Dunkirk and gallantly standing ready –
along with the Home Guard volunteers 'Dads Army' – to defend
the beaches and offer resistance, should Hitler still be minded to
invade. But there was a war to fight and an enemy, now joined by
Italy, to be defeated. On, above and under the surface of the
ocean, the Battle of the Atlantic was being fought to secure
Britain's strategic lifelines to the United States and the Empire;
the first faltering bomber attacks had begun against targets in
Germany; and the army in North Africa was enjoying some
surprising success against not the Germans, but the Italians, whose
military hubris had exceeded their capabilities.

The two dates that changed the course of the war were 22 June
1941 and 7 December 1941. From those moments onwards,

Churchill knew that Britain, her Empire and Commonwealth, were no longer fighting alone. When the Wehrmacht launched Hitler's ill-conceived strategic attempt to gain *lebensraum* (living room) in the west of the Soviet Union for the ethnic German people and secure the oil reserves of the Caucasus and the agricultural resources of Ukraine and Byelorussia, Churchill knew that Stalin and the Soviet Union had become allies in his fight against Germany. Although ideologically odd bedfellows, the old dictum that 'the enemy of my enemy is my friend' became the pragmatic foundation of a distrustful but mutually beneficial relationship between Stalin and Churchill. Or as Churchill put it to his Private Secretary, Jock Colville, 'If Hitler invaded Hell, I would at least make a favourable reference to the Devil in the House of Commons.'

Although Stalin, as well as Franklin Roosevelt later, were suspicious and, at times, critical of Britain's Mediterranean and imperial obligations, it was Hitler's decision to secure his southern flank before launching Operation Barbarossa that probably prevented Stalin's defeat in front of Moscow in the winter of 1941/42. The British were assisting the Greeks and an anti-Nazi coup took place in Yugoslavia. Hitler fatally delayed his attack on the Soviet Union from early to mid-summer, pausing to defeat Greece and Yugoslavia first. By the time his much-vaunted Panzer armies in their thin summer uniforms had reached the outskirts of Moscow, winter had set in, and the chance of an outright German strategic victory was gone. For Churchill this was the first of those two lifelines.

The second materialised out of a clear blue sky on the morning of Sunday 7 December 1941 when aircraft from the Imperial Japanese Naval Service attacked the US Pacific Fleet at their moorings in Pearl Harbor, causing catastrophic damage (though luckily the aircraft carriers were at sea). The next day, while the Japanese were also attacking the British colony of Hong Kong, the US declared war on Japan and by 11 December against Germany and Italy, made easier by Hitler's declaration of war against the United States. From Churchill's point of view, he had achieved what he had set out to do since becoming Prime Minister in May 1940 – to get the United States into the war against Germany, and Italy, for good measure.

It could be said that if the declarations of war were just the overture, the main movements were to be the agreements over strategy and the sequencing of campaigns to defeat Germany, Italy and Japan. However, as Churchill was about to discover, waging war with allies who had conflicting strategic objectives and time-tables demanded statesmanship of the highest order, ultimately to be played out on the world stage in major conferences over the course of the next three years. Yet, in December 1941, for Churchill and Roosevelt and their military staffs the initial priority was to hammer out an agreed Western position before sitting down with the Soviet Union's Joseph Stalin. That would come later.

Churchill and Roosevelt spoke on the phone in the immediate aftermath of Pearl Harbor. The American President confirmed events with the words, 'We are all in the same boat now.' Churchill later wrote that he 'slept the sleep of the saved and thankful', declaring:

> So we had won after all! Yes, after Dunkirk; after the fall of France; after the horrible episode of Oran [the attack on the French Fleet]; after the threat of invasion, when, apart from the Air and Navy, we were almost an unarmed people; after the deadly struggle of the U-boat war – the first Battle of the Atlantic, gained by a hand's-breadth; after seventeen months of lonely fighting and nineteen months of my responsibility in dire stress. We had won the war.

With the benefit of hindsight, he glossed over the many frustrations he had experienced in courting Roosevelt and the United States. Churchill was half American by birth – his beautiful mother was born in Brooklyn, New York – and he proudly asserted that 'American blood flowed in my veins'. He had visited the United States in 1895, 1900–01, 1929 and 1931–2, spending time touring its major cities, meetings its leading people and writing about its history, culture and customs. After 1940 he was determined to drag the Americans in, admitting that, 'No lover ever studied every whim of his mistress as I did those of President Roosevelt.'

He had always believed that this moment would come, that America would not abandon the Western democracies, but his faith had been sorely tested and it had proved a far more protracted and costly process than he had hoped. He had been forced to cede British bases for American destroyers, give up British gold reserves, and accept deferred payments for vital Lend-Lease supplies. Roosevelt had inched towards war, gradually assuming an ever-greater role in the defence of the Atlantic, but it was Japanese aggression rather than British diplomacy that had finally forced the United States onto the battlefield.

Churchill's relief at the materialisation of the Anglo-America alliance was no doubt real and palpable. It certainly changed the dynamic of the war, creating the grand alliance against fascism that would ultimately make Overlord possible, but it came with its own complications. His belief that now America was in the harem we could 'talk to her quite differently' would prove overconfident.

The Prime Minister certainly moved quickly. He lost no time in visiting Washington for Christmas, keen to argue that the highest priority for the Western Allies was a policy of Europe first, or more specifically, the defeat of Germany first. This was no easy case to make, given American anger against Japan, and was made even more difficult by the news that the Japanese had sunk the two British Royal Navy warships, HMS *Prince of Wales* and HMS *Repulse*, on 10 December 1941, when they were embarrassingly caught without air cover. This left Japan as masters of the Pacific and Britain's imperial possessions of Malaya, Singapore and Burma at great risk. A potential threat to India could not be discounted. At the ensuing Arcadia Conference between Britain and the United States, Churchill managed to achieve agreement that a holding action would be fought against Japan in the Pacific while the main effort of Allied forces would be concentrated against the defeat of Germany first. Thereafter all forces would be concentrated against Japan. For Churchill and the United Kingdom, after over two years of war, this was a strategic success of the utmost significance.

Yet, while that conference agreed the main muscle movements between the Western Allies, it did nothing to placate Stalin, who continued to argue strongly at every opportunity for a second front to be opened in Western Europe. He urged a return to France by the armies of the United Kingdom and the United States to take the pressure off the Red Army, which had been comprehensively mauled, but not beaten, in the early months of Barbarossa. Yet, in 1942 neither the US nor Britain was remotely capable of considering such an operation in strength. As in 1917, the US Army was faced with the challenge of expanding its size and capability ready to become a major participant in the war in Europe and elsewhere. It may already have been growing rapidly, with a million and a half officers and men by the middle of 1941, but it lacked training, combat experience and equipment. It would take time for the American economy to realise its full production potential. By 1942, the Americans were garrisoning Iceland, but they had fewer than five thousand men in the United Kingdom and only two divisions en route.

For the British, the problem was one of war weariness and imperial overstretch. They were already heavily committed in the Mediterranean and North Africa; stuck in a fight that had begun in late 1940 against the Italians. This had been the one theatre in which Churchill had been able to take the fight to the enemy. The Mediterranean Fleet under Admiral Cunningham and the army in Egypt under General Wavell had initially achieved significant successes against Mussolini's forces, and for a while it had looked as though North Africa might be cleared of the enemy by early 1941. In February, Lieutenant General Richard O'Connor had marked the defeat of Italian forces in the Libyan desert with a very British message (based on hunting terminology), signalling to his superior, General Sir Archibald Wavell: 'Fox killed in the open.' Perhaps O'Connor could have advanced further to Tripoli and finished off the war in North Africa for good, but Churchill's eyes had turned somewhat prematurely towards defending Greece and fighting in the eastern Mediterranean. During the operational pause in the desert after the Italian collapse, Hitler had despatched the Afrika Korps under Lieutenant General Erwin Rommel to prop up what remained of his Italian ally in North Africa. The success of Rommel in the desert during 1941 resulted in another torrid year for Churchill but it also set the scene for the emergence of one of the two leading British commanders in the Second World War: Bernard Law Montgomery. (For the curious, the other was William Joseph Slim, Commander of the Fourteenth Army in Burma.)

Of course, fighting in North Africa and the Mediterranean was also about defending the Empire. While Roosevelt and Marshall were wary of entangling American forces in a defence of the British Empire, Churchill's administration was an imperial government and had no option but to think in terms of imperial defence. Defeat and withdrawal in the Mediterranean threatened to further erode British supply lines to India and the Pacific (via the Suez Canal), risking vital oil supplies in Iran and Iraq, strengthening the Axis powers of Germany, Italy and Japan and – coming on top of earlier defeats – inflicting a potentially lethal blow on British morale. In the early months of 1942, there was a very real fear among British planners that if the Germans, Italians and Japanese coordinated their strategy, between them they might be able to besiege and close all the main imperial shipping routes and bring Britain to its knees.

The British were too heavily engaged elsewhere to simply break off and refocus on France.

The Allies, and particularly Britain, were still on the defensive, but the arrival of American men and material in the European theatre quickly reawakened the debate about the war in the West and the possibility of operations in France.

Churchill was fond of saying that the only thing worse than fighting with allies was fighting without them. By early 1942, he had not one but two powerful new allies, each coming to the top table with their own agendas and strategies for running and winning the war: the Russians desperate for help; the Americans keen to defeat Germany in Europe as quickly as possible so that they could turn against Japan in the Pacific. The British and Americans had agreed on a 'Germany First' strategy, and President Roosevelt was keen to see US troops in action, but the detail was lacking. Various operations had been discussed. Nothing had yet been decided.

It was at this moment that an important letter was handed to Churchill.

The White House
  Washington

April 3

11pm

Dear Winston

What Harry and Geo. Marshall will tell you about has my heart & mind in it. Your people & mine demand the establishment of a front to draw off pressure on the Russians, & these peoples are wise enough to see that the Russians are today killing more Germans & destroying more equipment than you and I put together. Even if full success is not attained, the big objective will be.

Go to it! Syria and Egypt will be made more secure, even if the Germans find out about our plans.

Best of luck. Make Harry go to bed early, and let him obey Dr Fulton, U.S.N. [US Navy], whom I am sending with him as super-nurse with full authority.

As ever
FDR

Most of the wartime communication between Churchill and Roosevelt was conducted by telegram, via trans-Atlantic telephone or through intermediaries. A handwritten missive from the President was rare and to be taken very seriously. Written out on green White House paper by the President at 11 p.m. on 3 April, it was hand-delivered to the British Prime Minister five days later by Harry Hopkins.

Hopkins was one of the President's closest advisers. Physically, he was not in good shape. Cancer had already led to the removal of most of his stomach. He looked gaunt and often dishevelled. To Mary Churchill, Winston's daughter, he appeared 'painfully thin with wispy hair'. Charles Wilson, Churchill's doctor, painted an even grimmer picture: 'his lips are blanched as if he had been bleeding internally, his skin yellow like stretched parchment and his eyelids contracted to a slit'. This is why Roosevelt had a US naval doctor accompany him on his mission to London.

But physical appearances can be deceptive. Hopkins was a man of incredible energy. He had worked with Roosevelt throughout the 1930s in combatting the great depression and since January 1941 had served as the President's main emissary to Winston Churchill, becoming a leading advocate of American support for Great Britain; famously winning the admiration of the British Prime Minister by expressing that support by quoting a biblical verse from the Book of Ruth . . . 'Whither thou goest, I will go and where thou lodgest I will lodge, thy people shall be my people, and thy God my God.'

This time, Hopkins did not arrive in London alone. He was accompanied on his mission by General George Marshall, Chief of Staff and military head of the United States Army. Six foot tall, smartly dressed, proper and precise, Marshall was very different to Hopkins, in character and temperament as well as appearance. To Joan Bright he was a 'very upright man' who would never 'have ever trimmed his sails or changed a little bit his position to accommodate the person he was talking to'. While the two Americans shared the view that the war would be won or lost in Europe, and that Hitler was the main enemy, their approach to Churchill and their British allies was very different. Hopkins used friendship, debate and humour to gain acceptance into Churchill's inner circle; Marshall maintained a deliberate distance. He arrived sceptical of British war strategy, defensive of American independence and determined to prioritise action in France.

OPERATIONS IN WESTERN EUROPE

1. Western Europe is favored as the theater in which to stage the first major offensive by the United States and Great Britain. By every applicable basis of comparison, it is definitely superior to any other. In point of time required to produce effective results, its selection will save many months. Through France passes our shortest route to the heart of Germany. In no other area can we attain the overwhelming air superiority vital to successful land attack; while here and here only can the bulk of the British air and ground forces be employed. In this area the United States can concentrate and maintain a larger force than it can in any other. A British-American attack through western Europe provides the only feasible method for employing the bulk of the combat power of the United States, the United Kingdom and Russia in a concerted effort against a single enemy.

Another, and most significant consideration is the unique opportunity to establish an active sector on this front this summer, through steadily increasing air operations and by raids or forays all along the coasts. This initial phase will be of some help to Russia and of immediate satisfaction to the public; but what is most important it will make experienced veterans of the air and ground units, and it will offset the tendency toward deterioration in morale which threaten the latter due to prolonged inactivity.

Finally, successful attack through Western Europe will afford the maximum possible support to Russia, whose continued participation in the war is essential to the defeat of Germany.

2. Decision as to the main effort must be made now. This is true even if the invasion cannot be launched during this year. A major attack must be preceded by a long period of intensive

- 1 -

American paper on operations in Western Europe, 1942

The President's letter was designed to open discussions that would lead to the establishment of a new front in Western Europe. It served as the preface to a second document, a secret memorandum. Entitled 'Operations in Western Europe', this American military plan – developed by Marshall and his protégé General Eisenhower, delivered by Hopkins and endorsed by Roosevelt – could not have been clearer. The United States wanted a cross-Channel operation and as quickly as possible. The language was unambiguous:

> Western Europe is favored as the theater in which to stage the first major offensive by the United States and Great Britain. By every applicable basis of comparison, it is definitely superior to any other. In point of time required to produce effective results, its selection will save many months. Through France passes our shortest route to Germany. In no other area can we attain the overwhelming air superiority vital to successful land attack; while here and here only can the bulk of the British air and ground forces be employed. In this area the United States can concentrate and maintain a larger force than it can in any other. A British American attack through Western Europe provides the only feasible method for employing the bulk of the combat power of the United States, the United Kingdom and Russia in a concerted effort against a single enemy.

The plan proposed immediate cross-Channel air operations and raids to allow troops to gain experience accompanied by an intensive effort to create an invasion force of 5,800 combat aeroplanes and 48 divisions, including some one million American troops. The objective was to seize the beaches between Le Havre and Boulogne. Recognising that it would take time to build up American forces in Britain, the earliest date for D-Day was estimated as 1 April 1943. But the plan also allowed for an earlier operation if the circumstances demanded. A more limited operation was also advocated to establish a beachhead in France in the event of a Russian collapse on the Eastern Front or a German disintegration.

The delivery of this letter and memorandum, and the discussions that followed, marked the arrival of the Americans in the European theatre. This was something that Churchill had been hoping for, and working towards, since May 1940. It might be assumed, therefore, that the contents of this letter would be music to his ears; after all, he had pledged himself very publicly to the restoration of France and the destruction of Nazism in Europe. But British weakness meant that he and the British Chiefs of Staff now favoured a very different policy.

In the short term Pearl Harbor had only exacerbated their weakness. This was no moment to risk a return across the Channel. In the Pacific, they had been relying on a strong American presence to deter and, if necessary, counter Japanese aggression. The loss of the American Fleet had left the British Empire in the East horribly exposed. Within weeks, this had resulted in the loss of Hong Kong, the capitulation of Singapore (the largest surrender in the history of the British Army) and a Japanese threat to the Indian Ocean and Australia. Worse still, the British were on the retreat again in North Africa. This was a bleak time. In July 1942, Harry Butcher, Eisenhower's naval aide, noted that, 'Rommel can almost smell the Suez and the Japs are knocking at the door of India.'

Defeat followed defeat, with insult added to injury by the escape of two German warships from France through the Channel to Germany. It was almost like a re-run of the disasters of 1940, occurring just at the moment that Churchill wanted to impress his new American and Soviet allies. Alexander Cadogan, Under-Secretary of State at the Foreign Office, confided his fears to his diary: 'our soldiers seem very incapable . . . Our generals are no use and do our men fight?' It was a refrain taken up by the Prime Minister. 'Have you not got a single general in that army who can win battles, have none of them any ideas, must we continually lose battles in this way?' Churchill fired these questions at General Brooke in front of the Cabinet. The Chief of the Imperial General Staff struggled to keep his temper and stiff upper lip, gripping his pencils so tightly that they sometimes snapped. In public, he made a robust defence: in private he too wondered why the troops were not fighting better and in a low moment conceded that half the corps and divisional commanders 'lack character, imagination, drive and power of leadership'.

Unsurprisingly, opposition to the government's management of the war effort was rising in the press. Churchill was forced to defend his administration's conduct of the war in Parliament. It was into this atmosphere of self-doubt and recrimination that Hopkins and Marshall breezed with their plan for attacking France.

Joan Bright observed it all from her office in Whitehall and would later recall:

> Well I think 1942 was a horrible year . . . I mean the Battle of the Atlantic was really nearly lost that year. It was a horrible year and things were going very badly in the Far East. We were losing all over the place, we were losing. And the Russians were screaming for us to go . . . and land . . . on the Continent, so the Americans and the Russians were sort of slightly anti our point of view.

British troops were desperately trying to hold their positions in North Africa and the Pacific. Seen from London, the strategy was clear: the Allies must weather the immediate storm, clear North Africa, secure the Mediterranean and only then could they contemplate a return to France. In the meantime, Combined Operations could continue to plan raids of increasing scale against the French shoreline. But Churchill was faced with a dilemma. Having worked hard to create the American alliance, and ultimately being dependent on American men and material for final victory, he could not risk alienating the President and Marshall. He could not simply ignore their plan. And so, an elaborate game of diplomacy began.

Tactically, the British decided to nominally accept the US strategy of focusing on France while simultaneously steering their new ally towards the Mediterranean. Hopkins and Marshall were exposed to the full force of Churchillian hospitality. They were wined and dined by the King and the Prime Minister. On the evening of 14 April, they were the guests at a specially convened meeting of the Defence Committee, called to consider the American plan, with key ministers and the Chiefs of Staff in attendance alongside the Prime Minister. Churchill opened proceedings by saying he had 'no hesitation in cordially accepting the plan' and he ended the meeting with the observation that 'It was clear that there was complete unanimity on the framework. The two nations would march ahead together in a noble brotherhood of arms.' But the devil was in the detail, and he also made a point of expressing one broad reservation: 'it was essential to carry on the defence of India and the Middle East' where Britain could not face the loss of an army of 600,000 men and the 'man power of India'. Nor, he pointed out, could Britain abandon the defence of Australia. Ominously, the Chief of the Air Staff, Charles Portal, felt that the British fighter force would be wiped out in a matter of months if used to support operations in heavily defended French air space alone, without support from American fighters.

So, behind the scenes Churchill and the British set about persuading, cajoling and convincing their American counterparts that any return to France could only happen after the completion of their preferred operations in North Africa. The Americans were initially intransigent. Marshall was insistent. If France was not possible then the Americans might turn east against Japan and fight in the Pacific instead. As Hopkins pointed out in the Defence Committee meeting, 'if public opinion in America had its way, the weight of American effort would be directed against Japan'.

In fact, anticipating the American position, Churchill had already instructed that plans be drawn up for possible operations in France. Suddenly new codewords abounded in Whitehall as possibilities were explored – Sledgehammer, for a limited operation against France, Bolero for a build-up of US forces in Britain. But, how would the necessary forces be assembled for a major assault on France? What would a large-scale operation look like? Might there be more immediate limited opportunities arising out of existing plans for raids against the continent?

In June, Churchill shot down plans to land a division and armoured units on the continent for a raid of just two to three days. While still in favour of small-scale raiding operations, he felt that there should be no substantial landing in France 'unless we are going to stay' and 'unless the Germans are demoralised by another failure against Russia'.

With regard to any major assault on France, the British commanders were divided as to where landings might take place – on the Normandy beaches (favoured by Mountbatten and the Combined Operations staff) or further north in the Pas-de-Calais (preferred by Fighter Command, as they would be able to operate more easily from British bases)? Churchill seemed to favour attacking everywhere simultaneously. He sent a minute to his Chiefs of Staff on 15 June expressing his view that the assault should take the form of at least six heavy disembarkations in the first wave, accompanied by at least half a dozen feints 'which, if luck favours them, may be exploited'. He was advocating attacks or diversions along a huge stretch of the Atlantic shoreline, in Norway, Denmark, Holland, Belgium, in the Pas-de-Calais, 'where the major Air battle will be fought', on the Cotentin Peninsula, at Brest, St Nazaire and the mouth of Gironde. Moreover, there should be at least three waves of assault. Perhaps he was being deliberately provocative, trying to flush out the objections of his Chiefs of Staff, because he concluded that

> Unless we are prepared to commit the immense forces comprised in the first three waves to a hostile shore with the certainty that many of our attacks will miscarry, and that if we fail the whole stake will be lost, we ought not to attempt such an extraordinary operation of war under modern conditions.

This essentially remained his view until well into 1943. The cross-Channel operation should only be mounted when the chances of success were overwhelming. When the paper was discussed, later that day, he told the chiefs that success 'would depend largely on the magnitude and the violence of the first assault, which should be carried out on the broadest possible front'. It fell upon the Commanders of Home Forces General Paget, Admiral Ramsay and Air Marshal Sholto Douglas and their Joint Planning Staff to investigate what was possible and respond. They pointed out that the scale and tempo of any operation would be limited by the lack of assault craft and shipping, by the difficulty of getting on and off the beaches, by the need to seize ports and airfields, and by the capacity of the ports in southern England to support the operation. The ports of Le Havre and Cherbourg would need to be seized in order to sustain supplies to the front. The Normandy beaches were identified as the most promising landing grounds, but German air power would need to be engaged over the Calais area, as it was nearer to UK air bases. They had identified the major challenges, all of which would continue to cause headaches for the planners over the course of the next two years, but little detailed planning could be done until the bigger strategic questions had been resolved with the Americans. Future plans were also being overtaken by current events.

Unfortunately, things were only getting worse for the British in the Mediterranean. While staying at the White House in June 1942, Churchill had to endure the humiliation of hearing about the fall of Tobruk (in Libya) from the mouths of President Roosevelt and General Marshall. This was not how he hoped to impress his American allies. Rommel was now once again threatening Egypt. Churchill returned to a storm of criticism in the British press and Parliament. On 2 July, he had to face down a confidence vote in his administration in the House of Commons in which the Labour MP Aneurin Bevan made the stinging rebuke that 'the Prime Minister wins Debate after Debate and loses battle after battle'.

The discussions about the Second Front raged in Washington in June and London in July. The fifty-one-year-old General Dwight D. Eisenhower arrived in the British capital to take up his position as American theatre commander. Like his mentor, General Marshall, Ike was a firm advocate for the cross-Channel assault. But he was also a good diplomat and a natural team builder.

In keeping with the sentiments expressed in the President's letter and accepting that a major invasion was not possible until 1943, the American military commanders continued to argue for some form of limited operation in 1942 to relieve pressure on the Russians. This was given more urgency by the fall of Sevastopol, the last Soviet bastion in Crimea. Harry Butcher, Eisenhower's aide, noted that 'The Red Army is carrying the brunt of the battle. The papers at home and in England are filled with demands for a second front.' An operation in France was needed 'to serve as life-saver to a drowning ally'. He also recognised that the British, having suffered a succession of defeats over a three-year period, were understandably more cautious and realistic, while the fresher Americans were 'perhaps inclined to take more chances'.

By July 1942, there was mounting confusion on both sides of the Atlantic over the various possibilities and their codenames, which the Prime Minister and President sought to codify in their trans-Atlantic telegram correspondence. Roosevelt set out their final agreement in his telegram of the 9th (see image on p. 63).

The codename for the full-scale assault would evolve over time. Roundup would become Super Roundup, which would ultimately become Overlord.

But in the short term the President accepted that Roundup could not be contemplated until after Bolero and the build-up of forces. He also recognised that Sledgehammer (the more limited operation) was only likely to take place in an emergency. But the nature of these operations still needed to be worked out. Plans were drawn up for a limited seizure of the Cotentin Peninsula, followed if successful by the liberation of the Channel Islands.

The British continued to push back, and Churchill was determined to be front and centre of the discussions. When General Marshall and Admiral King arrived in July 1942 and met with members of the British General Staff before seeing him, it invoked his fury. Butcher's account has him striding up and down the room at Chequers (the Prime Minister's official country residence)

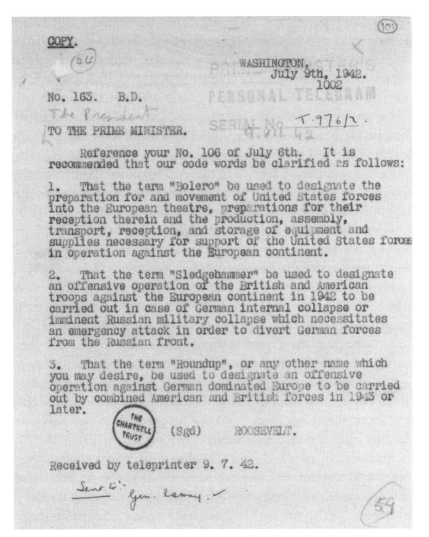

COPY.

WASHINGTON,
July 9th, 1942.
1002

No. 163.   B.D.

The President

TO THE PRIME MINISTER.

Reference your No. 106 of July 6th.   It is
recommended that our code words be clarified as follows:

1.   That the term "Bolero" be used to designate the
preparation for and movement of United States forces
into the European theatre, preparations for their
reception therein and the production, assembly,
transport, reception, and storage of equipment and
supplies necessary for support of the United States force
in operation against the European continent.

2.   That the term "Sledgehammer" be used to designate
an offensive operation of the British and American
troops against the European continent in 1942 to be
carried out in case of German internal collapse or
imminent Russian military collapse which necessitates
an emergency attack in order to divert German forces
from the Russian front.

3.   That the term "Roundup", or any other name which
you may desire, be used to designate an offensive
operation against German dominated Europe to be carried
out by combined American and British forces in 1943 or
later.

(Sgd)   ROOSEVELT.

Received by teleprinter 9. 7. 42.

Sent to Gen. Ismay.

Telegram from Roosevelt to Churchill, 9 July 1942

tearing pages from a book of British war laws and berating Harry
Hopkins while asserting in the most vigorous language that 'he
[Churchill] was the man to see first, that he was the man America
should deal with, and that the British Army-Navy chiefs were
under his command'. Resolving strategy with the Americans and
resisting their plans for any immediate lodgement in France were
a clear prime ministerial priority.

Logistical arguments were carefully deployed. The obvious weakness in the US conception of Sledgehammer was that it would take time to build up the required American forces in Britain. In 1942, the United States could only guarantee three and a half divisions. Even then complex questions arose as to how the US troops would cross the Atlantic and later the English channel, land on the beaches and be supplied once ashore. Escorts, tonnage and landing craft were going to take time to assemble in the right place and numbers. There were not enough landing craft available for a landing in force, and certainly not of the type to land sufficient quantities of tanks and armoured vehicles.

In the meantime, the Americans were expecting the British to provide the majority of the troops, the naval support and aerial protection for any operation. And, with all their other existing commitments, the British simply did not have the numbers. Nor did they have full control of the skies above the continent. Even the strategic value of establishing a limited presence across the Channel was questionable. It was not clear how much support it would give the Russians, as the Germans already had a strong presence in France and might not need to withdraw troops from the East. Ultimately, it was unlikely that any bridgehead could be held for long without the ability to feed in sustained reinforcements.

And then there was the risk of being seen to do nothing or too little. If Sledgehammer was not launched, and the Anglo-British forces concentrated instead only on Bolero, on building up forces in Britain for the later larger assault, this would offer no immediate support to the Russians and would see the Allies sitting idle in the West while the Red Army bore all fighting in the East, something both Churchill and Roosevelt were extremely reluctant to countenance. And time was against them. The window for any operation in France was rapidly closing, as the Atlantic winter weather and high tides meant that any cross-Channel operation was better conducted in spring or summer.

By July, Eisenhower was working on the detail for Sledgehammer with Paget, Douglas and Ramsay. Their report conceded that 'owing to a recent re-estimate of the number of landing craft that will be available this autumn, we do not consider the operation can be undertaken before 15th November'. Even then, they were unsure that they would have the necessary British gliders or American glider pilots, could not depend on the support of local resistance groups because of the extreme vigilance and activity of the Gestapo, and were clear that the operation could only be considered in the event of a crack in German morale. From the end of September, they could only rely on short periods of consecutive days of good weather, and, without a port, it was felt impossible to maintain the beachheads.

Churchill put his views succinctly in one of his celebrated 'Action This Day' telegrams to President Roosevelt on 14 July 1942. Styling himself 'Former Naval Person', a recognition of the fact that their wartime correspondence had begun in 1939 when he was still First Lord of the Admiralty, he wrote:

> I have found no one who regards 'SLEDGEHAMMER' as possible.
> I should like to see you do 'GYMNAST' as soon as possible. . . All this seems to me as clear as noonday.

Gymnast was the initial codename for an operation against French North Africa. It would later be rebranded as Operation Torch. Jupiter was an attack on German forces in Norway. The telegram is an expression of Churchill's desire to take the offensive, but not in France where the Germans were strongest and the risks greatest. It is a position he would continue to hold. In a more detailed telegram to the President, he expanded on some of his reasons: the diversion of shipping necessary for a limited Sledgehammer operation in France would damage British imports; even if successful, it would hinder, not help, the larger Roundup assault and the wider war effort by losing essential landing craft, disrupting the training of troops, creating a narrow front across the Channel that would have to be sustained to the detriment of the larger operation and by diverting planes away from the bombing of Germany. He chose not to mention the advantages to Britain

COPY

ACTION THIS DAY

PRIME MINISTER'S
PERSONAL TELEGRAM
SERIAL No. T.999/2.

FORMER NAVAL PERSON TO PRESIDENT
    Absolutely Personal and Secret

No. 114.

    I am most anxious for you to know where I stand
myself at the present time. I have found no one who
regards "SLEDGEHAMMER" as possible. I should like to
see you do "GYMNAST" as soon as possible, and that we in
concert with the Russians should try for "JUPITER".
Meanwhile all preparations for "ROUND-UP" in 1943 should
proceed at full blast, thus holding the maximum enemy
forces opposite England. All this seems to me as clear
as noonday.

        W.S.C.

        14. 7. 42.

Telegram from Churchill to Roosevelt, 14 July 1942

of securing North Africa and the Mediterranean, though he did
describe Gymnast as the best way of relieving pressure on the
Russians and as 'the true Second Front of 1942' and 'the safest and
most fruitful stroke that can be delivered this autumn'.

So, an attack on French North Africa was dangled as the best
alternative to Sledgehammer; an invasion of Vichy-held (and
nominally neutral) Morocco and Algeria. This would be an

American-led operation bringing the United States into the European theatre. After all, US forces might still be welcomed as liberators, while the British were yet to be forgiven for their action against the French Fleet at anchor in Algeria. If successful, it would relieve pressure on the British fighting in Egypt and Libya, open up a new front against Rommel's forces in the desert, facilitate a decisive end to the North African campaign and free up British forces for campaigning in France. It would enable the Allies to practise amphibious operations and landings on a less well-defended shoreline, where untried US troops would not face veteran German units. The operation could also take place relatively quickly with overwhelming Allied naval and air superiority.

It was these practical considerations that gradually tilted Roosevelt towards Churchill's preferred strategy. The process was helped by continued British weakness in North Africa. There was a dawning realisation by the Americans that they could not allow the British to lose in the Mediterranean. In any event, the US commanders were also divided among themselves. The Anglophobe Admiral Ernest J. King, Commander-in-Chief of the US Fleet, continued to demand greater resources for the Pacific theatre, which had an inevitable knock-on effect on any supplies for France.

Then came the ill-fated Dieppe raid of August 1942; the next step up in Churchill's strategy of escalating raids against France. The aim had been to capture and briefly hold the town of Dieppe on the French shoreline; a complex amphibious tri-service operation on a scale not yet attempted by Mountbatten and his Combined Operations team.

The operation was preceded by a fraught exchange in the Cabinet Room on 30 June. Captain John Hughes-Hallett, now the naval adviser at Combined Operations, was given the unenviable task of presenting the plans to the Prime Minister:

Mr. Churchill suddenly turned to me and asked whether I could guarantee success! The C.I.G.S. [General Brooke, later Lord Alanbrooke] interrupted and told me not to reply. 'If he, or anyone else, could guarantee success,' he said, 'there would indeed be no object in doing the operation. It is just because no-one has the slightest idea what the outcome will be that the operation is necessary.' Mr. Churchill then said that this was not a moment at which he wanted to be taught adversity. 'In that case,' said Alanbrooke, 'you must abandon the idea of invading France because no responsible General will be associated with any planning for invasion until we have an operation at least of the size of the Dieppe raid behind us to study and base our plans upon.'

Operation Jubilee – Disaster at Dieppe

'. . . the very last thing they'd (the Germans) ever imagine is that we would be so stupid as to lay on the same operation again'. With these words, Vice Admiral Louis Mountbatten, commanding the Combined Operations Headquarters, authorised the planning for Operation Jubilee – an attack on the port of Dieppe – to proceed. It was a successor to Operation Rutter, also a planned attack on Dieppe, called off the month before. Six thousand Allied troops had been briefed in great secrecy on 3 July 1942 aboard their landing ships that their objective was Dieppe. However, with a six-week delay, it is inconceivable when Operation Jubilee was launched on 19 August, towards the same objective, that the Germans did not know that Dieppe was the focus of the attack. In Dieppe both German soldiers and French civilians were on edge. '*Tommy kommt*' (Tommy is coming) was a frequent exchange. They were ready.

The butcher's bill on 19 August – 3,623 men killed, wounded or taken prisoner of the 6,086 men who landed, largely from the Canadian 2nd Infantry Division – confirms the scale of the disaster that was Operation Jubilee. Proportionally, this was one the highest casualty rates in Western Europe in the Second World War. To this must be added the loss of a Royal Navy destroyer and 33 landing craft with a further 550 killed and wounded, and 100 Allied aircraft lost, mostly Spitfires and Hurricanes, with 109 airmen killed, wounded or captured. For comparison, German losses, on land at 591 killed or wounded and 48 aircraft downed, were modest. For Winston Churchill in Cairo, recovering from a bruising summit with Stalin in Moscow, the news of the failure of Jubilee was another bitter pill to swallow, less than two months since the fall of Tobruk in North Africa.

The purpose of Operation Jubilee had been to launch an amphibious assault on the German-occupied port of Dieppe, to hold the town and port for a short time and thereby test the feasibility of mounting a direct attack on an enemy-held port, before conducting a fighting withdrawal. Within the plan, there were to be landings on six separate beaches, of which all except one failed. To take a positive from this negative, one of the conclusions drawn after Jubilee was that when the Second Front in Europe would eventually be mounted, the assault must be guarded by the highest level of operational security, be conducted over open beaches and that the logistics must be through ad hoc harbours, the genesis of the improvised Mulberry harbours.

But if there were failings at the operational and tactical levels of war, Jubilee must be seen in the wider strategic context of the overall conduct of the war. Churchill was under huge pressure from both the Americans and the Russians to agree an early return to France, but the failure of Jubilee proved conclusively that Operation Sledgehammer – a return in force to northern Europe in 1942 – would fail and cast severe doubt that Operation Roundup – an invasion in 1943 – was also too risky to be contemplated. Although Churchill had hoped for more local success from Jubilee – largely to quell Stalin's complaints about British unwillingness to confront the Germans on land – he was next able to propose Operation Torch, an Anglo-American assault on the western North Africa coast. This, and the subsequent invasions of Sicily and southern Italy, bought time for a thorough analysis of the failings of Jubilee and for far better preparations to be made for Operation Overlord in 1944.

Having won the strategic argument with the Americans that although a policy of the defeat of Germany first had primacy, Churchill had also persuaded them that the route to success was via the Mediterranean and only later to return to France. Meanwhile, Stalin would have to be content with the diversion of German divisions away from Russia that the Mediterranean demanded, the round-the-clock bombing of Germany from English airfields and the supply of weapons delivered by the Arctic convoys. This all provided breathing space for the lessons of Jubilee to be analysed and absorbed.

Intelligence was a major failing. The reconnaissance and knowledge of the German dispositions at Dieppe was poor. Although the 10th Panzer Division was thought to be in reserve around Amiens, this was uncertain. The fighting capability of the defending German 302nd Static Division was unknown. Study of the topography, especially the nature of the beaches, was poor. The shingle beaches led to the bogging down and stranding of many of the tanks and other armoured vehicles. Cooperation between the landing and the air forces was inadequate and the fear of the loss of a capital ship meant that the Royal Navy refused to commit a battleship to onshore bombardment. Given the loss of the HMS *Prince of Wales* and HMS *Repulse* off Singapore the previous year, this was understandable, but the solution for the future was air superiority over the battlefield, not a refusal to commit valuable firepower. In 1942 there was much to learn. Mercifully, by Operation Overlord in 1944, these lessons had been learnt. However, the shadows of Gallipoli, Norway and now Jubilee did nothing to lessen Churchill's 'Black Dog' (the Victorian term he used for his depressive moods).

In the event, there was much to study. The failed operation was a stark reminder of the difficulties of conducting such an amphibious assault and consequently another nail in the coffin of Sledgehammer. Seizing an enemy-held port by frontal assault would not be easy. Brooke saw it as a lesson 'to the people who are clamouring for an invasion of France'. Churchill also preferred to view it as a lesson and would not 'hear of the word "failure"', but the lesson was surely that the Allies were not yet ready for a return to France. In the words of Professor Paul Kennedy, the psychological lesson of Dieppe was that when the Allies did come ashore in France, 'they were going to have to be very, very good'.

Hughes-Hallett observed it all from one of the accompanying naval ships. It fell on him to implement some of the lessons learnt. His key recommendation was the creation of a permanent assault force, to support further raiding and to commence the detailed training and preparation that would be needed for a return to the continent. As a result, he was ordered to form and command Force J – J for 'Jubilee', the codename for the Dieppe operation. Establishing his headquarters in Cowes on the Isle of Wight, he began with a handful of assault ships and a few flotillas of landing craft. This was an essential early step in creating the professional force for D-Day.

Churchill learnt of the outcome of the Dieppe raid while in the Middle East. He was about to return from his latest overseas trip. His mission had been twofold: to remove General Auchinleck from his command in North Africa and to meet for the first time with Marshal Stalin in Moscow. These two events were not unconnected. The change in command in Egypt was seen by Churchill as vital for restoring morale and re-energising the conflict against Rommel. Responsibility passed to General Alexander as the overall theatre commander, with General Montgomery – after the death of General 'Strafer' Gott when the plane carrying him was shot down – assuming command of the Eighth Army. Victory in the desert remained the immediate British priority. They needed to win the battle they were already fighting before they could focus on other fronts.

This was also the crux of the message that Churchill took to Moscow: namely that there would be no Second Front in France in 1942 and that the Anglo-American Allies had decided to prioritise

Operation Torch and attack French North Africa. The British Prime Minister would later compare taking this news to the Kremlin as like 'carrying a large lump of ice to the North Pole'.

> I do not like the job I have to do.
> I cannot think my views will go down well.
> Can I convince them of our settled view?
> Will Stalin use Caucasian oaths and yell?
> Or can I bind him with my midnight spell?
> I'm really feeling rather in a stew.
> It's not so hot a thing to have to sell.
> No Second Front in 1942.

Those lines form part of a poem called the 'Ballade of the Second Front', which was written out by General Wavell while sitting on the floor of the Liberator B-24 bomber carrying the British party back from Moscow to Tehran. In it, Wavell gives humorous voice to Churchill's anxieties going into the meeting. Despite an initial warm welcome, described by Churchill as 'totalitarian lavishness', the timing of a Second Front in France quickly dominated the discussions, with Stalin using a key meeting in his office in the Kremlin on 13 August to make his views only too clear.

According to Ian Jacob, one of Churchill's military advisers, who was brought in to take the minutes: 'Stalin appeared quite at home, and made his remarks in a very low, gentle, voice, with an occasional gesture of the right hand, and never looked the Prime Minister in the face.' But what Stalin said in his quiet measured tones was calculated to cut Churchill to the quick. The Germans were not supermen; the British Army lacked the courage to face them. Roosevelt and Churchill should honour their plans to seize the Cotentin Peninsula now. Ultimately, it took a Churchillian threat to leave Russia early, coupled with promises of a Second Front in 1943 and a private late-night eating-and-drinking session with Stalin (more totalitarian lavishness during which Stalin devoured a suckling pig) to ensure a cordial end to proceedings, but the British left with no doubts as to Soviet wishes.

And those wishes were shared by large sections of the British Parliament, press and public, who also felt that the country needed to do more to support their Soviet allies. From the autumn of 1942, this only intensified against the backdrop of the Battle of Stalingrad, which featured week after week in newspapers and cinemas as a heroic Russian defence against the German invaders, and one that contrasted with British surrender in Libya and Singapore. As Roosevelt had put it back in April: 'Your people & mine demand the establishment of a front to draw off pressure on the Russians, & these peoples are wise enough to see that the Russians are today killing more Germans & destroying more equipment than you and I put together.' The Red Cross Aid to Russia Fund raised its first million pounds for essential supplies and medical equipment from the British people in just three months between October and December 1941. And this in spite of all the domestic shortages. It would go on raising money for the rest of the war, through individual donations, flag days, concerts and a range of high-profile fundraising activities. Churchill could not ignore the groundswell of support for Russia at home, not least because it was very close to home indeed – with his wife Clementine chairing the Fund. He insisted on sending vital supplies to Russia via the dangerous Arctic convoy route to Archangel and Murmansk, he supported the Allied bombing of Germany, and he threw his weight behind Torch, but many – in Russia, America and Britain – continued to press for more. His friend and erstwhile rival, the media magnate Lord Beaverbrook, resigned from the Cabinet in February 1942 and used his newspapers to lead a campaign calling for a Second Front Now.

By the end of 1942, Churchill had secured the preferred British strategy of fighting in North Africa rather than France. He had done so in spite of opposition from both his American and Soviet allies and in the teeth of significant criticism and pressure at home. In reality, the adoption of the strategy was a recognition of British weakness and imperial overstretch. Both Roosevelt and Stalin ultimately had no option but to go along with it, as the Americans were not yet strong enough to invade France on their own (and were ultimately reliant on use of the United Kingdom as a forward base in order to do so), while the Russians – for all their hard words – were under attack and had no option but to accept any assistance that their Western allies could offer.

It is easy to see why D-Day gets knocked back to 1943. Neither the British nor the Americans believed a large-scale assault was feasible and Sledgehammer was seen as too limited and too risky. But it is less obvious why the Allied invasion of France does not happen until 1944. The answer lies partly in the law of unintended consequences. The decision to proceed with Operation Torch, and the operations that then flow from it, further delayed the build-up of forces in the United Kingdom. This was not immediately apparent to Churchill at the time. November 1942 was a good month for the Anglo-American armies. General Montgomery finally defeated Rommel at the Second Battle of El Alamein, achieving that long-awaited British victory, and began to advance across the Libyan desert from the east. Meanwhile, at the other end of North Africa, General Eisenhower landed in Morocco and Algeria and deployed eastwards. The Germans were now caught in a pincer movement.

This initial success led Churchill to resurvey the big picture. In a note to his Chiefs of Staff in early December he felt that the most important new factor was the impending German defeat in Russia, which might reduce 180 German divisions to 'little more than brigades', and which was likely to prevent the transfer of enemy troops from the Eastern to the Western theatre. It led him to produce an optimistic target schedule for 1943 that predicted the clearing of the North African shoreline by the end of January, the opening up of the Mediterranean by March, the assembly of the necessary landing craft for the cross-Channel operation in Britain by June, the completion of preparations for Roundup by July, and the liberation of France in August or September.

Unfortunately, it quickly became clear that those American and British pincers in North Africa would take much longer to close. The American-led ground troops in the west faced more initial opposition from Vichy French forces than anticipated, the political situation remained volatile, and their attempts to push towards Tunis were soon bogged down in wet weather and impassable roads. The British Eighth Army were initially able to exploit their victory in Egypt by crossing the Libyan desert, recapturing the port of Tobruk and advancing as far as the coastal city of Agheila. But thereafter, their advance was stalled by the difficulties of supply over such vast distances, the Germans having left the key port of Benghazi severely damaged. German resistance in Tunisia remained determined and stubborn, and in Rommel the Allies faced a capable commander with a sizeable army. Intelligence estimates were that he had fifty thousand Germans and thirty thousand Italians. Even allowing for the fact that they were not all frontline troops and lacked tanks and artillery, this was still a considerable obstacle and one that would take several months to defeat.

Meanwhile, in France, Hitler had responded to events by ending all vestiges of Vichy independence and further strengthen-ing his grip on the country. He was now busy fortifying the French coastline. In March 1942, Führer Directive 40 had recog-nised that Allied landings were now likely and correctly identified the risk of the British using landing craft, paratroopers and airborne forces to land on the beaches. It called for the defence of the more probable target areas and resulted in the building, between 1942 and 1944, of thousands of concrete gun emplace-ments, anti-aircraft batteries, and command and observation posts along the Atlantic shoreline. All of which would make a cross-Channel assault progressively more difficult. Meanwhile, continu-ing losses to U-boats in the Battle of the Atlantic were threatening British supply lines, and the war in the Pacific was eating into American shipping quotas. Churchill's schedule quickly looked unrealistic.

It was against this backdrop that Churchill and Roosevelt and their Combined Anglo-American Chiefs of Staff met again to consider their next steps. The conference took place in Anfa, on the outskirts of the Moroccan port city of Casablanca, between 14 and 24 January 1943. Symbolically this was an important moment. The American Commander-in-Chief, in spite of his disability (he was unable to walk unaided as a result of polio), had travelled across the Atlantic Ocean to meet with the British Prime Minister in the theatre where their troops were now fighting side by side. Harold Macmillan, the British Resident Minister in Algiers, likened it to the meeting of two great Roman Emperors. For both Churchill and Roosevelt, this was an escape from the routine of Washington and Whitehall, but it was also the moment to determine their joint war strategy going forward.

According to Ian Jacob, a key member of the British team, Churchill wanted to have his cake and eat it. He wanted to exploit success in as many theatres as possible, with the cleansing of the North African shoreline to be followed by the capture of Sicily and accompanied by the reconquest of Burma and a moderate invasion of France. He was determined to resist American demands for the primacy of France and prepared his team for a continuation of their strategy of gradual persuasion of the Americans, which he said must be like 'the dripping of water on stone'. He knew that General Marshall still favoured conducting Operation Roundup, the full-scale invasion of France, at the earliest opportunity. The head of the US Army remained convinced that the quickest way to Berlin lay through western France.

The issues were now extensively debated. The Anglo-American Combined Chiefs of Staff gathered in conference once or twice a day to thrash out a joint military strategy, while the President and Prime Minister used their rather more luxurious villas to host less formal meetings with key advisers concentrating on the big political issues. The recommendations of the Chiefs of Staff were then discussed and ratified at three plenary sessions attended by Churchill and Roosevelt on 15, 18 and 23 January. What emerged was a more or less complete acceptance of the preferred British viewpoint; the large-scale cross-Channel assault was to be further delayed, subordinated to further operations designed to secure the Mediterranean and reduce German strength before undertaking any major operation in France.

By the plenary meeting of 18 January, General Alan Brooke was able to report that after 'days of argument' the Combined Chiefs had now agreed the outline of a document 'setting forth the general strategic policy for 1943'. The priority was seen as dealing with the U-boat menace. This was to be the first charge on Allied resources, as it would 'provide security for all our operations'. Thereafter, the primacy of the war against Germany was confirmed over and above that against Japan, with the aim of forcing the enemy to withdraw ground and air forces from the Russian front. But this was to be accomplished by operations from North Africa, not the United Kingdom. The next target had been identified as the Italian island of Sicily. It was agreed that the Allies would continue 'preparing forces and assembling landing craft in England for a thrust across the Channel' but only 'in the event that the German strength in France decreases, either through withdrawal of her troops or because of an internal collapse'. The green light was given to specific operations in the Pacific, including the capture of Rabaul and Eastern New Guinea (a province in Papua New Guinea), and plans were laid for an end-of-year offensive in Burma and for bridgeheads across the Chindwin River. The maximum Combined Air Offensive was to be conducted against Germany from the United Kingdom, with a view to breaking German morale, and every effort was to be made to induce Turkey to enter the war on the Allied side.

General Brooke could hardly believe his luck. Churchill felt the same. This was an almost wholesale acceptance of their preferred British strategy. It was no doubt helped by the fact that the Americans were not as prepared or united in their views going into the meetings. Admiral King remained determined to see US naval operations in the Pacific, and these continued to draw heavily on American production quotas, especially for shipping and landing craft. The Americans would later complain that they were both outnumbered and outmanoeuvred by the British at Casablanca, but the records of the Casablanca meetings reveal many sound reasons why the President, Marshall and the Americans had little choice but to agree the joint strategy.

There were certainly lessons to be learnt from Torch that suggested further preparations were needed before attacking in France. The landings in Morocco had been hampered by the size of the Atlantic waves. Resistance in Algeria had been heavier than anticipated. And this had been an assault against a less well-defended shoreline. First contact with the Germans in Tunisia had highlighted the continued difficulty of facing a battle-hardened enemy. Operations in the Pacific could not simply be abandoned and were now competing for resources. The U-boat menace in the Atlantic made it more difficult to bring men and materials across the ocean in the numbers that would be required for a cross-Channel assault, especially while destroyers and escorts were committed to convoy duties, both across the Atlantic and to Russia. There remained huge logistical difficulties. The Americans did not yet have enough divisions available to secure and hold the North African shoreline, fight in the Pacific and countenance a major invasion of north-western Europe. There was still a shortage of shipping and of landing craft, especially tank-carrying craft. In contrast, a move against Sicily was easier to mount from North Africa, might knock Italy out of the war and would help the Allies secure the Mediterranean, reopening a faster shipping route from Europe to the Pacific and thereby releasing the necessary shipping for other theatres.

For Roosevelt and Churchill, delay remained another major political consideration. If the Allies simply stopped after securing North Africa and switched to building up forces for an assault on western France, there would be a considerable gap – while the required forces were assembled in Britain – during which their armies would not be engaging the enemy anywhere in Europe. At Casablanca, they were already concerned at the prospect of even a few months' delay between operations in Tunisia and Sicily. The optimum time for a cross-Channel operation, in terms of weather and tides, was between May and September. Issues of shipping and production meant that the requisite forces and landing craft could not be assembled in the UK in time for a spring or summer offensive. These factors, when taken together, made a large-scale assault in 1943 almost impossible. Better therefore to use the existing momentum in the Mediterranean and to prepare the ground for a major operation in 1944.

There was also a natural caution, arising from the level of complexity and the associated risk of failure, which led the Allied military planners towards building their relationship and refining their tactics in what was believed to be a safer theatre of operations. Dennis Wheatley, best known as a writer of thrillers and novels about the occult, was working just a few rooms away from the Prime Minister in the Treasury building as part of wartime intelligence, a member of the London Controlling Section charged with creating elaborate deception plans to protect British operations. As such, he was one of the few people allowed to read all of the War Cabinet, Defence Committee and Chiefs of Staff minutes. His view, admittedly expressed later with the benefit of hindsight, was that Churchill's perception of Roundup was not a mighty invasion, but 'as the codeword implies, a landing to "round up" any German units that might still be resisting after the defeat and disintegration of the German Army had been achieved by some other means'.

The Prime Minister's level of support for the cross-Channel operation certainly shifted from one moment to the next, depending on events and to whom he was speaking. Brooke became incensed in May 1943 at what he saw as the Prime Minister's inconsistency and his maddening desire 'to carry out ALL operations simultaneously irrespective of shortages of shipping!' Churchill wanted the flexibility to be able to exploit success when and where it happened, especially given how rare it had been before 1942, and he saw huge risks in putting all the British eggs in one basket. Hence, he was prepared to prod his commanders and to explore all options. It was also in his nature to constantly seek new outlets for action.

But after Casablanca, he was certainly not alone or at odds with Brooke in advocating further delay in France. This was the accepted strategy of the British Chiefs of Staff. In May 1943, at much the same time as Brooke was complaining about Churchill, Eisenhower recalled the British CIGS saying that 'he would be glad to reconsider the cross-Channel project, even to the extent of eliminating that bold concept from Allied strategy'. Brooke's diary from the same month records his exasperation with General Marshall for still wanting to push straight into France, prompting his later reflection that 'the Americans still failed to grasp how we were preparing for a re-entry into France through our actions in the Mediterranean'. There was an undeniable difference in emphasis between the Allies, though the debate was far more complex than it is sometimes now portrayed.

What Churchill and Roosevelt did agree on at Casablanca was the need to impose unconditional surrender on Germany. This sent a clear signal to their absent Soviet ally, to neutral powers and to their opponents that they were going to see things through to the end.

By 1943, the main steps on that long road had been agreed. The Mediterranean would be the immediate priority, but preparations would be stepped up for a larger entry into France in early 1944. It was a compromise, but the fact that the President, Marshall and Eisenhower all ultimately agreed on it was a recognition that this provided the surest and safest way to victory at what they believed would be the lowest cost. With hindsight and our knowledge of the success of Overlord, it is a decision that has been and can be challenged, but from the military perspective there were clearly a number of obstacles that had to be overcome before any large-scale cross-Channel operation could be launched.

Yet this does not mean that Churchill was prepared to abandon operations in France altogether. At the plenary meeting of the Casablanca Conference on 18 January he returned to the idea of a more limited assault, advocating seizing and holding a bridgehead across the Channel. In 1942 he had opposed Operation Sledgehammer; now, in 1943, he told the Combined Chiefs of Staff that he looked more favourably on it and that he thought it should be given a 'sharper point', including a commander and a target date. The President agreed and suggested preparing a schedule for the build-up of forces month by month. He also suggested there should be a British commander. Churchill replied that the question of command should be determined later but that they should designate a British commander at this time 'who could undertake the planning of the operation'. Ultimately, he felt that command of such an operation should be held by an officer of the country furnishing the largest number of troops. In January 1943, it was clear that any limited cross-Channel operation conducted in the short term would have to be a primarily British affair as there was only one American division in the UK.

The speed of any American build-up was revisited in the final plenary meeting of 23 January. When Churchill expressed disappointment that there would only be four fully equipped American divisions in the United Kingdom by 15 August 1943, he was told by Marshall that the figure would probably be five and that by the end of the year there might be as many as nineteen. Churchill wondered whether this could be speeded up by using the luxury trans-Atlantic liners as troop carriers, or by reducing the amount of equipment needed to support the troops, estimated at an initial 8 tons per man with a further 1.3 tons per man per month. He also questioned whether savings could be made on vehicles and reserves, stating that 'Fighting men for the beaches were the prime essential.' His comments must have raised eyebrows among the military commanders, but here was a theme to which Churchill would return. He remained a product of the Victorian army and was not always capable of grasping the enormous logistical tail required by a modern army.

As 1943 began, the invasion of France had been deferred, not cancelled. Principles had been laid down for its command and planning. Many of the challenges identified at Casablanca would now influence its development. For Churchill, it was about seizing the immediate opportunity. There was an obvious advantage in going into Sicily and securing the Mediterranean. France remained a far riskier proposition and he preferred to hold back, to see the enemy weakened, to build up forces and to be ready to move across the Channel if and when circumstances changed.

GO HOME.

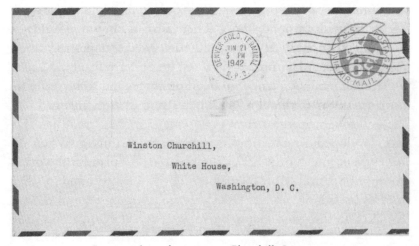

Letter and envelope sent to Churchill, June 1942

4

It Won't Work, But You Must
Bloody Well Make It

'. . . all right if you won't play with us in the Mediterranean
we won't play with you in the English Channel'.

IT WAS THE year 1943 that made D-Day possible. In January, at
the Casablanca Conference, it still seemed a remote possibility;
an operation to be planned for but not necessarily undertaken.
Churchill and Roosevelt had taken the decision to appoint a
commander, but as of yet there was no real plan and no troops to
command. As a result, it was agreed not to appoint a Supreme
Commander but, in their stead, to have someone charged with
producing the detailed planning. General Frederick Morgan was
given the role and designated Chief of Staff to the (non-existent)
Supreme Allied Commander (COSSAC). His interview was a
'delightful visit for lunch at Chequers' on 4 April with the Prime
Minister. Churchill duly reported back that Morgan seemed 'a
capable and sensible officer'.

Morgan was not a battlefield commander. He had served as an
artillery officer in the First World War and subsequently in India.
He had fought in the retreat from France in 1940 and thereafter
had developed a reputation for operational planning. When the
Allies went into North Africa, he was asked to plan for the occupation of Spanish Morocco; when they looked to build on their
success in Tunisia, he was tasked with considering an invasion of
Sardinia. In the event, neither plan was needed. Morgan was used

to his projects going nowhere and was under no illusions about the strange and uncertain nature of his latest role. His Staff College Report from 1928 noted that he 'Has a keen but kindly sense of humour which should prove a great asset to him.' He was going to need it. Upon his appointment General Brooke told him, 'Well, there it is. It won't work, but you must bloody well make it.' Morgan later wrote that, 'There followed months of toil in an atmosphere of persisting doubt and uncertainty. Not until the last moment could I be sure that I had not laboured in vain, had not merely contributed one more project to the vast library of rejects.'

Churchill minuted his Chiefs of Staff on 18 April 1943 regarding the new COSSAC role. At Casablanca he had indicated that he was prepared to revisit Sledgehammer and might be in favour of a limited assault on France within the next year, especially in the light of a German defeat on the Eastern Front. Now, he reversed that view, writing: 'A German collapse being extremely unlikely and not to be counted upon this year, and neither American reinforcements nor landing-craft being available, we cannot do "Sledgehammer" in 1943.' Instead, General Morgan should work with Fighter Command and Combined Operations to prepare an 'amphibious feint' designed to bring about a major air battle and reduce the power of the Luftwaffe. He should deploy 'Camouflage and pretence on the most elaborate scale' to keep alive the threat of the invasion and pin the enemy in the west, and only finally should he continue Bolero, the gradual build-up of forces, and the 'long-term study' for Roundup, the major cross-Channel assault, while also making 'Month-to-month arrangements in case of a German collapse.' In case there was any doubt about the level of priority Churchill was applying to this new role, the Prime Minister then specified that 'General Morgan's organisation does not require to be very large or numerous'. In an earlier minute to Brooke, he had made clear that there was no use in proceeding with 'the creation of this vast complicated staff when so far only one American division has reached this country and there are no immediate prospects of heavy reinforcements'.

Churchill's focus was clearly on the Mediterranean and on the forthcoming operation against Sicily. The orders that were then issued to General Morgan by the Chiefs of Staff were more diplomatically phrased but amounted to much the same. The Allied object was the defeat of the German fighting forces in north-west Europe:

> To this end the Combined Chiefs of Staff will endeavour to assemble the strongest possible forces (subject to prior commitment in other theatres) in constant readiness to re-enter the Continent if German resistance is weakened to the required extent in 1943. In the meantime, the Combined Chiefs of Staff must be prepared to order such limited operations as may be practical with the forces and material available.

In particular, Morgan and his team were tasked with preparing three sets of plans. First, was the elaborate camouflage and deception scheme, designed to extend over the entire summer and keep alive the German expectation of a cross-Channel assault in 1943. This was intended to pin down enemy forces in France, thereby easing pressure on the Russians on the Eastern Front and the British-American armies in the Mediterranean. The need to undertake Churchill's amphibious feint was specified. Second, there was to be a plan for a return to the continent in the event of German disintegration 'at any time from now onwards with whatever forces may be available at the time'. And third, Morgan was to plan for a full-scale assault against the continent in 1944 'as early as possible'.

Morgan was hampered by the fact that his was an administrative headquarters with no operational forces under its direct command and reliant on cooperation with others. The army forces earmarked for the invasion of Europe were the First Canadian and Second British Armies, together forming the Twenty-First Army Group, but these were under the control of General Paget as Commander-in-Chief Home Forces; a situation mirrored in the American Army where General Devers commanded the forces in the UK being built up for a campaign in France. Air Marshal Leigh-Mallory would soon assume command for the Allied Expeditionary Air Force and Admiral Little was Commander-in-Chief, Portsmouth. Cutting across all of this was the role already given to Mountbatten and his Combined Operations HQ, which effectively gave them an interest in any amphibious operation. This was the strange new world that Hughes-Hallett found himself navigating. In charge of the naval assault force for any operation against France, he was reporting to Combined Operations, while drawing on naval resources from Portsmouth and working with Morgan's new team, for which he was soon acting as the naval chief of staff. In his words, 'a good deal of "Coffee-housing" went on between General Morgan and senior officers at COHQ'.

It is from this point, as Morgan's team gets to work in May 1943, that Operation Roundup – the invasion of northern France – is renamed as Overlord. But its development still had a long way to go. The last chapter has shown that its planning could not be considered in isolation. It was part of a global war that saw Churchill and Roosevelt struggling to manage limited resources, to balance the competing demands upon them and to respond to ever-changing events. Delay and slow progress were in part the result of prioritising the war in North Africa and the Mediterranean, but the reason for that prioritisation was that a number of preconditions had to be met before the Allied liberation of France could be seriously contemplated. These might be summarised as follows:

- A sophisticated level of British and American inter-service cooperation
- Control of the seas
- Mastery of the air
- A huge build-up of men and materials
- A greatly weakened and overstretched enemy
- The existence of enough landing craft to get the army safely ashore and keep them supplied
- The development of officers and troops with real combat experience and high morale

It is worth looking at each one of these in turn. Could any of these preconditions have been met before the spring of 1944?

A sophisticated level of British and American inter-service cooperation

John Martin was Churchill's Principal Private Secretary and accompanied his boss to Washington DC in June 1942. The visit was not low key and the presence of the British Prime Minister as a guest of the President in the White House was well known. A letter, postmarked from Denver, Colorado, survives in Martin's papers. It was simply addressed to 'Winston Churchill, White House, Washington D.C.' Once opened, its contents were even more succinct. Just two anonymous type-script words on an otherwise blank sheet of paper: 'Go Home'. With the benefit of hindsight, much of what has been written about the wartime partnership between Britain and America has focused on its closeness, on the creation of a special rela-tionship (a term that was coined by Churchill but not popular-ised by him until after the war when he delivered his famous iron curtain speech at Westminster College, Fulton, Missouri, in 1946). We tend to forget that these sentiments of brother-hood were far from universally shared on either side of the Atlantic in 1942. Elements of American public opinion were still fiercely isolationist and anti-British, just as elements in Britain were pro-Russian and anti-American.

From the top down, from the Prime Minister and President, it took time to build the close political and military ties and develop the trust and teamwork that underpinned the alliance and made Overlord possible. The Anglo-American and inter-service coop-eration, planning and staff work needed to make an assault against Hitler's Fortress Europe was never going to be produced by desk clerks working in offices; it had to be forged and tested in war. There had been some secret British–American staff talks prior to Pearl Harbor. Immediately afterwards, a clear partnership framework had been established with the creation of the Combined Chiefs of Staff Committee. This brought together the Joint Service Chiefs of each country (the military heads of their respective army, air and naval forces) and gave the British Chiefs of Staff permanent representation in Washington DC, establishing a constant communication channel with their American counterparts. The big strategic decisions concerning Overlord and D-Day were taken at a series of major conferences throughout 1943, culminating in the Tehran Conference in November attended by Marshal Stalin for the Soviet Union. (For more information about these conferences, see pp. 116–118.) These meetings were often difficult, but they allowed a common strategy to be hammered out. Central to Allied cooperation was the principle, adopted from early 1942, that British forces would serve under an American theatre commander and vice versa. Whichever country had the largest forces in the theatre would have the command. Churchill played a clear role in creating this framework, but it was one thing to establish a structure, another to build trust and allay national suspicions and rivalries.

Back at COSSAC, General Morgan and his American deputy General Barker inevitably found themselves at the centre of these mutual national suspicions. General Barker 'earned for himself the reputation in his own service of being "sold out to the British"', while General Morgan's 'own efforts at internationality soon caused me to be regarded . . . as "sold out to the Yanks"'. Generally, Morgan found that when meeting the British authorities about Overlord 'one had to be conscious of their scepticism towards the whole affair' and 'their idea of co-operation was that others should co-operate with them and not vice-versa'. There were moments when he felt that 'it was not easy to convince oneself of British bona fides'. With the Americans 'it was more a matter of keeping bubbling enthusiasm within practical bounds' while managing their reservations about British adventuring in the Mediterranean, the Balkans and the Aegean. To the British, Eisenhower was just a 'politico-military figurehead'; to the Americans, Montgomery was massively over-rated.

At the highest levels, Churchill, Eisenhower and Morgan all

sought to combat these national prejudices by bringing people together. Churchill led by example, entertaining British and American commanders at Downing Street and Chequers. He also gave his blessing to a Churchill Club, which was created in central London in one of the evacuated houses of Westminster School. Elaborately decorated by Robert Lutyens and managed by Pamela Churchill (later Harriman), the Prime Minister's daughter-in-law and a consummate hostess and networker, it was open to all American and Dominion officers and other ranks with a university education; running concerts and lectures to expose them to British history, culture and society. On a more practical level, General Morgan made good use of the restaurant and bar at his Norfolk House headquarters in St James's Square to bring together British and American team members and visitors. It set the precedent for later developments. Come April 1944, Harry Butcher would report that camaraderie was 'helped a lot by the fact that we have American coffee at our desks around eleven each morning and British tea around five'.

When Eisenhower was given command of Torch, a British admiral, Andrew Cunningham, was appointed as his naval commander for the operation. After Casablanca, when he became the Allied Supreme Commander in North Africa, Ike had British deputies for all three services – Cunningham for the navy, Tedder for the air and Alexander for the army. When Cunningham was recalled to London as the new First Sea Lord, he was replaced by another Brit, Admiral Ramsay, architect of the Dunkirk evacuation, who had worked on the initial plans for Roundup and coordinated the naval aspect of the Sicilian campaign. In North Africa and Sicily, US Generals Bradley and Patton served alongside British Generals Montgomery and Anderson. Alexander would go on to become the theatre commander in Italy, but Eisenhower took Montgomery, Ramsay and Tedder with him when he became the Overlord commander. They may not have always agreed, and elements of personal rivalry and competition undoubtedly remained and sometimes loomed large (with Montgomery and Patton the worst offenders), but they knew each other well and – for the most part – could work together well.

This bond was not forged instantaneously. In 1942 Eisenhower was acutely aware that the

> whole basis of our higher organization was new. Time and again during the summer old army friends warned me that the conception of Allied unity which we took as the foundation of our command scheme was impracticable and impossible; that any commander placed in my position was foredoomed to failure and could become nothing but a scapegoat to carry the odium of defeat for the whole operation.

And there were certainly incidents. During the final stages of the Tunisian campaign in March 1943, the British corps commander, General Sir John Crocker, was highly critical of the performance of an American division when talking to the press, prompting much British and American antagonism and bad blood. However, by June 1943, with North Africa cleared and the Allies poised to invade Sicily, Churchill was praising Eisenhower's leadership and General Marshall was prepared to argue that the Germans' greatest discomfort now came not so much from their loss of troops as 'from the fact that the United States and Great Britain have worked so well as a team'. It was in North Africa in 1942–43 that the commanders for Overlord gained their first experience of working together against the common enemy: the same enemy commander in General Erwin Rommel that they would face one and a half years later in Normandy.

The common language no doubt made things easier, but cultural differences remained. When Eisenhower supported a plan for the British to open up their homes to Americans, he was told by Mr Stevenson, head of the American Red Cross, that it would typically take two or three years before a British family would invite a stranger in! Tensions grew in proportion to the increasing number of American troops in Britain. The racist treatment of Black American service personnel by their White American counterparts led to objections from some British citizens. Churchill dodged questions on the issue in the House of Commons in September 1942 and the matter soon ended up before the British War Cabinet on 13 October. It was decided that while the UK authorities would do nothing to interfere with segregation within the American Army, they would not allow it to be enforced within British military or civil establishments. Instead – in papers that certainly seem racist today – they suggested explaining the White American viewpoint to British audiences while urging the British to avoid contact with Black African Americans. The Cabinet emphasis was clearly on trying to avoid conflict with their US allies. This did not stop other quarrels arising between British and American soldiers, young men with pent-up energy, who routinely fought one another on the streets of the southern port towns, like Southampton, in which they were now garrisoned. Dinners and drinks for officers only went so far. The special relationship was real and worked, but like all relationships it needed time and always had its limits.

Control of the seas

In his own words, the only thing that ever really frightened Churchill during the war was the U-boat peril: 'I was even more anxious about this battle than I had been about the glorious air fight called the Battle of Britain.'

He had served twice as First Lord of the Admiralty, the civilian minister with responsibility for the British Royal Navy; first in 1911–15 at the beginning of the First World War and then again for a similar period at the beginning of the Second in 1939–40. While neither tenure had been a universal success, with both marked by friction with his admirals, Churchill remained supremely confident in his own understanding and knowledge of naval matters. By the end of 1942, it was clear to him and to the

President that the Battle of the Atlantic would have to take precedence over all other theatres of operation, including any cross-Channel assault.

It was a battle that was expressed in figures – Allied merchant shipping losses in one column, numbers of German U-boats (submarines) sunk in another; production numbers versus losses on both sides. Churchill was self-deprecating about his own mathematical abilities. In his autobiographical memoir *My Early Life*, written in 1930, he described how:

> I had a feeling once about Mathematics, that I saw it all – Depth beyond depth was revealed to me – the Byss and Abyss. I saw, as one might see the transit of Venus – or even the Lord Mayor's show, a quantity passing through infinity and changing its sign from plus to minus. I saw exactly how it happened and why the tergiversation was inevitable: and how the one step involved all the others. It was like politics. But it was after dinner and I let it go!

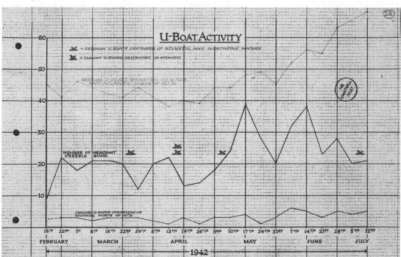

Chart showing U-Boat activity, February – July 1942

One way in which Churchill digested the huge amount of information arriving on his desk was to have the complex figures and statistics converted into graphs and charts. Hand-drawn specially for him, these colourful documents presented the realities behind the figures in a highly visual and easily comprehensible manner. The message they were conveying about the loss of Allied merchant shipping in the Atlantic was unmistakable, and Churchill would later write: 'How willingly would I have exchanged a full-scale attempt at invasion for this shapeless, measureless peril, expressed in charts, curves and statistics!'

The backdrop to the Casablanca Conference in January 1943 was a crisis in the Atlantic. The Germans now had more than two hundred operational U-boats hunting in wolf packs and concentrating their efforts in the gap that existed mid-ocean where their submarines could not be harried by air attack, the Allies lacking the range to reach them from their bases in Newfoundland and Iceland. The preceding year, 1942, had seen the loss of 1,664 Allied merchant ships, nearly 8 million tons. Despite the huge production capacity of the United States, the Germans were still sinking ships faster than the Allies could construct them while simultaneously building U-boats faster than they were being lost. Imports were falling and oil supplies, on which the Allied war effort ultimately depended, were dangerously low.

Britain was an island, cut off from most of neighbouring mainland Europe by Hitler's occupation, and dependent – in an age before large-scale commercial air freight – on imports by sea for her survival. With traffic through the Mediterranean almost impossible, her main supply routes were now coming across the Atlantic Ocean. If these could not be maintained, the country might be brought to its knees and forced to negotiate. In any event, a heavily besieged country would not be in a position to act as a forward base for an Allied liberation of France. Not only did the German U-boat campaign threaten the American ability to assemble troops and materials in Britain, it also diverted British and US naval resources into defending the merchant convoys, thereby hampering their ability to take the offensive in the Channel.

It was a battle that the young Christian Oldham watched

unfold. Born in 1920, she had felt compelled to do her bit and, as the daughter of an admiral, quickly realised that she had no real option but to join the Wrens (the Women's Royal Naval Service). After basic training, she took an administrative post at the Wrens HQ near London's Admiralty Arch. Like Joan Bright she worked through the Blitz, stealing moments of pleasure attending concerts and theatre performances as the bombs fell. A period in charge of a degaussing range in East Tilbury soon followed, demagnetising the hulls of merchant ships so that they would not fall prey to magnetic mines. As Christian grew in confidence, so she sought more responsibility.

In early 1942 she qualified as an officer. Her job was to oversee the accurate plotting of the movement of ships at sea and she assumed responsibility for teams of Wrens, first in Plymouth, then Edinburgh and ultimately Belfast – all vital control centres in the battle for the Atlantic. The work could involve fifteen-hour shifts relaying the latest radar sightings and signals intelligence information, mapping the progress of the Allied convoys and recording the sinkings. It left her in no doubt that, 'We had to win the Battle of the Atlantic. Losing it would mean losing the war altogether.'

Small wonder then that at Casablanca this threat was recognised by the combined Allied leadership, who stated that 'measures to be taken to combat the submarine menace are a first charge on the resources of the United Nations [the preferred US term for all countries fighting the Axis powers] and provide security for all our operations'.

It took the first half of 1943 to win the Battle of the Atlantic and establish command of the seas. This was achieved by a combination of resources, tactics, technology and intelligence. Churchill used the convening power of his office to bring together the relevant authorities in a new Anti-U-boat Committee that helped coordinate the British response across the armed services and government departments. He ordered the suspension of the Arctic convoys, carrying much-needed supplies to Russia, and concentrated all British naval escorts in the Atlantic. Pressure was applied to speed up delivery of Liberator aircraft with very long-range capabilities, thereby helping to close the gaps in air cover. New technology was introduced. Short-wave radar, undetectable by the U-boats, allowed British planes to detect enemy submarines on the surface. New forward-throwing anti-submarine mortars were introduced. Efforts to bomb U-boat docks and production facilities were largely unsuccessful due to the strength of the concrete pens, but the introduction of new 'Support Groups' of naval ships, independent of the convoys, dedicated to hunting, locating and destroying U-boats, made a huge impact, especially when accompanied by escort carriers (normally merchant ships converted to carry planes), effectively eliminating all air gaps and allowing aircraft to put up defensive screens around convoys and take the fight directly to the enemy.

What was not apparent at the time, nor allowed to be included in the early histories of the war at sea, was the complementary role played by intelligence. The change in British cyphers helped hide the convoys from the sharp eyes of German codebreakers, while the British breaking of the German naval Shark settings for U-boat traffic by the team at Bletchley Park is what helped guide the new support groups to their targets. By May 1943, the situation in the Atlantic was in the process of being transformed.

Not that this was immediately obvious at the time. In Belfast, Christian anxiously plotted the course of ONS-5, a slow convoy of forty-three ships bound for North America, following its tortuous progress through heavy Atlantic seas and then watching in alarm as a huge U-boat wolf pack closed in and began to cause havoc. 'Signal after signal came in and the teleprinter buzzed on relentlessly.' On this occasion, her professionalism masked a specific personal agony. Her new fiancé John was the First Lieutenant on board the destroyer HMS *Oribi*. At one point his ship rammed U 125. Fortunately, *Oribi* remained afloat and John was unscathed (and would go on to marry Christian). The U-boat went down.

This convoy sailed at a turning point. The Germans were now taking heavy losses and Admiral Dönitz withdrew his submarines from the Atlantic, an essential prerequisite to Overlord. It still took time to confirm the success and then capitalise on it by building up forces and supplies in Britain, but the Allies were now in a position to divert naval resources to offensive operations against the continent. Yet considerable risks remained. The U-boats, safe in their heavily protected pens on the French coast, might still play a role in trying to prevent any cross-Channel attack. They could also rely on support from the flotillas of small, fast, torpedo-wielding E-boats operating out of Cherbourg or Le Havre; ships that were capable of both defensive minelaying and attacks on Allied landing craft.

Mastery of the air

Mastery of the air was just as important to the success of Overlord as command of the seas. In 1942 the British had pushed back against Sledgehammer, the more limited operation in Brittany or Normandy, on the grounds that their fighter force would be eaten up very quickly by continual engagement with the enemy above the continent. These fears had seemed justified by the strength of the German Air Force over Dieppe during the subsequent raid in August. In any air battle over France, the Germans would enjoy the home advantage of being closer to their bases and being able to refuel more quickly. Air supremacy was therefore felt to be an important prerequisite to a successful invasion of Europe, particularly one that was intended to push on into Germany. One of Churchill's essential preconditions for Overlord was 'That there must be a substantial reduction in the strength of the German fighter aircraft in North-West Europe before the assault took place.'

The Allied strategy was built around a policy of attrition and dispersal, accompanied by huge production. The aim was to build up British and American capacity while systematically reducing that of Germany and Italy through sustained bombing of industrial centres, including the synthetic oil plants and ball-bearing factories that provided the Luftwaffe with their aviation fuel and vital components. In so doing, Churchill and Roosevelt initially also hoped to demonstrate to Stalin that they were diverting German air forces away from the Eastern Front.

The Allied strategy that emerged from the Casablanca Conference was to intensify the bombing of Germany to destroy enemy morale and production capacity, while maintaining operations in the Mediterranean and the threat of operations against France from Britain. Churchill's orders to General Morgan were that he should prioritise deception operations designed to lure the Luftwaffe from France into a general air battle that would reduce their strength. Some of the resulting deception measures and plans would prove far more successful than others, but it was not over the Channel but rather on the Russian front that the power of the German Air Force was ultimately broken.

Indeed, it is somewhat ironic, given that the Western Allies had hoped to use air power to relieve pressure on the Soviet Union, that the supposedly far inferior Red Air Force now played a key role in reducing German air power. In part, this was by sheer weight of numbers. By the summer of 1943 the Soviets were able to mobilise about 10,000 frontline aircraft, while the total German forces in the West and the East only numbered 3,551 serviceable combat planes. Both Soviet and American production capacity was far greater than that of Germany, and their production centres were out of the range of possible German attacks. The fall of Mussolini and the Italian armistice of September 1943 further increased the pressure on the Luftwaffe, removing the Italian air force, the Regia Aeronautica, from the Mediterranean theatre. The Germans were increasingly unable to compete, but it took time to build Allied forces up while grinding the Luftwaffe down. As with the war at sea, 1943 witnessed the decisive shift in the balance of power.

Yet another factor was the relentless bombing of Germany by the Allies. It was a strategy that Churchill had endorsed from the moment he became Prime Minister, one of the few ways in which he had been able to take the fight to the enemy. But again, it took time. Nineteen forty-two saw both the arrival of the American 8th Air Force in Britain and the appointment of the single-minded

Air Marshal Arthur Harris as head of British Bomber Command. Harris favoured the area bombing of German cities and production centres, and introduced larger-scale raids. The Casablanca Conference further increased the tempo, unleashing Operation Pointblank against German military and industrial targets. With the Americans bombing Germany by day and the RAF at night, the Luftwaffe were forced to divert more and more resources to the defence of the German homeland.

By February 1944, the Allies' own analysis was that the completion of Operation Pointblank was in sight. The American Economic Warfare Division calculated that German single-engine fighter production had been reduced from 950 per month down to 250, with twin-engine fighter production down from 225 to 50, and output of crucial ball-bearings cut by 40–50 per cent.

But it was not all about numbers. Allied tactics were also more flexible; allowing air resources to be switched more easily between theatres and operations – playing a strategic role in bombing one moment and a tactical one in supporting ground troops the next. Each theatre had an independent air command working alongside the army theatre commander. This is not to say that all was peace and harmony. In a future chapter we will look at the intense debate that raged around bombing strategy in the immediate prelude to D-Day, but the international and inter-service Allied command structures allowed these issues to be discussed and resolved. Suffice it to say that by the end of 1943, the Allies had the numbers, the experience and the confidence in the air to contemplate Overlord.

That grand narrative is reflected in the personal stories of countless individuals, many of them now lost to history. On 3 July 1941, Roland MacKenzie walked into a recruiting office in Calgary and volunteered for the Royal Canadian Air Force. A banker by profession for the last thirteen years, having left school at sixteen, he was described by his interviewing officer as: '29 years old, 5 foot ten, 145 lbs, confident, easy, upright, neat, conservative, clean, slender, of clear speech, quick, deliberate, alert, sincere and reserved'. He had no prior flying experience but was one of many Canadians who still felt a sufficiently strong connection with Britain to put his life on hold and in danger for the next four years. By September 1942, he had literally graduated with flying colours from the pilot training school in Saskatoon and was soon entrusted with training others, itself an often-dangerous task. Roland was part of the huge expansion in men and materials that made Overlord possible. In June 1943 he was sent to the United Kingdom and began to train on bombers. A poignant manuscript note in his logbook survives: 'Through Adversity to the Stars – 6 weeks of life in Bomber Command 1 in 3 chance to survive.' He was now preparing for the role he would play in supporting D-Day and was only too aware of the risks.

The Allies certainly had a large pool from which to draw. Their bomber and fighter crews came from around the Empire and Commonwealth; from Canada to the Caribbean. David Olusoga, in his book *Black and British*, has reminded us that over one hundred men from the West Indies were decorated for their service with the RAF or Royal Canadian Air Force.

A huge build-up of men and materials

The build-up of American and other national forces in Britain had started in the immediate aftermath of Pearl Harbor, but it had initially been small. The 34th American Division had arrived in Northern Ireland in January 1942, followed by the first detachments of the United States 8th Air Force in southern England the following month. A year later, there were over a thousand American aircraft in the country, many engaged in the bombing of Germany. It had taken longer to assemble substantial ground forces. Operation Torch and the diversion of the American troops to North Africa had meant that, as late as early 1943, there was only one US division in the UK. Nor was it possible simply to transfer large numbers across the Atlantic without putting in place the substantial infrastructure that would be needed to sustain them.

In May 1942, Churchill authorised the creation of a Bolero

Committee in London to consider the requirements of an increased American presence. This involved taking agricultural land for the building of aerodromes and training areas. The British were already anticipating receiving over one million American service personnel and having to build in excess of seven hundred aerodromes. With manpower resources already stretched, this was not something that could be achieved immediately, especially while shipping remained under threat in the Atlantic. It took time to build up the Allied forces, just as it took time to wear the enemy down.

A greatly weakened and overstretched enemy

Yet perhaps the real turning of the tide was one that Churchill himself chose to largely downplay in his Cold War-era history of the Second World War, and that was the smashing of the German Army on the Eastern Front in Russia in 1943. It is noticeable that he devotes only six pages to the siege of Stalingrad (now Volgograd) in Volume IV and just three pages to the Battle of Kursk in Volume V. Yet these huge land battles, fought by enormous armies, far larger than those deployed by the British and Americans in North Africa or the Mediterranean, accounted for the vast majority of German combat losses. By the autumn, the Red Army had pushed the Wehrmacht back hundreds of miles on a huge front and had retaken Kiev in the Ukraine.

It is easy to see why Churchill might not want to focus attention on the scale of the Russian success. Much of the original rationale for attacking in France had been to relieve pressure on the Russians. Throughout 1942, he remained acutely conscious that the Russians were still killing more Germans and destroying more equipment than the British and Americans put together. In early 1943, when Moscow was informed of the decision taken at Casablanca to attack Sicily rather than France, it caused a near breakdown in British relations with the Soviet Union. In March, Stalin denounced Churchill for reneging on repeated promises to establish a Second Front in Western Europe in 1943, writing: 'I deem it my duty to warn you in the strongest possible manner how dangerous would be from the viewpoint of our common cause further delay in the opening of the second front in France . . . about which I feel I cannot be silent.' In private, Churchill was prepared to admit that he felt 'so very conscious of the poor contribution the British and American armies are making in only engaging perhaps a dozen German divisions during the greater part of this year'.

But the nature of the Allied fear about the Soviet Union was also changing. In 1942 their worry had been that the Russians might collapse and that a limited intervention in France might be required as a last-ditch measure to divert German attention and help prop them up. By the middle of 1943, the tables had turned. The sheer scale of Soviet success on the battlefield introduced a new element into Allied planning, namely the fear that Germany might collapse completely leaving the Soviets in possession of large swathes of the continent. That was not the outcome that Britain had gone to war for in 1939.

The Germans were certainly becoming increasingly stretched. In February 1943, British military intelligence was observing the withdrawal of troops from France to the Russian and North African theatres and concluded that thirty enemy divisions had been lost or capitulated at Stalingrad. Of equal significance was the dilution in quality of the German Army, which hitherto had seemed so strong. Divisions were being re-formed and sent into battle with untrained troops, a shortfall of numbers and a lack of equipment, while the transfer of forces from one operational theatre to another suggested that their reserves were running low.

Another of Churchill's preconditions for D-Day was 'That there should not be more than twelve mobile German divisions in Northern France at the time the operation was launched, and that it must not be possible for the Germans to build up more than fifteen divisions in the succeeding two months.' The numbers were going in the right direction, especially when size and quality of German divisions was taken into account, but in February

1943, British intelligence was still indicating that the Germans had thirty operational divisions in France and the Low Countries. Unfortunately, this number would rise as the Germans began to anticipate the Allied offensive in France.

Should the Allies have gone into France in strength in 1943, as some American commentators clearly felt at the time, and some historians have argued since? It is of course impossible to know what the result would have been, but looked at from Westminster or the White House it remained a very risky proposition. Until at least halfway through 1943, Germany still threatened Britain's supply lines across the Atlantic, had the ability to mount a significant air defence over France, and might still have been able to transfer large numbers of troops from Russia and the Mediterranean – especially as the price for a cross-Channel assault in 1943 would have been the Allies stopping after their victory in Tunisia and leaving Italy as an enemy power and the Mediterranean as a contested sea. Even then, it was uncertain that they would have been able to build up sufficient forces fast enough to take on a less-weakened enemy at an earlier date in France. There would have been a period of inactivity that might have jarred with British and American public opinion at home, simultaneously allowing the Germans to further strengthen their defences in France. The result of a repulsed invasion – a Dieppe on a far grander scale – would have had huge repercussions for Allied war strategy. It seems unlikely that Churchill's government would have been able to survive such a catastrophic defeat. Roosevelt, too, would have come under increased political pressure and might have had to refocus American efforts on the Pacific. The morale of the Allies and the countries of the Empire and Commonwealth would have been severely shaken, that of Germany strengthened, perhaps allowing her to regroup and stabilise on the Eastern Front. All this is of course in the realm of the counter-factual, but it is the sort of speculation that Churchill, the President, the Combined Chiefs of Staff and their joint planners were obliged to engage in on a daily basis.

The existence of enough landing craft to get the army safely ashore and keep them supplied

The ability to deliver the troops and their equipment onto the beaches is an often-overlooked factor in the success of D-Day. Britain and the United States had large navies and could get their armies across the Channel, but without the control of large deep-water ports (which were inevitably going to be heavily defended) they had no way of getting them ashore. Planning for D-Day was dependent upon securing the necessary number and variety of landing ships and craft. These were essential for any amphibious operation, and they simply did not exist in any significant numbers at the beginning of the war. A report of April 1939 concluded that Britain would not have the landing craft to put a single brigade ashore for six months and would not be able to contemplate capturing and holding enemy territory for two years. Once the war started, production of such craft accelerated. By the end of 1941 the number under construction in Britain was 348, while the 1942 programme planned to deliver 1,168 by May 1943. The Americans also threw themselves into large-scale production.

But it was not just a matter of building the landing craft. You also had to have a small, specialised navy to operate them. As early as October 1941, Mountbatten was talking about the need to train 16,000 men.

Churchill, Roosevelt, the Combined Chiefs of Staff and their planning teams spent huge amounts of time wrestling with the logistics of the landing craft. They were needed for North Africa, Sicily and Italy, and in large numbers in the Pacific. They had to be maintained and moved. They also had to be available in Normandy in sufficient numbers not just for the initial assault, but for the crucial days thereafter when the beachheads needed to be reinforced and supplied from the sea. Such planning had to factor in losses through bad weather or enemy action.

The final Overlord operation would involve a staggering 4,126 landing ships and craft, including 55 large infantry-landing ships,

236 tank-landing ships, 248 smaller infantry- and 837 tank-landing craft, 502 assault craft and 464 craft for mechanised equipment, as well as a range of more specialised vessels. It inevitably took time to assemble, to recruit and train the crews, and develop the procedures and tactics for such an armada.

The development of officers and troops with real combat experience and high morale

And then there was the issue of morale. The Allied forces might have had an increasing advantage in terms of quantity and quality of arms, but prior to 1943 they had yet to develop the ability and cultivate the self-belief to use them effectively. Up until the Second Battle of El Alamein in November 1942, the British Army had not had a large-scale, decisive victory against the Germans. Small wonder then that Churchill wanted to savour and celebrate the moment, ordering the ringing of British church bells and proudly announcing at the annual Lord Mayor's luncheon in London's Mansion House that 'We have victory – a remarkable and definite victory. The bright gleam has caught the helmets of our soldiers and warmed and cheered all our hearts.' American troops had to suffer their own baptism of fire at the Battle of the Kasserine Pass in Tunisia in February 1943, before they too gained in experience and became more battle-hardened.

Churchill, Eisenhower and Montgomery were all great believers in the value of high morale. Winston would certainly have been aware of Napoleon's dictum that 'The moral [sic] is to the physical, as three is to one.' All three believed that commanders should be seen by their men. Eisenhower felt that it paid big dividends in terms of morale, which 'given rough equality in other things, is supreme on the battlefield'. Montgomery felt that 'One of the chief factors for success in battle is the human factor.' Churchill maintained that 'battles were not won by arithmetical calculations of the strength of the opposing forces'. Having put himself centre stage in 1940, becoming the main voice and image of the British war effort,

Winston knew that he had a role to play in building and sustaining that confidence. Search the internet and you can find a wonderful period piece of Pathé News footage of Churchill visiting the troops in North Africa in June of 1943. Dressed eccentrically but distinctively in his zip-up siren suit and a pith helmet, complete with dark glasses, walking cane and cigar, the Prime Minister is clearly the star attraction as he travels from unit to unit and from one photo opportunity to another. He is pictured talking to a huge audience in the amphitheatre at Carthage, visiting an American unit, driving past cheering troops while flashing his signature V for Victory salute and addressing others from the back of a lorry. It is a role that he clearly relished. This was deliberate leadership from the front by a natural showman who enjoyed the limelight.

Morale is a difficult quality to define, but it depended on having the right training and equipment, on having experience of victory, and confidence in commanders and colleagues.

By the end of 1943, the essential preconditions for Overlord had largely been met. The Allies had secured control of the sea and were increasingly dominant in the air. Germany had lost her European ally and was massively overextended, fighting on several fronts and unable to keep pace with Allied production. The British and Americans had developed and tested their system of combined command. Their troops had fought side by side in North Africa and Sicily and had gained valuable experience of planning and executing amphibious landings on enemy-defended shorelines in both. None of this meant that the attack on France was a *fait accompli*. It was clear to all involved in its planning that this was an operation of an entirely different magnitude.

For a start, the invasions of North Africa and Sicily had confirmed the difficulties inherent in such amphibious operations. In Sicily, in July 1943, the Allies had overwhelming numerical superiority and were facing an already demoralised Italian Army and a German force of little more than two divisions, far smaller than that in France. Yet they still encountered difficulties and took significant casualties. The weather once again caused problems, with the initial airborne assault running into high winds. Paratroopers were scattered and gliders lost at sea. Problems coordinating the naval and air bombardments with the landings on the beaches resulted in aircraft being lost through 'friendly' fire and troops put ashore in the wrong places. Though the beaches were secured, the Germans subsequently held up the advance of Montgomery's troops and ultimately evaded capture and escaped from the island.

Thomas Rodgers, known as TL, from Andalusia, Alabama, was a member of C Company of the 504th Parachute Regiment, part of the United States 82nd Airborne Division. Described by one of his comrades as, 'Quiet, unobtrusive and retiring', TL was a big man, but one who 'smoked little and [perhaps unusually for an American paratrooper] never drank or cursed'. He was dropped into Sicily in the darkness of 10 July, the second night of the operation, and was lucky to make it safely to the ground. Twenty-three aircraft and some of the descending paratroopers were shot down by their own side. It highlighted a problem that needed to be fixed and led directly to the creation of a special unit of Pathfinders, specially trained volunteers who would parachute behind enemy-held lines ahead of the main force and use lights and radar to guide the others safely in. Characteristically, TL was one of those who stepped forward for this special training. 'When asked to accept a dangerous assignment, he would reflect a moment and then answer quietly, "I'll go."' Volunteering to be a Pathfinder would prove a fateful decision that would lead him to play a key role in Operation Overlord.

In the short term, however, Sicily had highlighted just how difficult Normandy might be. The northern French shoreline formed the most heavily defended section of Hitler's Atlantic Wall – a huge series of concrete fortifications intended to stretch from the French frontier with Spain all the way up to northern Norway. Plus, there was still the risk of U-boats, E-boats (armed motor boats) and mines in the Channel. The Luftwaffe was down but not out, and the German Army still maintained a large number of divisions in France (including formidable Panzer divisions).

Success could not be taken for granted. There were still lessons that needed to be learnt. John Selwyn Lloyd, a young staff officer for the Second Army and future British Foreign Secretary, was just one of those charged with studying these beach landings and developing new techniques for moving troops on and off the shoreline. He visited Sicily in July 1943, testing out landing craft and examining beach obstacles.

The war also had a momentum of its own. Just as North Africa led to Sicily, success in Sicily culminated in the overthrow of Mussolini and to the Anglo-American Allies moving belatedly onto the Italian mainland in an unsuccessful attempt to forestall German control of the country. Churchill was certainly a leading advocate of following up on Sicilian success by moving into Italy and stubbornly remained so in spite of the continuing build-up of American forces in Britain for Overlord. Even before the invasion of Sicily, and while protesting that he had no intention of interfering with plans for the cross-Channel operation, he was urging Eisenhower to quickly exploit any opportunity arising out of the fall of the island and expressing his fear that Ike would interpret his mission in too narrow a fashion. By July, he was convinced that the right strategy for 1944 was a maximum effort in Italy, advancing to the line of the River Po and preserving options to seize Vienna or turn against the south of France. Thereafter, he became the biggest advocate for two successive amphibious operations, designed to leapfrog enemy forces on the peninsula. The first, with landings at Salerno in September 1943, aimed to seize Naples; the second at Anzio in January 1944 was designed to facilitate the capture of Rome. Both landings were heavily contested, and the Allies faced strong German counter-attacks intended to force them back into the sea. The forces at Anzio struggled to break out of the beachheads. In a frank letter to General MacArthur, the American general commanding Allied forces in the south-west Pacific, Churchill admitted that what he had hoped would be a wildcat looked in danger of becoming a 'stranded whale'.

Far from being the soft underbelly of Europe, as described by

Churchill, Italy was to prove a hard, mountainous spine and one that was extremely costly in men and materials. Churchill specifically asked that some American paratroopers be kept back from France for use in Italy. As a result, T. L. Rodgers and the 504th would go into Salerno and Anzio and would spend the next few months slowly fighting their way up the peninsula. One of their number would angrily reply with a roll-call of battlefields when told that the paratroopers had it easy and were the glamour boys of the army: 'Sicily, Salerno, Shrapnel Pass, the Plains of Naples, the Volturno, Cassino and sixty-three days on Anzio. Now go goof your gums on a clam, you silly bastard!' But, as time went on and losses mounted, the American military leadership increasingly looked at these operations as pulling resources away from the main battle in France. To Brooke and the British Chiefs of Staff, Salerno and Anzio were salutary warnings of the difficulties that would be encountered in storming the Normandy beaches.

But it was the natural momentum of war, and the difficulty of disengaging from operations once started, that helped keep the Allies away from the northern French coastline.

As the second half of 1943 unfolded, as American forces began to arrive in Britain in strength, and as the preconditions for a cross-Channel assault were steadily met, Churchill fell into line and supported Overlord as the primary joint operation for 1944. But this did not mean he saw it as the only operation.

He undoubtedly had one eye on the post-war situation. If Britain were to remain an imperial power, which was certainly his hope, then she needed to control the eastern Mediterranean. Winston was wary of instability in the Balkans or Soviet domination in Greece, especially after the Italian surrender, and was furious when Eisenhower refused to divert resources from his Mediterranean command to enable the British to occupy the Greek Dodecanese Islands formerly held by Italy and now seized by Germany. Foremost among these was Rhodes. He appealed to Roosevelt in a telegram of 8 October 1943, earnestly praying that his views might receive some consideration at this critical juncture and stressing that 'this operation could be fitted in to our plan without detriment either to the advance in Italy of which as you know I have always been an advocate, or of the build-up of Overlord which I am prepared faithfully to support'. Notice the revealing contrast between his active promotion of campaigns in the Mediterranean with his passive endorsement of Normandy. Unsurprisingly, it prompted a quick slap-down from the President, who had no intention of being diverted into what he viewed as a Greek sideshow, arguing: 'Strategically, if we get the Aegean Islands [including Rhodes], I ask myself where do we go from there and vice-versa where would the Germans go if for some time they retain possession of the Islands.'

Churchill's telegram to British Foreign Secretary Anthony Eden, who was visiting Moscow, captures his position. Written on 29 October, it confirms that he still wanted the best of both worlds. (See telegram on p. 110.)

Churchill was trying to maintain as much equipment, including vital landing craft, in the Italian theatre for as long as possible. Rebuffed by Roosevelt, he was also trying to enlist the Soviet Union and Turkey in his plans for an offensive against the Dodecanese Islands. The Turks had spent much blood, time and effort on seizing Rhodes from Europeans in the fifteenth and sixteenth centuries; now Churchill wanted them to abandon their neutrality and help the British hold it against the Germans by providing air and naval bases. Perhaps unsurprisingly, they refused.

For Churchill, these Italian and Mediterranean campaigns were also about winning laurels. It was now obvious that the Americans would contribute the largest forces for Overlord and that the commander in France would therefore be American – either Marshall or Eisenhower. Ike got the job in December 1943 and the British general, 'Jumbo' Wilson, replaced him as Supreme Commander in the Mediterranean. This left Brooke very disappointed, as Churchill had implied to him that the job might be his.

Yet Churchill still had to fight a rearguard action throughout the autumn to quash American suggestions that the Overlord and

OUTWARD TELEGRAM

[This Document is the Property of His Britannic Majesty's Government, and should be kept under Lock and Key.]

[This telegram is of particular secrecy and should be retained by the authorised recipient and not passed on]

[Cypher]   SPECIAL (EXTRA)

FROM FOREIGN OFFICE TO MOSCOW

No. 174 Extra
29th October, 1943   D: 2.20 p.m. 29th October,1943.

                    p p p p

MOST IMMEDIATE

DEDIP

Most Secret and Personal

Following from Prime Minister for Secretary of State.

1. There is of course no question of abandoning Overlord which will remain our principal operation for 1944. The retention of landing-craft in the Mediterranean in order not to lose the battle of Rome may cause a slight delay, perhaps till July, as the smaller class of landing-craft cannot cross the Bay of Biscay in the winter months and would have to make the passage in the Spring. The delay would however mean that the blow when struck would be with somewhat heavier forces, and also that the full bombing /effort on Germany would not be damped down so soon. We are also ready at any time to push across and profit by a German collapse. These arguments may be of use to you in discussion.

2. See also my telegram No. 171 Extra. I see you have discouraged the Turkish Foreign Secretary from coming to see you in Cairo on your way home, but of course if U.J. liked the idea about the Submarines it might be very convenient for you to handle the matter yourself in Cairo. At the same time you would of course ask for facilities for the use of the Air bases from which the Aegean islands can be defended and attacked. Should action be found possible we will send a precise military statement of what we want.

O.T.P.

Telegram from Churchill to Eden, 29 October 1943

Mediterranean theatres be combined into a giant European super Command. He clearly feared that the result would be a single all-powerful American Commander-in-Chief, most probably General George Marshall. Whereas, with Wilson as the Supreme Commander in the Mediterranean and Alexander commanding the 15th Army Group fighting in Italy, he could at least claim that the British were still in charge on one battle-front. The capture of Rome seemed a particularly glittering prize and Churchill was not ready to give up on it.

It was in this spirit that the British Prime Minister approached the Tehran Conference, the first meeting of the 'Big Three' – of himself, Roosevelt and Stalin – held in the Iranian capital in November 1943. En route to see the US President for a pre-meeting in Cairo, he fumed about the 'evils of Americans'. He was clearly very animated and Brooke was worried about the line his boss might take in the conference, with Churchill inclined to say to the President, 'all right if you won't play with us in the Mediterranean we won't play with you in the English Channel', and being prepared to let the United States direct their main effort to the Pacific. His mood cannot have been made any easier by poor health, exacerbated by the strain of travel. It was no doubt further tested by Roosevelt's refusal to discuss the European strategy with him at their pre-meeting in Egypt. The presence of Chiang Kai-shek, the Chinese nationalist leader, meant that their Cairo discussions focused primarily on the war in East Asia and the Pacific.

On 26 November, Winston sent a long letter to Clementine from Cairo. Key passages are revealing of his frustrations:

> We have now been five days here and so far have only really tackled the Chinese end of the business. However a good deal has gone on behind the scenes in the sense of bringing the British and Americans nearer together on the great and grim issues with which we are confronted. Tomorrow at first screech of cock we start for CAIRO THREE [Tehran] and we shall stay there I hope three of four nights. U.J. [Uncle Joe, Churchill's nickname for

Stalin] meets us on the evening of the 28th. It has not been possible to come to grips with our main problems without knowing what are his views and wishes.

. . .

Let me know how public opinion is going on different things. Of course I know it is said in London that I was frustrated in my conduct of the war in the Mediterranean during the last two months. It is not for me to challenge this. I cannot pretend to have an adequate defence of what actually occurred. I have been fighting with my hands tied behind my back, but now I hope to get better arrangements and procure the necessary decisions for future blows on a good scale . . .

I have not yet succeeded in gripping affairs as I hope and mean to out here, but I have a feeling things will go the way I want. Tomorrow we start so very early that I am now going to sleep for an hour before dining with the Embassy in Cairo.

Tender love my darling Clemmie. How I wish you were out here w[ith] me to see the variegated show.

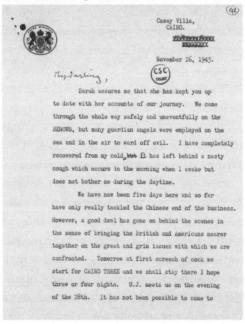

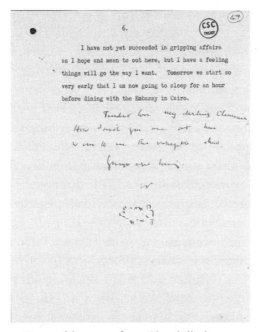

*First and last page from Churchill's letter to
Clementine Churchill, 26 November 1943*

At Tehran, Churchill was to be disappointed. Roosevelt went out of his way to establish a bilateral relationship with Stalin, and Uncle Joe's views and wishes on Overlord were in harmony with the President's. The Russian and American leaders were now united in their clear desire for a cross-Channel assault in the late spring of 1944. This would be supported by a simultaneous Soviet offensive on the Eastern Front and by an Allied invasion of southern France, drawing on troops from Italy. In breach of the security principle that codenames should have no discernible connection with their operation, the attack in the south was to be codenamed Anvil, presumably because it would be the anvil on which the hammer of Overlord would break the enemy. Churchill tried to stress the importance of continuing to fight in Italy and the Balkans, arguing that in the short term such operations would continue to draw forces from the Russian front and that later they would divert German forces from Overlord. Success in the

Mediterranean might yet bring Turkey into the war on the Allied side. Ultimately, however, the die was cast. A date of May 1944 was set for the invasion of France (Brooke's diary indicates by 1 June 1944), and the primacy – Churchill called it 'tyranny' – of Overlord was established.

Prior to the 'Big Three' meeting with Roosevelt and Stalin, Churchill's old friend Field Marshal Jan Smuts, the Prime Minister of South Africa, had advised him to secure the Italian flank before embarking on these new operations in France. Churchill had replied, 'I hope you will realize that British loyalty to OVERLORD is keystone of arch of Anglo-American co-operation. Personally I think enough forces exist for both hands to be played and I believe this to be the right strategy.'

But the reality was that his hands were increasingly tied. Negotiations with Turkey had failed. Progress in Italy was slow, and more resources would now be siphoned off for France, including for operations against the south of the country. The Balkans were a dead end, Italy a secondary theatre. Regardless of Churchill's doubts, the way home now lay firmly through France to Berlin.

His response, according to his long-standing friend, Violet Bonham Carter, was to ruefully remark:

> There I sat with the great Russian bear on one side of me with paws outstretched, and, on the other side, the great American buffalo, and between the two sat the poor little English donkey, who was the only one, the only one of the three, who knew the right way home.

In the context of the convoluted path that the Western Allies trod to be poised to invade Western Europe in June 1944, many steps were taken. Under Montgomery, Stan Hollis fought with his 6th Green Howards comrades from El Alamein through the western desert to Tunisia, eventually linking up with the first US troops to see combat after their landings in November 1942 in French Morocco and Algeria. With North Africa cleared of all Axis forces, Stan Hollis was part of Montgomery's next strategic move in the Allied invasion of Sicily beginning on 9 July 1943. While Stan was fighting, and nearly dying, at Primosole Bridge on the Catanian Plain, General Montgomery could be said to be consolidating his understanding of how to fight and win on the mid-twentieth-century battlefield. He had observed and learnt in the closing months of the First World War that the skilful coordination of armour, infantry, artillery and airpower with sufficient and massive stocks of ammunition could break well-defended positions and restore manoeuvrability to the battlefield. He eventually achieved this at El Alamein – albeit at some considerable human cost – in the invasion of Sicily and the consequent invasion of Italy, before being withdrawn on 23 December 1943 to prepare for the invasion of Europe.

On arrival back in London, Montgomery found himself once more under the overall command of General Dwight D. Eisenhower, but responsible for developing the plans for what became Operation Overlord, the invasion of Europe. He inherited the aftermath of the disastrous assault on the port of Dieppe, Operation Jubilee, in which almost a thousand Canadian soldiers had been killed and nearly two thousand taken prisoner in demonstrating that capturing a well-defended port on the French coast was somewhere between very dangerous and impossible. He resolved that the future invasion was to be across the beaches. His old adversary, Erwin Rommel, now in command of the western defences in France, had come to much the same conclusion. Construction of the Atlantic Wall, largely by forced labour, was accelerated. The stage was being set for the final showdown between the Western Allies and Germany, somewhere, sometime, on the coast of France. But where? And when? Stan Hollis, now withdrawn with his 6th Green Howards battalion from Italy to prepare for the battle for Europe, wondered much the same!

The International Road to D-Day: A Timeline of the Key Conferences in 1943

The President, Prime Minister and their Combined Chiefs of Staff met regularly during 1943 to develop their joint strategy. These meetings all had a bearing on the timing and nature of Overlord.

The Casablanca Conference

The year began with the Casablanca Conference (codename Symbol), held between 14 and 24 January 1943, in French Morocco. The immediate priority was to resolve the next political and military steps, coordinating the American and British advances from west and east into Tunisia and dealing with arrangements for the administration of French North Africa. Thereafter, the conference took the decision that the next Allied objective would be against Sicily. This was a recognition that they were not yet strong enough to move against the heavily fortified Atlantic shoreline of France and it effectively pushed D-Day back to 1944. The conference recognised that the defeat of the U-boats in the Atlantic and the further bombing of Germany were necessary precursors to a cross-Channel assault. However, the decision was taken to appoint a British general to further develop plans for operations against France.

The Third Washington Conference

May saw Churchill engage in shuttle diplomacy. In Washington DC (codename Trident, 12–25 May) he met with the President and Combined Chiefs. Thereafter, he flew to Algiers (29 May–4 June) accompanied by Generals Marshall and Brooke, where he was joined by Foreign Secretary Eden and met with Eisenhower and the military commanders about to engage in Operation Husky, the invasion of Sicily. These meetings finalised the arrangements for the assault on Sicily but left open the question of moving into Italy thereafter. The decision was taken to postpone the cross-Channel assault until May 1944, as, given other operations, it would not be possible to build up the required forces and equipment prior to that date. Churchill was particularly keen to exploit success in Sicily with attacks against the Italian mainland, while Marshall argued strongly for the primacy of Overlord. Eisenhower was prepared to contemplate some further action in Italy while forces continued to be assembled in the United Kingdom for the assault on France.

The Quebec Conference

The Quebec Conference (codename Quadrant, 17–24 August) took place in Canada in the aftermath of the fall of Mussolini and against the backdrop of the successful Allied invasion of Sicily. Churchill and Roosevelt were hosted by the Canadian Prime Minister, William Lyon Mackenzie King, though he was excluded from the key Allied discussions. Churchill accepted the principle of the primacy of Overlord over the Mediterranean, though he continued to urge operations in Italy, in part as a means of diverting German forces from France. He advocated seizing Sardinia and Corsica. The conference also discussed the plan to simultaneously attack southern France (Operation Anvil) in May 1944 as a further means of occupying the Germans and preventing them amassing forces against Overlord. Discussion took place too concerning the war in the Pacific and future cooperation regarding the atomic weapons that the Allies were developing.

The Tehran Conference

The year ended with the Tehran Conference (codename Eureka, 28 November–1 December), which was itself sandwiched between two meetings of Churchill, Roosevelt and their staffs at Cairo, 23–26 November and 4–6 December).

Churchill had hoped to use the first Cairo Conference to coordinate European strategy with Roosevelt ahead of the Tehran meeting with Stalin, but in this he was thwarted by Roosevelt's reluctance to engage in bilateral diplomacy before his first meeting with the Soviet leader and by the presence of the Chinese nationalist leader Chiang Kai-shek, which meant that discussions focused largely on the Pacific. At Tehran itself, Churchill had to accept the clear American and Russian decision to prioritise Overlord over operations in Italy. The Soviets agreed to launch their own simultaneous offensive on the Eastern Front (Operation Bagration), while deception measures were discussed, along with the plans for the attack on the south of France (Anvil, now given the codename Dragoon). There was also much discussion of the importance of Turkey joining the war on the Allied side, though at the subsequent second Cairo Conference President İnönü of Turkey refused to abandon his country's policy of neutrality.

These conferences punctuated the debate on the timing of D-Day, but by the end of 1943 the stage was set for Overlord. Churchill, Roosevelt and their Combined Chiefs would not meet again until after 6 June.

TOP SECRET

Supreme Headquarters
ALLIED EXPEDITIONARY FORCE
Office of the Chief of Staff

SHAEF/18231/Ops

25 March 1944

Dear *Prime Minister*

I do not know whether the suggestion I am going to make is practicable or whether it will be repugnant to you personally.

The large scale exercise which it is necessary to carry out about 3rd - 5th May, will seriously detract from the degree of surprise that Plan 'FORTITUDE' is designed to achieve, if the enemy should interpret it in the true sense, as our final rehearsal. Accordingly everything possible must be done to convince the enemy that this exercise is the first, and that Operation 'OVERLORD' is the second of a series of exercises which must be carried out before D day.

I, therefore, submit for your considered opinion the proposal that when you next address the Nation you include a statement somewhat in the following terms: "It will be necessary to hold a series of exercises during the next few months which, being unprecedented in scale, will call for many restrictions on the public. These must be borne with patience and it is the duty of every citizen to refrain from speculation." I consider that such an address, framed in your own words, would greatly assist in concealing from the enemy the date of 'OVERLORD'.

It is intended that after your statement a similar warning will be given to the DUTCH, BELGIAN and FRENCH peoples through the medium of the BBC, primarily with the object of preventing untimely uprising in their countries.

Faithfully
Dwight D Eisenhower

The Right Honourable Winston Churchill,
"Chequers".

TOP SECRET

Letter from Eisenhower to Churchill, 25 March 1944

5

Bodyguard of Lies

'In wartime . . . truth is so precious that she should
always be attended by a bodyguard of lies.'

THE LATE AFTERNOON of 30 November 1943 found Winston
Churchill celebrating his 69th birthday in the unlikely
surroundings of the Soviet Legation in Tehran, the capital city of
Iran. Here, he was taking part in a plenary meeting of the first
'Big Three' conference with President Roosevelt and Marshal
Stalin. The British Prime Minister and the American President
were accompanied by their leading political and military advisers
– Hopkins, Harriman, Marshall, King, Eden, Dill, Brooke,
Cunningham, Portal and Ismay were all present. Stalin was there
with Molotov, his Minister of Foreign Affairs, and the Soviet military hero Marshal Voroshilov. Agreement had already been
reached on launching Operation Overlord in May 1944. Whatever
the precise date, the British and Americans were now committed
to a cross-Channel operation within the next six months 'on the
largest scale that would be permitted by the landing craft available
at that time'.

Towards the end of the meeting, the conversation turned to the
difficulties of hiding the preparations for such an offensive from
the enemy. Churchill referred to the number of depots for equipment being constructed in southern England and the changing
appearance of the coastline, as more and more military installa-
tions appeared. He asked Stalin about making arrangements for a

combined cover plan, prompting the Russian leader to describe how on 'such occasions, the Soviets had achieved success by the construction of false tanks, airplanes and airfields' in sectors where no operations were planned, knowing that they would be picked up by German intelligence. This had sometimes been done on a huge scale and been accompanied by the deliberate use of radio signals to lure the enemy into attacking the wrong targets. In response, Churchill observed that 'In wartime . . . truth is so precious that she should always be attended by a bodyguard of lies.' The full quote appears in his war memoirs, the contemporary minutes simply record him saying 'truth deserves a bodyguard of lies'.

As Churchill conversed with Stalin in Tehran, he knew that deception was but one part of the intelligence armoury that would be crucial to success on D-Day. In order to deceive the enemy, it was essential to know what they were thinking and planning. In order to measure success, it was imperative to see their responses in real time to Allied actions. And at all times it was essential to guard against enemy espionage and to make sure that the Allied plans were adequately protected. Put simply, intelligence and deception were two sides of the same coin and Churchill knew that one of the key prerequisites for deception planning was to try to discover through intelligence what the enemy thought you were going to do. If successful, one could then construct a deception plan to reinforce the enemy's (wrong) convictions about your future intentions. Though of course the enemy would be trying to do the same thing.

The area of intelligence and counter intelligence, deception and espionage, is one in which Churchill had a long-standing interest. He relished hearing about covert missions and successful spying operations, and by 1944 he already had a long history of personal involvement with the security services. Indeed, as Warren Dockter has pointed out in his recent essay for the *Cambridge Companion to Winston Churchill*, his very first military adventure in Cuba, between November and December 1895, around the time of his twenty-first birthday, had been officially sanctioned by the

War Office precisely because it had a clear intelligence value. Churchill and his friend and fellow officer Reginald Barnes used their army leave to take the role of British military observers, accompanying a Spanish column engaged in suppressing a Cuban national uprising. But they had also been charged with gathering information on Spanish weaponry and tactics. Before departure, the two young subalterns had been summoned to a meeting with General Chapman, the army's Director of Military Intelligence, who furnished them with 'maps and much valuable information' and requested that they 'collect information and statistics on various points', including the effect of the new Mauser bullet being used by the Spanish.

Young Churchill had seen for himself the value of military intelligence as a war correspondent and then soldier in the Second Boer War. And once in Parliament, as the newly elected MP for Oldham, he called for the reorganisation and additional funding of the Intelligence Division of the army, which he described as being starved 'for want of both money and brains'.

As Home Secretary in the Edwardian era, he had strengthened the creation of the new home security and foreign intelligence services (which would become MI5 and MI6), supporting the clandestine examination of mail and the introduction of a register of resident aliens. As First Lord of the Admiralty in 1914–15 he had supported the signals interception, code-breaking and analysis work of the Royal Navy's room 40, the precursor to Bletchley Park. In the 1920s he had used his intelligence community contacts to inform his campaign against communism, before switching his focus in the following decade to Nazi Germany, and on becoming Prime Minister in 1940 he had insisted on seeing as much raw intelligence as possible, setting up his own statistical unit within the Admiralty and then Downing Street to help him make his own interpretations, and analysis.

Information flowed into Churchill's office from a huge range of civilian and military channels. His own daughter Sarah was a section officer in the Photographic Interpretation Unit of the

RAF Intelligence Branch at Medmenham, where she sometimes worked twelve-hour overnight shifts looking at aerial reconnaissance photos in support of European and North African operations, later writing: 'Puzzling and tedious as it often was, there were moments of terrific excitement and discovery.' Human intelligence was collected from interrogated prisoners and from the network of agents overseas operated by the Secret Intelligence Service (SIS, also known as MI6). German radio traffic was intercepted and analysed to identify the location of enemy units. But Churchill quite rightly attached the greatest significance to the special signals intelligence work of the Government Code and Cypher School at Bletchley Park, code-named Ultra. Hidden in plain sight in the heart of the Buckinghamshire countryside, a team of codebreakers and analysts was engaged in breaking encoded enemy communications, including the fiendishly complex Enigma cypher machines used by the Germans to protect their most secret diplomatic and military messages.

By the end of 1943, Churchill was sitting like a spider at the heart of his own worldwide intelligence web. MI5, the Home Intelligence Service, was responsible for rounding up German spies in Britain and had been successful in turning almost all of them into double agents. This was coordinated through the Twenty Committee, so named because the roman numerals for twenty were XX, a double cross. The Special Operations Executive (SOE) was smuggling agents into occupied countries to support sabotage and guerrilla operations. The Political Warfare Executive (PWE) was disseminating covert propaganda to undermine enemy morale and encourage resistance. Deception plans to protect military operations were being devised and coordinated by the London Controlling Section (LCS), a clandestine military operation that worked alongside the Joint Planning Staff. These organisations had all been developed or expanded during the war and now enjoyed levels of manpower, resource, funding and power that would have been inconceivable in peacetime.

Coordinating this complex structure of overlapping and sometimes rival secret organisations was not easy. The Joint Intelligence Committee reported directly to the Prime Minister and the Chiefs of Staff. But Churchill also had his own liaison officer to the security services, in the form of his trusted aide Desmond Morton. Morton, like many of those involved in wartime intelligence, had served with distinction in the First World War, acquiring a bullet that was still lodged somewhere dangerously near his heart, and was the sort of buccaneering personality whose company the Prime Minister particularly appreciated. Meanwhile, Sir Stewart Menzies, the head of SIS and known as 'C', supplied Churchill with his daily diet of selected raw intelligence derived from Bletchley Park. Access to this material was understandably extremely tightly controlled. It was brought to Churchill in a special locked buff box for his eyes only and for which he kept the key. His Private Secretary Jock Colville made the mistake of recording this secret in his diary in October 1940, only to realise his error and cross the whole page through. When the leading codebreakers asked for more resources in October 1941, Churchill immediately issued an order that their requests should be met 'on extreme priority'. The work of Bletchley Park did not become public knowledge until 1974. This meant that its role was not evident in early histories of the Second World War, including Churchill's own memoirs and the British official histories of the conflict. Yet it underpinned all intelligence activities. The letter on p. 126 is a rare wartime example of Churchill mentioning the establishment at Bletchley and shows his continued patronage of the organisation.

The British Prime Minister made a point of meeting with many of those involved in clandestine war work, and clearly enjoyed hearing at first hand the details of secret operations. No previous occupant of 10 Downing Street had ever been as informed on intelligence issues. But this created its own problems. Churchill had to adjudicate on competing demands and rivalries between the different organisations, and to decide what could be revealed,

(201)

October 16, 1943.

Personal and Confidential.

My dear Postmaster-General,

I am glad to learn from the Director of the
establishment at Bletchley of the very valuable assistance
which your Department is affording him, particularly with
regard to satisfying the vast communication needs and in
the provision of certain highly technical and delicate
machinery.

You are at liberty to convey, confidentially, my
appreciation of this invaluable contribution to the war
effort to those officials who are directly engaged in
assisting this organization.

Yours very sincerely,

Captain the Rt. Hon. Harry F.C. Crookshank, M.P.

Letter from Churchill to Postmaster-General, 16 October 1943

when and to whom. He regularly bombarded his commanders in
the field with 'most secret' information, sometimes referred to by
the codename Boniface, derived from his secret intelligence
sources, but had to be careful not to do so in a way that endangered agents or compromised the material derived from the breaking of the German codes. A principle was established that no

Allied operation could be undertaken in response to Ultra information if to do so might reveal to the Germans that their codes
had been broken; there must always be some plausible alternative
cover story for how the information had been obtained. This
might take the form of a plane being hastily despatched to overfly
a newly revealed enemy location as if it were conducting photographic reconnaissance.

The reproduced telegram is an example of Churchill using
the Boniface information to inform his commander in the field;
in this case the recipient is Montgomery in Tunisia in the closing
stages of the North African campaign in March 1943. (See
p. 128.)

By the time of the Tehran Conference, the British had rounded
up the German agents in Britain, had developed a comprehensive
network of double agents to feed back misinformation, were
listening in real time to German communications and had established a network of guerrilla groups and agents within occupied
France, ready to undertake sabotage operations.

It was a world that Joan Bright had become very familiar with.
Her calm efficiency and engaging manner had brought her to the
notice of General 'Pug' Ismay, Churchill's military adviser and
Chief of Staff, and she had been brought upstairs to the 'principal'
floor within Whitehall, where she was running a Special
Information Centre for the British military commanders and
maintaining the registry for the Chiefs of Staff. In her words: 'I
was given a carpet, a long polished table, wall maps, an easy chair
and some official secrets.' In fact, she was now one of the best-
informed people in Britain: a keeper of the official secrets. As
such she was also one of a very few who were aware of the final
piece in the intelligence jigsaw – the deception planning that
would provide Churchill's bodyguard of lies.

For, even as Churchill joked with Stalin at Tehran, he already
knew better than most that the British were well versed in such
deception operations. In April 1942, when first considering
American plans for an assault against the continent, he had
prefigured his 'bodyguard of lies' quote by telling Hopkins and

Scrambled to C.'s office 4 p.m.
28.3.43.

CLEAR THE LINE. PRIME MINISTER'S
PERSONAL TELEGRAM
SERIAL No. T·391|3

PRIME MINISTER TO GENERAL MONTGOMERY.
Personal and Secret.

(To be transmitted through 'C').

1.   Bravo: I was sure of it. Now the question is
the cop.

2.   Presume you know all Boniface, viz: Firstly,
164th Division has lost nearly all its vehicles and heavy
weapons.   Secondly, 21st and 15th Panzers are regathering
on heights south-east of El Hamma.   Thirdly, Italian
Commander-in-Chief (quote) of Mareth garrisons (unquote)
asked 15th Panzer Division to provide a battle group to
cover his last retreat at Zouitinat, a point about 13
miles south-east of El Hamma and 13 miles south-west of
Gabes.   You should have received all this through other
channels, but to make sure I repeat it.

God bless you.

W.S.C.

28.3.43

Telegram from Churchill to Montgomery, 28 March 1943

Marshall that 'The true objectives could . . . be obscured in a cloud of rumours.' In fact, the British were already masters of the dark arts.

When fighting superior numbers of Italians in North Africa in 1940, General Wavell had created a special 'A' Force to trick the Italians in the desert. It was led by Lieutenant Colonel Dudley

Clarke. Dennis Wheatley, who regarded Clarke as the 'Father of Deception', described him as small and fair-haired 'but with a strange quietness about his movements and an uncanny habit of suddenly appearing in a room without anyone having noticed him enter it'. He built up a formidable network of secret agents and undertook deception operations throughout the huge Mediterranean theatre, including the Middle East and Africa. Subsequently, as Commander-in-Chief India, Wavell employed Major Peter Fleming, the brother of the James Bond creator, Ian Fleming (who was himself working in naval intelligence), to head up his deception section in the sub-continent. So successful were these overseas operations that they led in October 1941 to the creation of the London Controlling Section (LCS) with a mandate to coordinate Allied deception worldwide and to lead deception planning in the European theatre.

Wavell wrote to Churchill urging that the unit be strengthened. It began to assume a greater prominence from June 1942, partly because the Allies were now finally in a position to contemplate more offensive operations in Europe, which would require deception plans, but also because of the appointment of Lieutenant Colonel John Bevan as the Controlling Officer. Bevan was far from a standard career soldier. In 1918, he had been given the task of establishing the German Order of Battle for their spring offensive. This work had brought him to the attention of Churchill, then Minister of Munitions. Thereafter, Bevan had spent the interwar period running the family firm of stockbrokers and was well connected in military and political circles, being the brother-in-law of General Alexander. He quickly developed a good personal relationship with General Brooke, thereby ensuring that LCS's voice was heard by the Chiefs of Staff at the very summit of Allied decision-making.

Bevan surrounded himself with other well-connected, intelligent, slightly unorthodox and creative individuals such as the author Dennis Wheatley, whose scarlet-lined RAF greatcoat and cane must have made him look like a creation from one of his own horror novels, or Bevan's deputy Major Ronald Wingate, a Double First from Balliol who had served as a political officer

COPY

(68)

IZ 354
TOO 1230/21
TOR 1415Z/21

MOST SECRET.

MOST IMMEDIATE.

From: Armindia.

To: Air Ministry.

18461/C   21.5.42.

Private for Prime Minister from General Wavell.

I have always had considerable belief in deceiving
and disturbing enemy by false information. C in C Mideast
instituted special Branch Staff under selected officer charged
with deception enemy and it has had considerable success. I
have similar branch in India and am already involved in
several deception plans. These however can have local and
ephemeral effect only, unless part of general deception plan
on wide scale. This can only be provided from place where
main strategical policy is decided and Principal Intelligence
Centre is located. Coherent and long term planning of
deception must be centred there. Fully appreciate value of
work done by I S S B and Controlling Officer but have
impression the approach is defensive rather than aggressive and
confined mainly to cover plans for particular operations.
May I suggest for your personal consideration that policy
of bold imaginative deception worked between London,
Washington and Commanders in the field by only officers with
special qualifications might shew good dividend, particularly
in case of Japanese.

TOO 1230/21

THE
CHARTWELL
TRUST

(Circulation)

Col. Jacob.

Telegram from General Wavell to Churchill, 21 May 1942

in Aden during the First World War, before spending much of his career in India and becoming Governor of Baluchistan. The section was strategically located within the Treasury buildings, close to Churchill's own offices, and not far from where Joan Bright was working with General Ismay and the Chiefs of Staff. This meant that LCS was well placed to work with the wartime planning staffs and the other intelligence agencies. Indeed, in its early days the unit lacked its own secretarial assistance and Dennis Wheatley was obliged to turn to Joan Bright for help with typing out one top-secret deception plan. Of course, the central London location was also ideal for conducting clandestine business over alcohol-fuelled dinners in the privacy of Pall Mall clubland.

LCS's first experience was gained in protecting Operation Torch, the landings in Morocco and Algeria. There was a very real fear among the Allied planners that the build-up of forces in Britain or in the tiny British enclave of Gibraltar would be seen by enemy agents from Spain and that they would be targeted by Luftwaffe bombers or U-boats as they assembled for the assault on the beaches. The initial LCS cover story for the build-up in Britain was that forces were being assembled for a possible attack against Norway or France. This was not easy. For the story to be convincing, there had to be troops available and equipped for such operations in the United Kingdom, and those troops had to believe that they might be about to be sent across the North Sea or Channel. With all available resources being diverted towards supporting Torch, and towards finding equipment for fighting in North Africa, it was obviously going to be difficult to persuade the authorities to provide Arctic clothing and supplies! As Wheatley put it, 'nearly everyone we approached scarcely bothered to conceal the fact that he thought this new-fangled deception racket a lot of nonsense'.

More successful were the cover plans for the converging of the Allied forces on North Africa. Information was put out that they were going to reinforce Malta, or invade the south of France, or attack Italy or Greece. This information was fed to the enemy by double agents, through diplomatic channels, by misleading the troops involved and by planting false intelligence. The aim was to create uncertainty and at the very least contribute to enemy caution. The fact that German air and submarine forces were held back further east of the actual objectives suggests that it enjoyed some success. These were all lessons that were learnt and applied for D-Day. Similar measures were applied in the following spring when the Allies made their next major move into Sicily.

One particular deception – Operation Mincemeat – has since gained a particular notoriety. In a plot that would later become the subject of a bestselling book and successful film, the aptly named *The Man Who Never Was* (remade in 2021 as the film *Operation Mincemeat*), the body of a Welsh drifter was given the identity of a British staff officer and dropped into the Mediterranean off the coast of Spain. The false plans carried by the corpse suggested that the British were going to attack in the eastern Mediterranean or Sardinia rather than in North Africa. When the body was recovered, the false despatches were passed to the Germans. Even if they did not swallow them 'rod, line and sinker' (as Wheatley certainly believed), enough uncertainty was caused to prevent them moving more troops to the west. The brainchild of a flight-lieutenant in MI5 (the Home Intelligence Service) but carried out largely by a team from within MI6 (the overseas intelligence service) and supported by Bevan's LCS, Mincemeat demonstrates the complex inter-departmental nature of these operations. It is also a good example of creating a credible plan, as the Allies had indeed debated attacking Sardinia. Indeed, some on the British planning staff continued to believe that it would have been a less costly operation than Sicily and more effective in reasserting control of the Mediterranean. Churchill received a personal bedside briefing on Mincemeat from Bevan.

After the appointment of General Morgan, Colonel Bevan and his team worked with COSSAC to maintain the pressure on the Germans in France through several further, if ultimately less successful, deceptions involving supposed operations against Norway or the French shoreline. As specified by Churchill in his directive to Morgan, these were designed to keep the enemy in France occupied and unsettled, to draw Luftwaffe forces out into combat and, most importantly, to prevent the reinforcement of Italy. This led inevitably to further codenames as a succession of interrelated deception operations were concocted to keep the Germans guessing. Under the overall designation of Cockade, there was Tindall, the notional sailing of five divisions from Scotland against Stavanger in Norway that would then be called off to release forces for Starkey, a feigned attack with fourteen British and Canadian divisions on Boulogne, supposedly to be followed almost immediately by Wadham, an assault by two American Army divisions on Brittany, both of which would also be called off at the last minute.

In his memoirs, General Morgan was open about the difficulties faced in mounting these deceptions. It was not always possible to get the resources to make them convincing. Perhaps unsurprisingly, the Admiralty refused to loan him their obsolete battleships to impersonate an invasion fleet, nor would the RAF Fighter Command allow enemy reconnaissance aircraft access to British airspace in order to overfly and photograph his dummy aeroplanes and airfields.

Yet these fake operations were undertaken with increasing scale and sophistication, involving real troop and ship movements, and supported by actual air attacks on enemy positions. Operation Starkey was the largest. It took place in late August and early September 1943; a feint against the French coast around Calais by a genuine naval force, designed to test the German response and draw the Luftwaffe into a real air battle with the RAF. A huge force was assembled in the waters between Gravesend and Southampton, comprising 100 major and 260 minor landing craft, plus a further 175 dummy landing craft and 95 coastal vessels. There was a special fleet of twenty oceangoing ships, designed to test the sailing of a convoy through the Channel – something that had not been attempted since the fall of France. This was a naval force three times larger than that which had been used in the raid on Dieppe.

A full-scale movement exercise was undertaken by the army to create the impression that several divisions were being concentrated in the south of England. Commandos launched a number of raids on the French coast. The Twenty Committee used its network of double agents to feed false intelligence to the Germans, suggesting that an assault was imminent. Three days were spent minesweeping and clearing a path for the force in the Channel. Anti-aircraft units were installed on the ships, and tanks were loaded into landing craft at Dover. German airfields in the Pas-de-Calais region were heavily bombed. Few of those involved would have been aware that they were taking part in a grand deception.

Churchill followed the progress with great interest, sending a good-luck telegram as the operation launched. For him, its primary importance was almost certainly as a diversion for the Allied landings at Salerno in Italy, pulling German air forces away from the Mediterranean.

Hughes-Hallett, now a commodore, was responsible for the naval planning. On 8 September, the ships sailed from their anchorages around the Solent towards Dover, before turning towards Boulogne and the beaches around Fécamp. Hallett was on board the destroyer HMS *Albrighton* as the fake force sailed out into the Channel, maintaining close contact by means of a scrambled VHF link with Air Marshal Leigh-Mallory, who was providing fighter cover and standing ready with his forces should the German Air Force respond to this bait. A smokescreen was provided from coastal and landing craft, while radio jamming was provided by mobile units driving along the cliffs of the British south coast. The ships got to within ten miles of the French coast before turning back. All ships were safely back in port by 9 September.

In the event, Starkey failed to bring about the hoped-for air battle. Intercepted radio traffic indicated that the Germans suspected it was a feint and held back their forces. The operation was regarded by those who planned it as a failure. Yet there were some positives. The ships were able to sail down the Channel largely unopposed. The enemy coastal batteries around Calais did open fire, but without result. In so doing, they revealed their location and were exposed to attack by American bombers. Overall, the operation contributed to the general German uncertainty about Allied intentions, and reinforced the view that Calais was where the Allied attack would ultimately come. It also proved a most valuable training exercise for the navy and army, testing the inter-service and international coop- eration that would be vital for successful landings and confirm- ing that the United States Air Force and the RAF could work well together. It highlighted the difficulty of assembling landing craft in sufficient numbers and led to loading procedures being refined and improved. Most importantly perhaps, it provided valuable lessons for the bigger deception that would accompany Overlord itself.

Churchill's quote about 'bodyguard of lies' was seen by the members of LCS, who had access to all the War Cabinet papers. John Bevan's response was to pay homage and name their deception operation for Overlord Bodyguard; a codename that would once again seem to breach basic security protocol by being too revealing of its purpose. All the techniques developed by the unit since 1942 now came into play and on a much grander scale. By early 1944, it was clear to the Germans that Allied forces were being assembled in huge numbers in Britain and that an invasion of the continent must soon be attempted. Suggestions that these troops were going to the Mediterranean or Pacific would no longer be convincing. The decision had been taken to land on the Normandy beaches. Now it was vital to trick the enemy into believing that the Allies were plan- ning to land elsewhere in northern Europe, and – once the landings had taken place – to convince them that Normandy was just a feint and that the main assault was still to come at a different location. If this could be done, then the Germans might hold back some of their forces for a few weeks, buying the Allies vital time to establish, secure and reinforce their bridgehead.

The plan, developed by Bevan and the LCS, and refined by Lieutenant Colonel David Strangeways, who was brought from Italy by Montgomery, did this by playing on existing German fears. It was clear that Rommel had identified the Pas-de-Calais region as being a likely invasion site. It was the closest point to Britain, and therefore easy for the Allies to reinforce by sea and protect by air. A successful landing and breakout would open the road to Paris. To reinforce this impression, an illusion on an enormous scale was needed. Nothing less than an entire fake army group would suffice. Thus, while the real invasion forces were assembling in the south of the country, a fictional First United States Army Group (FUSAG) was being created in Kent and Essex on either side of the Thames Estuary. This was done by taking real army units, known to be in England, and generating fake radio traffic that indicated they were now being assembled and trained in the east of the country (even though in most cases they were not). The signals were accompanied by the presence of dummy landing craft, the appearance of troops and vehicles with fake insignia and by false intelligence from a range of double-cross agents. There was even a notional Commander-in-Chief in the person of General George Patton, recently disgraced after an incident in Sicily when he had slapped two soldiers suffering from battle fatigue. Patton was known to be feared by the Germans, who correctly assumed that he would ultimately play a role in any French campaign. This part of the overall Bodyguard plan was intended both to deceive the Germans and to hide and protect the real invasion build-up. It was known as Fortitude South. But it was not the whole plan.

Fortitude North was the simultaneous attempt to use further deception measures to keep the Germans guessing in Scandinavia. Hitler was known to fear that the Allies might attack in Norway. Again, this was seen as a credible threat. The British were holding troops in Scotland, they had attacked Narvik in 1940, and had been encouraging guerilla operations within Norway ever since. Geoffrey Pyke, working for Mountbatten and Combined Operations, had spent time working on new vehicles mounted on skis to traverse ice and snow. Indeed, Churchill had repeatedly pressed his Chiefs of Staff to mount just such an attack, while previous deception operations, such as Tindall, had deliberately seeded this possibility. Now the Allies were able to play on these fears by creating a notional British Fourth Army under the command of Lieutenant General Sir Andrew Thorne, who was the genuine commander of British forces in Scotland, and by falsely suggesting that he would lead an assault against Stavanger, in conjunction with a simultaneous Soviet attack against Norway. The usual range of deception tactics were deployed to reinforce this impression: troop exercises, fake wireless traffic and dummy equipment. But they were also accompanied by a novel diplomatic initiative. The British authorities now began to imply to the government in neutral Sweden that they might be about to liberate neighbouring Norway. As part of this exercise an entirely fictional scenario was put to Sweden that they might want to offer humanitarian assistance to Norway and help police the country in the event of a German collapse following an Allied attack. It was correctly assumed that the news would leak back to Berlin from pro-German elements in the Swedish government.

There is not space here to do justice to the full complexity of the deceivers' plans. A huge range of channels were utilised to suggest that the Allies were facing delays in assembling their forces, or were waiting on a Soviet offensive, or on further results of their bombing campaign. There was even a suggestion that there might be an attack in the Bay of Biscay. Just before D-Day, the actor Clifton James, a double for Montgomery, put on an incredible public performance in Gibraltar, playing the British general in front of enemy agents to convince the Germans that an attack in France could not be imminent while one of the senior commanders was in the Mediterranean. The idea was to keep the enemy guessing. There is an irony here. In 1942, Churchill had advocated attacking occupied Europe at multiple locations on the Atlantic shoreline from Norway to the mouth of the Gironde, utilising at least half a dozen feints 'which, if luck favours them, may be exploited'. This had never seemed feasible and would have divided Allied resources – Eisenhower and Montgomery were clear that the actual military blow needed to be concentrated for maximum impact – but it was of course possible to create multiple diversions and threats. The enemy was to be kept confused and guessing.

The Bodyguard was now in place, on a scale and level of sophistication that was only possible in 1944 after years of experimentation, practice and building of networks. Deception had proved its value and was now a fully integrated part of the planning process. Churchill was not directly involved in developing these decoy operations, but he loved this type of subterfuge and acted as a consistent patron and advocate for the work.

Suggestions that he announce a fake summit with Roosevelt came to nothing, but there was one small role for the Prime Minister. On 26 March, he broadcast to the British nation and in his final remarks he warned his audience that 'in order to deceive and baffle the enemy as well as to exercise the forces there will be many false alarms, many feints and many dress rehearsals'. These lines were put in at the request of Eisenhower, who had sent a 'Top Secret' message to Churchill the previous day, keen to convince the Germans that his planned major dress rehearsal on the south coast on 3–5 May was just one of a series of such exercises, and in the hope that Overlord itself might be initially seen as just such a feint.

Churchill knew of course that the deception plan was inevitably the shadow of the actual plan, and that both had to work. The early signs were positive. As preparations began in earnest, the German military remained spread along the French coast. They knew the blow was coming, but not where or when the hammer would fall.

Piers for Use on Beaches

CONDITIONS OF BEACH

Average gradient is 1 in 200 and beaches are open to the south west.

CONDITIONS OF TIDE

2. Range of spring tides is 30 feet and the strength of the tide parallel to the beach is 4 knots at springs.

SCAFFOLDING PIERS

3. A pier to be of use for unloading ships of 20 foot draught would have to be 1 mile in length and 40 foot in height at the seaward end. The present type of scaffolding pier does not exceed 20 foot in height. It is doubtful whether a pier of these large dimensions could be made with scaffolding, but in any case the amount of material required would be prohibitive.

PONTOON PIERS

4. A pontoon pier would have to be similar in length. All floating piers suffer from the disadvantage of having to be securely moored with heavy anchors. Even then they are most vulnerable and will not stand up to a gale of wind. The strength of the tide is so great that the moorings will have to be very large. If large pontoons were moored, 20 yards apart, at least 200 anchors would be required. The sea-ward end of a floating pier must be particularly well moored and the mooring chains form an obstacle to ships coming alongside. Owing to the poor ratio between the weight of a floating pontoons and the weight they can carry, and to their vulnerability to sea wind and tide, they are not favoured in comparison with scaffolding piers on open beaches.

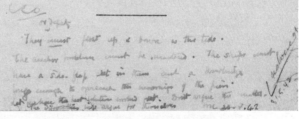

Minute on 'Piers for Use on Beaches', annotated by Churchill, 26 May 1942

6

Mulberries and Gooseberries

'Gentlemen, I am hardening on this operation.'

IN MILITARY PLANNING, especially at the operational – the campaign – level in war, there is a very close relationship between the commander, the staff, the plan and the outcome. This is essential because the plan, and its outcome, are the personal responsibility of the commander. The staff deal with much of the detail but the essence of the plan – the operational idea – belongs to the commander. The buck starts and stops with the boss.

Although General Dwight D. Eisenhower, Ike, was to be in overall command in Europe, General Bernard Montgomery was to be the land forces commander for the assault phase, and it was he who was responsible for delivering the overall success of Operation Overlord and the Normandy campaign. This, in turn, led to the defeat of the Germans in the West in 1944/45 and contained Stalin's Red Army's further expansion into Europe. In the final analysis, it was the boots on the ground of the land forces that determined the successful outcome, enabled, of course, by the inestimable contributions of the naval and air forces, in support. Bernard Montgomery was the architect of the foundation of that success, Operation Overlord.

As we have seen, by 1944 the planning for the return to north-western France had passed through many hands and changes of codename. Mountbatten and his Combined Operations team had been charged with making the initial preparations but were confined by lack of resources. Things then changed with the arrival of the Americans, and plans for a large-scale attack (code-named Roundup) had been developed in 1942 by Eisenhower and the British commanders of Home Forces – Paget, Douglas and Ramsay.

The Allied sequence of conferences had resolved at the Trident or Third Washington Conference in DC in May 1943 that the Western Allies would open the Second Front in Europe in 1944. Ike – the consummate convenor of Allied cooperation – had been appointed Commander of the Supreme Headquarters Allied Expeditionary Force, while Monty – the war fighter – was to be commander of the 21st Army Group charged with delivering the success of the overall plan. However, in 1943, both Ike and Monty had been heavily engaged in operations in North Africa, Sicily and Italy. To get planning for the re-entry in Europe underway, and to plan for a number of other potential contingencies in Europe, Lieutenant General Frederick Morgan had been appointed as Chief of Staff to the (unnamed) Supreme Allied Commander (COSSAC). As we have seen, his was an ultimately thankless job but nevertheless he had produced a draft plan for Operation Overlord.

Morgan's initial plan was for a three-divisional assault aimed on a narrow front directly at Caen in Normandy, the other main option of an attack on the Pas-de-Calais having been argued out (the coast was felt to be too heavily defended and more difficult to land on). When Eisenhower was shown the COSSAC plan in Algiers in October 1943 he was appalled and expressed his doubts at wanting to be the overall commander. 'Not enough wallop in the initial attack' was his much-quoted comment. Ike was not alone in his criticism of the draft plan. Churchill and CIGS Brooke had little faith in the COSSAC plan, which perhaps explains at least part of their lack of initial enthusiasm for Overlord.

Ike asked to see Monty in Algiers on 27 December to discuss Overlord. At this meeting both men agreed that the COSSAC plan needed strengthening and that the price to pay for this was potentially a month's delay from May to June 1944. The two generals then met again in Marrakech, Morocco, where Churchill was recovering from a near-death experience.

By December 1943, the British Prime Minister was running on empty. Completely exhausted after the Allied conferences in Tehran and Cairo, he travelled to Tunisia to see Eisenhower. It was one journey too many, and he collapsed with pneumonia. The attack was life-threatening. The crisis occurred on 14 December, when his doctor, Lord Moran, recorded:

> He was very breathless and anxious-looking. I felt his pulse: it was racing and very irregular. The bases of his lungs were congested, and the edge of his liver could be felt below the ribs . . . As I sat by his bedside listening to his quick breathing, I knew that we were at last right up against things. It was four hours before the heart resumed its normal rhythm, and I was relieved to count a regular pulse of 120.

Moran called for medical back-up. A team of experts was hastily assembled. Digitalis, used to treat heart conditions, was administered. Sulfadiazine, an antibacterial drug, was used to fight the pneumonia. The War Cabinet was informed, and Clementine Churchill flew in from Britain. Meanwhile, Churchill spoke of being prepared to die in Carthage, telling his daughter Sarah, who was travelling with him, that, 'Don't worry, it doesn't matter if I die now, the plans for victory have been laid, it is only a matter of time.' A recent study of this episode by two eminently qualified medical consultants, Allister Vale and John Scadding, has concluded that fear of his death was not an exaggeration, and that the overall mortality from pneumonia of this type in the early 1940s was higher than 40 per cent for someone of his age with a related heart condition.

With the benefit of the best care available, sustained by the presence of his wife and daughter, and protected by a detachment of the Coldstream Guards, Churchill pulled through. After Christmas, he left for a period of recovery in Marrakech, a favourite haunt from his pre-war days. He took with him the plans for

Overlord, and it was from his convalescent bed that he began to engage with the detail of an operation that was now just six months away.

On New Year's Eve, Eisenhower and Montgomery both flew into Morocco. Churchill rang in the changes by celebrating with the newly appointed Overlord commanders. Ike had just relinquished his position as Supreme Commander in the Mediterranean Theatre and was returning to the United States for a brief period of rest before taking up his new role. Montgomery was heading straight for Britain.

A well-timed German strike on Churchill's villa in Marrakech could have ruined the Allies' new year and seriously disrupted the liberation of France! Instead, Montgomery recalled an amusing dinner with Mrs Churchill and Lord Beaverbrook. Churchill was well enough to engage in some intensive lobbying of the two generals. He bombarded Eisenhower with demands and questions regarding the pending Allied landings at Anzio in Italy and took the opportunity to share with Montgomery the plan for Overlord. This was the first time Monty had seen it in full and Churchill was keen to get his first impressions. Not one to join the Prime Minister's post-midnight celebrations, the famously austere Montgomery retired to bed early and used the time to write down his first reactions. His main point was that the initial landing was on too narrow a front and confined to too small an area. This would lead to confusion getting on and off the beaches. There needed to be clearer and greater separation between the British and American areas of landing. According to Montgomery, Churchill received this information in bed the following morning, though Winston's recollection of their conversation was more colourful. In his version, the key exchange happened later in the day:

When he [Montgomery] arrived at Marrakesh we had a two hours' drive out to our picnic at the foot of the Atlas. I had given him early in the morning the plan prepared over so many months by General Morgan and the Anglo-American Joint Staffs in London.

After he had read it in summary he said at once "This will not do. I must have more in the initial punch."

As Montgomery was not yet acting in an official capacity and had not yet had the opportunity to consult Air Marshal Tedder or Admiral Ramsay, who were commanding the air and naval forces for the Normandy landings, he asked for his written response back. Churchill replied that he would keep it for his personal information. Instead, he made immediate use of it, firing off a multi-page telegram to the Chiefs of Staff via General Ismay on 2 January in which he cited Montgomery's 'very serious criticism that the proposal to move so many divisions in over the same narrow strip of beaches would be quite impracticable and would lead to inextricable confusion'. On the first page of his telegram, Churchill also emphasised the need to replace words like 'assault' or 'invasion' with 'enter' and 'liberation'. He was at pains to get the tone as well as the detail of the operation correct. 'Invasion' was to be reserved for Germany. It was an important distinction. Back in London, Brooke – about to be appointed a field marshal – noted that the PM 'is now becoming very active again!' He was not the only one. Montgomery quickly got to work on reshaping the plan.

From the moment that Churchill showed Montgomery the plan, matters began to change. Montgomery knew that if he was to take charge, he needed to craft the plan, own the plan and then ensure its success. To Montgomery, the initial landings of three divisions, through which another thirteen would pass by D+12 (days), under the COSSAC plan, would replicate the chaos and confusion that characterised the Salerno landings in southern Italy in September 1943, and, as it turned out, would do so again at Anzio in January 1944. For Montgomery the campaign plan required:

- The initial landings to be made on the widest possible front.
- Corps to develop their own operations, within the overall plan, from their own beaches with no other corps landing on those beaches.

- British and American armies to be kept separate.
- Operations to be developed such that a good port be secured for the British and American forces to have their own port.

With these general thoughts expressed, the scene was set for three extraordinary days of conference in London when Montgomery was formally briefed by the COSSAC staff on their plan. At 9 a.m. on 3 January Monty convened his first Overlord conference. Perhaps sensing the inadequacies of his plan, Morgan allowed his two senior planners to conduct the briefing, explaining as best they could how they had reached the decisions they had. When complete, Monty announced a twenty-minute break in proceedings before he would give his views. When he took to the floor, he expressed his complete disagreement with the COSSAC proposals. He wanted a focus on a very wide bridgehead, perhaps as far west as St Malo and as far east as Dieppe. He certainly did not want just a narrow axis towards Caen. He wanted more troops in the initial assault. He gave the planners twenty-four hours to think again.

The next day the conference reassembled. Monty challenged all the figures that had led to the three-division plan, insisting instead that five divisions should make the initial landings. He accepted that attacking on the west side of the Cotentin Peninsula was an ambition too far but insisted a landing must be made on the east side – on what became Utah beach. He questioned the command-and-control structure that was proposed. Under the COSSAC plan, the initial assault would be commanded by the 1st US Army for the first week with one American, one British and one Canadian corps under command. Then the British and Canadian troops would go under the command of the 1st Canadian Army with the British commander of the 21st Army Group assuming overall command. While Morgan may have thought that this multi-national mishmash might have appealed to Eisenhower, to Monty it was a recipe for confusion and disaster.

By the third day of the conference, the main issues were settled. It was to be a five-division assault and more landing craft must be found. The bridgehead would be fifty miles wide. (For more information on the individual beaches, see pp. 167–8.) Airborne troops would not focus on the early capture of Caen but on the flanks from the Orne River in the east to the southern end of the Cotentin in the west, especially to facilitate an early capture of the port of Cherbourg from the land side. It also became clear at that stage that Monty was sceptical about the concept of using an artificial harbour, code-named Mulberry. However, all present at the conference were transformed by the decisiveness and energy that Monty now injected into the planning process. As Eisenhower's representative in London and as the commander of land forces, all concerned recognised Montgomery's authority. From 6 January 1944, five months before D-Day itself, there began to grow a sense of optimism in the 21st Army Group, in sharp contrast to the defeatist atmosphere that had characterised the COSSAC organisation. Monty made it quite clear that there would be no more 'bellyaching'!

From the descriptions of Montgomery's galvanising actions during the first week of January, it would be wrong to ignore the role of Eisenhower in this initial planning. Despite originally preferring the more congenial General Harold Alexander to be commander of the 21st Army group, rather than Monty, Eisenhower understood that this was a British decision, and when CIGS Brooke persuaded Churchill that Monty was the correct choice, Eisenhower accepted the decision. He may have felt challenged by Monty. Indeed, Churchill may have initially thought the same. After all, Brooke was frequently challenging him at home. Did he need another awkward general? But Brooke knew that Monty, for all his bombastic and self-enhancing habits, was a fighter and a winner. From his First World War experiences, Monty had learnt the importance of identifying the risks in battle and mitigating them with thorough preparation and planning, including the building up of adequate logistic stocks. He liked a 'tidy battlefield'.

Montgomery outlined the revised plan to Eisenhower on 21 January. The price of the enlarged landing force and the wider bridgehead was indeed to be a month's delay. The other issue that was finally settled was that Morgan's command-and-control plans were rejected and that Monty would command all land forces on the ground from the start of Overlord until Eisenhower decided to formally activate the US 12th Army Group under General Omar Bradley. He did this on 1 August 1944, assuming overall command himself, as the Normandy campaign was coming to a close. From that moment the British and Churchill's influence on the conduct of operations in the West would begin to wane.

With control of the military operation passing to Montgomery, who was reporting to Eisenhower, Churchill's ability to influence the military strategy effectively disappeared. Instead, he threw himself into overseeing the delivery of the practical elements that were needed to support the operation's success.

A key problem facing Montgomery and his planning staff was how to sustain the beachheads in the absence of a port. Since 1942, the Normandy beaches had been consistently identified as the best landing grounds for the Allied forces. They were sheltered from the Atlantic swell and were less well defended than the shoreline around the Pas-de-Calais, while still remaining within the range of Allied air cover. But – crucially – they lacked a deep-water anchorage by which the necessary supplies could be brought in to maintain the troops in a rapidly expanding theatre. Cherbourg, at the tip of the Cotentin Peninsula, was expected to be taken quickly but it would not be large enough on its own to sustain an army of over one million men, while it might take several weeks to capture Le Havre.

The answer to this problem had emerged over the course of the previous two years and had proved to be rather fruity. It lay in the creation of Mulberries, artificial harbours to allow for the unloading and protection from the weather of larger ships, and Gooseberries, man-made breakwaters at shallower depths, to ensure calmer waters for smaller vessels and the all-important landing craft. The walls of these artificial ports were to be created from a number of specialist concrete and steel elements. Churchill was fascinated by the potential of science and technology and took a keen interest in these details.

A good idea often has many parents, and it is certainly true that the design, creation and operation of these D-Day ports involved an enormous number of specialist teams. Churchill could claim a role as their godfather. For, as he was later very keen to point out, his paper on future naval policy for Lloyd George in 1917 had foreseen some of these very developments. In it, he had proposed the creation of an artificial base on the shallow sandbanks of the Horn Reef, off the Danish coast, which could be created from

A sufficient number of flat-bottomed barges or caissons made, not of steel but of concrete . . . They would float when empty of water and could thus be towed across to the site of the artificial island . . . By this means a torpedo and weather-proof harbour, like an atoll, would be created in the open sea, with regular pens for the destroyers and submarines, and alighting platforms for aeroplanes.

Churchill was clearly not the only one to be thinking along these lines, either in 1917 or later, and there is no suggestion he circulated or published his First World War naval policy paper after becoming Prime Minister in 1940. It fell upon those charged with delivering the return to France to reach the same conclusions when faced with a similar problem. The solution came in stages, but Churchill was there to provide support and patronage at every step. First came the idea for the construction *in situ* of a temporary pontoon pier, to allow unloading of ships onto the beaches. It was promoted by Mountbatten at Combined Operations and developed by the leading military engineer, Colonel Bruce White. The problems were formidable. Any structures would need to be able to cope with rising Channel tides of up to 30 feet and 4 knots in strength, as well as batterings from the Atlantic storms. If floating pontoons were used, they would have to be very securely moored.

The concept was approved by the Prime Minister at the end of May 1942. He used his red pen to annotate the paper with his response:

> They <u>must</u> float up & down on the tide. The anchor problem must be mastered. The ships must have a side-flap cut in them, and a drawbridge long enough to overreach the moorings of the piers. Let me have the best solution worked out. Don't argue the matter. The difficulties will argue for themselves.

This document was subsequently reproduced as a facsimile in his war memoirs and framed and hung on his study wall at Chartwell. It was the start of a concerted campaign by the Prime Minister to get action on the issue. On 26 September he sent a minute to the Chiefs of Staff and the Minister of Production, expressing his belief that 'we ought to have three or four miles of this pier tackle. It could of course be used in many places in short sections. Pray do not hastily turn this aside.'

Delivery fell to Mountbatten, as Chief of Combined Operations. By the end of October, he was wrestling with the logistics, reporting back that a major operation on the French beaches would require a sustained lift of 10,000 to 12,000 tons of supplies every day and that four piers would be needed to handle 50 per cent of the total. Three potential designs were being investigated. Churchill kept the matter on the agenda of the Chiefs of Staff Committee, insisting on regular progress reports and sending repeated missives to Mountbatten encouraging him to 'press on'. Inevitably, the Prime Minister sought the advice of his scientific adviser Lord Cherwell, who in turn brought in Brigadier Jefferis of MD1, the head of a specialist weapons research unit established with prime ministerial patronage and often referred to as 'Churchill's Toyshop'. He wanted the best brains working on the problem and was not prepared to let the matter drop.

By March 1943, he was back on the attack. He wanted to know if the piers could be used to save on landing craft in Operation

Husky, the invasion of Sicily, complaining that 'This matter is being much neglected. Dilatory experiments with varying types and patterns have resulted in our having nothing. It is now nearly six months since I urged the construction of several miles of piers. Was Brigadier Jefferis consulted?' Churchill insisted on writing to General Eisenhower, pointing out that, 'the conditions are incomparably more favourable to the use of quickly constructed piers in the "Husky" area than in the English Channel'. This, in spite of the fact that Mountbatten had already reported to him that there were enough landing craft to maintain the required forces in Sicily, where they were only contemplating supplies through the beaches for one month for one and a half divisions; a tiny fraction of the scale of what would be needed in Normandy. Meanwhile, the trials continued.

The issue was also on the agenda of General Morgan as part of his Overlord planning. But the difficulties remained. The pontoon piers might allow for unloading directly onto the beaches, but they would need protecting against the sustained rough seas that would be expected by autumn. Without some protection that could be put in place very quickly, it was also feared that the smaller landing craft used for the initial assault could suffer very heavy casualties in rough seas. This called for the creation of complete self-contained harbours and barriers on a huge scale and threatened to derail the entire operation. It was at this point that Hughes-Hallett, the naval commodore commanding the assault force, had his brainwave:

> On Sunday, June 20, I went with Brian Egerton and Richard Fenning, as was our custom, to attend the morning service at the Abbey, and throughout most of the service I turned the whole matter over and over again in my mind. During the singing of the Anthem, it suddenly came to me in a flash that we must, and could, create an artificial area of sheltered water on a Napoleonic scale by sinking a host of block-ships so as to create vast breakwaters within perhaps 12 hours of the original landing.

Given his religious location, he could put this down to divine inspiration. The use of blockships enabled the nucleus of the Mulberry harbour to be established quickly, as they could sail themselves into position before scuttling. The site could then be strengthened by the addition of all the other elements – the huge concrete blocks and steel structures that would take longer to assemble. It allowed planning for the harbours to proceed at full speed. It was agreed at the first Quebec Conference that there should be two Mulberries, one American off Omaha Beach and one British at Arromanches. Hughes-Hallett worried that the American port was being constructed purely for political reasons, having been told by an American colleague that 'Our Army boys . . . are determined to have a port of their own.' When he warned that it was a technical impossibility because there was no convenient shoal of water on which to sink the blockships and caissons off the American beaches, he was told: 'but they have set their hearts on an artificial harbour of their own – almost as if it were a status symbol – they will have their way whatever you or I say, so we might as well string along with them'. Its British counterpart would later become unofficially known as Port Winston (Churchill declining the official designation of 'Port Churchill').

It was a fitting name. Churchill grasped the need for these artificial harbours and now took it upon himself to oversee their delivery in time for D-Day in June. Having recovered from his illness in North Africa, and aware that the date for Overlord was now set, he threw himself into the preparations. Given the competing demands for wartime production, he was worried that targets were not being met and that some of the innovations he favoured were not being pursued.

The result was a call for immediate action. Upon returning from Morocco in January 1944, he fired off a minute to Cherwell, Ismay and General Laycock, Mountbatten's successor as Head of Combined Operations, expressing his concern at 'the continued failures on the Synthetic Harbour business'. He then took the chair at a late-night meeting in the Cabinet War Rooms on

Monday 24 January, using the convening power of his office to bring together the key military and political departments for a conference at which 'everything connected with the Synthetic Harbours and with the piers and landing stages should be considered'. It was a case of 'Action this Day'.

The ministers in charge of Production, War Transport and Supply were brought together with some of the senior military commanders for Overlord. Bruce White, the designer of the artificial piers, now a brigadier, was present. Eisenhower was represented by his Chief of Staff, the American general, Walter Bedell Smith. Cherwell was there to support Churchill on the technical issues.

The Prime Minister kicked things off by stating that he was 'disturbed by recent reports about the "Mulberry" position and feared some of the projects were lagging behind schedule'. There followed a frank discussion. The Admiralty made clear that, in addition to the two Mulberry harbours, which might take three or four weeks to establish, another five Gooseberry breakwaters would be required to provide immediate protection for shipping in the shallower water off the beaches. Rear Admiral Tennant of the Allied Expeditionary Naval Force confirmed that without them casualties to landing craft might be as high as 20 to 30 per cent per day if there was not reasonably calm water on the landing beaches. The Prime Minister was playing his role as a prodding stick and demanding action. What was the latest progress on the different elements required for building these harbours and how could their construction and delivery 'be pressed forward with the utmost energy'? Were there enough tugs to tow them across the Channel? How many blockships would be needed and where would they come from? What could the Americans provide?

Those present were left in no doubt about the urgency of the issue and what was at stake. The scale of what was being contemplated was immense. The creation of the two Mulberries and five Gooseberries required 25,000 feet of blockships plus the towing of nearly one million tons of material across one hundred miles of open sea from British harbours. Those assembled were given just

THIS DOCUMENT IS THE PROPERTY OF HIS BRITANNIC MAJESTY'S GOVERNMENT

● The circulation of this paper has been strictly limited.

It is issued for the personal use of...

● **MOST SECRET.**   Copy No......4.4

C.O.S.(44) 53 (0)

20TH JANUARY, 1944

WAR CABINET

CHIEFS OF STAFF COMMITTEE

MERCHANT SHIPPING REQUIRED FOR MULBERRIES

Memorandum by the First Sea Lord

At Quadrant+ the Combined Chiefs of Staff were informed
that the provision of Artificial Harbours was necessary to the
success of OVERLORD.   After QUADRANT the Combined Chiefs of
Staff were informed

    (i) that two harbours were required

        (a) An American Harbour assigned to American Forces

(W.S.C.) (b) A British Harbour assigned to British and
            Canadian Forces.

   (ii) that sunken ships should be used as possible components
       for the shallow water Breakwater to the full extent
       of their availability.

2.   On the 9th October the Chiefs of Staff took note that an
American Mulberry and a British Mulberry would be required for
OVERLORD and on the 12th January that, in addition to two
Mulberries, shelters would be required for landing craft which
have been given the name "Gooseberries".

3.   As instructed the Admiralty has examined the operational
requirement for the composition of the Breakwater in conjunction
with S.A.C. and the War Office.   It has been established that
the most satisfactory solution will be a combination of
Bombardon and Phoenix in water of over 2 fathams and blockships
in water of under 2 fathoms.

        + C.C.S. 307, C.C.S. 108th Mtg. and C.O.S.(Q) 8
        x C.C.S. 117th Mtg and C.C.S. 307/2
        / C.O.S.(43) 243rd Mtg. (0)
        / C.O.S.(44) 9th Mtg. (0) and C.O.S.(44) 17 (0)
        ≠ C.O.S.(44) 1st Mtg. (0) and
           C.O.S.(43) 776 (0) 2nd Revise

..1..

*Paper prepared for Chiefs of Staff, outlining requirements
for constructing artificial harbours, 20 January 1944*

seven days to report back. When they reconvened in the same place at the same time, 22.00 hours in the Cabinet War Rooms, on the following Monday, it was clear that the prime ministerial prod had worked. The latest production estimates for the steel pierheads and floating roadways (Whales), for the reinforced concrete caissons (Phoenixes) and the huge interlocking steel crosses (Bombardons) were reported and the Prime Minister expressed himself satisfied that 'a very substantial part of the requirement would be met in adequate time'. (For more information on the different elements used in the Mulberries, see pp. 166–7.) The number of tugs remained a potential bottleneck, but priority would be given to shipping extra numbers from the United States.

The meeting of 24 January also acknowledged some failures. Not all the bright schemes of the scientists and engineers had come to fruition. It was announced that plans to create barriers against the waves using pipes discharging a constant stream of air bubbles, or inflated airbags carrying curtains of concrete (code-name Lilo) had been abandoned. There was more of a discussion about the viability of the temporary air strips (Tentacles). Churchill expressed himself 'very disturbed' that the one existing prototype in America was being broken up for other uses. He saw a potential win in using these structures to guarantee the vital air mastery over the beaches, but reluctantly gave way when Air Marshal Leigh-Mallory, the Air Commander-in-Chief for the Allied Expeditionary Force, confirmed that 'our' fighters would have sufficient range from the UK to maintain complete cover over the beaches, while the artificial airfield would take at least forty-eight hours to erect, by which time the RAF expected to have constructed two airfields on shore.

Of course, if things had developed slightly differently, they might have been discussing using an aircraft carrier made of ice! While this sounds preposterous, it was a genuine idea from the fertile mind of Geoffrey Pyke. He had been studying the molecular qualities of pure ice and had discovered that if small particles of some other substance, such as wood pulp, were suspended in water and then frozen, the resulting material had an incredible tensile strength. Moreover, it could not be easily melted and was very easily repaired. In September 1942 he sent a memorandum of over two hundred pages to Mountbatten explaining how this new material would win the war and change the world. It opened with a Pykeism, a quote from *The Scandal of Father Brown* by G. K. Chesterton: 'Father Brown laid down his cigar and said carefully: "It isn't that they can't see the solution. It is that they can't see the problem."'

The paper proposed an incredible number of uses for the new material, which became known as 'Pykrete', suggesting that it could effectively win the war on its own, but the one that grabbed the attention of Admiral Mountbatten was the possibility of unsinkable ship bergs that could be used to carry aircraft around the globe. Extensive tests were carried out. The codename suggested by Pyke was Habbakuk, a misspelling of Habakkuk, a minor prophet from the Hebrew scriptures (Pyke was Jewish).

Mountbatten clearly relished demonstrating the properties of the reinforced ice. He is supposed to have won over the Prime Minister by dropping a block into Churchill's hot bath to show it did not melt. At the Quebec Conference in August 1943, he called for a block to be brought into a meeting of the Combined Chiefs of Staff and then proceeded to open fire on it with his revolver. Brooke watched in horror as 'the bullet rebounded out of the block and buzzed round our legs like an angry bee'. Those waiting outside thought that their Chiefs had reached such a level of disagreement that they had started shooting one another, causing Churchill to note dryly in his later war memoirs, 'But who in war will not have his laugh amid the skulls? – and here was one.'

In the end, the ice carriers proved too difficult and perhaps too revolutionary to develop, especially at a time when resources were stretched, and more conventional weapons were needed in such huge numbers. But as late as June 1943, Churchill still harboured hopes that something might be brought on stream in time to 'play a decisive part against the war in Japan' or that the Pykrete be used for static platforms – 'seadromes' – to help with the invasion of France. It was not to be.

MULBERRIES AND GOOSEBERRIES

Another related problem for D-Day was how to deliver the Allied forces onto the beaches in the face of obstacles and heavy defending fire. The beaches were protected by several layers of defence. These began with sunken obstacles, submerged at high tide, including jagged steel structures and wooden stakes with mounted mines designed to knock out landing craft or vehicles coming ashore. Once on the beach the assault troops faced barbed wire, further obstructions and land mines, while being subjected to a sweeping crossfire from overlooking gun emplacements, pill boxes and strongholds. To get off the beach, they needed to break through the concrete sea wall. Bombardment from the air and sea would be vital in softening these defences but it would not eliminate them. Success was dependent upon having sufficient mobile heavy armour to provide close support for the infantry along with specialist teams to clear a path off the beach as quickly as possible. The Dieppe raid had shown the difficulty of landing tanks on an enemy-held shore and provided a horrible illustration of the vulnerability of infantry if trapped on the beach. This was a nightmare scenario for Churchill, and it is not surprising therefore that he took a keen interest in developing solutions.

Churchill's association with the development of the tank takes us back – once again – to the First World War. As First Lord of the Admiralty in 1914–15 he had refused to restrict himself to purely naval matters and had embraced the development of new technologies that might help break the trench stalemate on the Western Front. The same motivation that led him to advocate for the Dardanelles operation had also caused him to support the development of the Royal Naval Air Service (even taking flying lessons himself) and to sponsor early research into heavily fortified 'land ships' that would allow British troops to retake the offensive. In a memorandum to Prime Minister Asquith, written in January 1915, he outlined the problem as the 'getting across of 100 or 200 yards of open space and wire entanglements' and suggested that the solution would be:

to fit up a number of steam tractors with small, armoured shelters, in which men and machine guns could be placed, which would be bullet proof . . . The caterpillar system would enable trenches to be crossed quite easily, and the weight of the machine would destroy all wire entanglements.

In the same paper, he had gone on to call for the production of large shields and for the use of smokescreens to provide cover for attacking troops. Once again, then, by the time of the Second World War he was already familiar with the challenge faced by the D-Day planners and willing to support technical innovation. This led him to identify a kindred spirit in Major General Percy Cleghorn Stanley Hobart.

Hobart was one of the pioneers of modern tank warfare: a passionate believer in a mobile, mechanised army, he was an uncompromising figure who spent most of his career at odds with the military establishment. The historian and strategist, Basil Liddell Hart, compared him to Guderian or Rommel, who developed the German Panzer forces and principles of *blitzkrieg* warfare, while noting that 'in the British way, he [Hobart] was never given such opportunity of command in war as they obtained'. He was first brought to Churchill's attention by the author and independent MP Alan Herbert, who wrote to Winston in October 1936 referring to Hobart as 'top dog, I think (or very nearly so) of Tanks' who 'has a lot of interesting things he wants to say to someone who like you knows about Defence'. Hobart was then commanding the 1st Tank Brigade, while Churchill was conducting his campaign for British rearmament and opposing the appeasement of Hitler. It is clear that they met and that Hobart warned Churchill of the need for more tanks. At that time, like many others, Churchill had not appreciated the full extent to which armoured forces might transform modern warfare. Once installed as Prime Minister, and faced with the success of the German Panzer forces in Western Europe in 1940, he realised that he needed to play catch-up and massively scale up British tank numbers.

By this time Hobart had been forcibly retired from the army. He had been sent to Egypt to form a mobile force for desert warfare (what would later become the 7th Armoured Division, famous under Montgomery for their victories in North Africa as the 'Desert Rats') but had fallen out with his Commander-in-Chief, who described him as 'Unduly optimistic' about the capacities of the Royal Armoured Corps. During the summer of 1940, he was living in Chipping Campden in the Cotswolds, brooding on his dismissal and playing a role in the local defence volunteers known as the Home Guard. Fortunately, he still had friends in high places, who brought his predicament to the ear of the Prime Minister. Following a meeting at Chequers in October, Churchill was adamant that Hobart was exactly the sort of tank commander he now needed, sending a minute to General Dill, the then Chief of the Imperial General Staff (head of the army), confirming that Hobart should be given command of one of the new tank divisions.

Hobart assumed responsibility for raising and training the 11th Armoured Division, but by September 1942 his abrasive personality, strong views on tank warfare, ill health and age (at fifty-seven he was now considered too old to command the division in combat) were continuing to cause frictions and Churchill had to step in and save his career for a second time, writing to the Secretary of State for War, describing Hobart as:

> A man of quite exceptional mental attainments with great strength of character, and although he does not work easily with others, it is a great pity we have not more of his like in the Service. I have been shocked at the persecution to which he has been subjected . . . The High Commands of the Army are not a club.

The timing was fortunate. General Alan Brooke was now Chief of the Imperial General Staff and prepared to support Hobart, while preparation for the invasion of France, though subordinate in the short term to the war in the Mediterranean, was firmly back on the agenda. It was clear that heavy armour was going to be needed to clear the beaches and General Hobart seemed the man most experienced to deliver it. He was given command of the new and innovative 79th Division – a name continued in today's army for the unit charged with original thinking – and moreover the freedom, with the patronage of Churchill and Brooke, to develop a force that was capable of leading the assault onto the Normandy beaches.

As foreseen by Churchill in 1915, the tank had already been adapted to clear obstacles, and tanks with specially mounted flails had been used to clear minefields at the Battle of El Alamein, but Hobart was able to take their modification to another level. Every likely German obstacle was studied, and solutions put in place. Special hull-like screens were developed allowing tanks to sail onto the beaches; there were bomb-firing tanks that could blast open concrete fortifications; track-laying tanks that could lay down a route over areas of soft sand; tanks with bridges that could overcome obstacles; and others with flame-throwers or wire-cutters. Crucial to Hobart's thinking was that these specialist tanks should also be able to fire and fight, thereby allowing them both to defend themselves and to play an offensive role beyond the clearing of obstacles.

Nor was Hobart working in isolation on innovation for the landings. Combined Operations and MD1 were also involved in developing new weaponry and equipment. The Prime Minister's scientific adviser, Lord Cherwell, maintained a watching brief on it all and his support for particular projects was often vital in getting the Prime Minister's attention. Meanwhile, Churchill loved nothing more than escaping London to watch the latest demonstration. Not every innovation worked or proved useful. Tanks carrying bright lighting for night attack were not needed once it had been decided to attack in daylight (and were of course themselves potential targets for enemy fire). A proposal for a cliff-bridging device that would take the tanks and mechanised transport directly from the ships and place them on top of the cliffs was felt to be 'technically feasible' but not 'tactically applicable' to the Normandy coastline. A vital innovation installed soon after the landings was the laying of a pipeline under the ocean (Pluto), which ultimately provided a constant source of fuel from the Isle of Wight across to Normandy.

The tactics mattered too. To land tanks on the beaches ahead of infantry in rolling seas required an incredible amount of coordination. The production in sufficient numbers of landing craft, especially the larger tank-landing craft, was a bottleneck and a source of serious concern right up until early 1944. Their use also required the development of special operational procedures. Tank-landing craft were heavier and travelled more slowly than lighter troop-carrying craft. This meant that all craft had to be carefully brought together at sea off the beaches, with their release towards shore carefully timed by the responsible naval officers. Once on the beaches, the assault had to be directed so that the specialist teams and tanks could work together to clear the obstacles and minefields quickly and efficiently, otherwise the constant flow of troops onto the beaches would quickly become backed up and provide easy targets for enemy fire. Once a beach had been seized, beachmasters, specially trained naval officers, would be needed to direct traffic on and off the landing sites.

This all required considerable training. The Prime Minister continued to maintain a watching brief over it all. He spent time visiting British and American forces, including US paratroopers near Winchester, telling them that they had a 'great part to play', and that they were the 'most modern expression of war'. The morning of 31 March 1944 found him in Yorkshire, where he visited the Guards Armoured Division and watched a lorry being driven through water. Elsewhere, others were making their preparations.

Hughes-Hallett, as the naval assault force commander, had worked hard on growing his command. By the end of 1943, Force J numbered 15,000 officers and men and was capable of landing a full division of troops on the various beaches. Hallett had 28 assault ships, 200 tank-landing craft and a much larger number of infantry-landing craft, motor gunboats, steam gunboats, motor launches and support craft under his direct control, while other British and American naval resources were being assembled elsewhere around the English shoreline. He had also developed, trialled and trained his force in procedures for assembling, transporting and launching the assault. His reward was command of the heavy cruiser HMS *Jamaica*, which – probably much to his regret – did not participate in D-Day.

Having helped train others in Canada, Roland MacKenzie's journey now took him to Scotland. Arriving in July 1943 he spent time at Banff and Edzell, familiarising himself with the tactics and equipment in use in the European theatre. Then to Staffordshire to join his crew and to undertake intensive operational training ahead of combat sorties. By January 1944 he was graded 'above average' and considered ready.

T. L. Rodgers and the 504th Parachute Infantry Regiment arrived in Liverpool and transferred to Camp Stoughton in Leicestershire. As his unit began to settle in and, according to one of their own – Ross Carter – began to familiarise themselves with local women and beer, it fell to teetotaller TL to look after them. As the rest of Ross's unit behaved, in his words, as 'uncouth barbarians', TL and twenty-four others volunteered for detached service as Pathfinders in Normandy. Rodgers' parting words to his friend Ross Carter were, 'I'll be as careful as I can, Ross, but I may not be careful enough this time.'

Christian Oldham (now married as Mrs Christian Lamb) was also doing her bit. Recruited in February 1944 for a piece of top-secret work, she now found herself alone in a tiny room in a central Whitehall basement surrounded by detailed maps of the Normandy coastline. Her job was to painstakingly 'delineate everything that could be seen on every compass bearing from each landing position, visible from the bridge of an approaching Landing Craft for identifiable confirmation'. She was only in her early twenties and privy to one of the greatest secrets of the war. She knew the actual landing beaches. Sometimes she would see Churchill on the stairs. For him, those same secrets made this a time of particular worry.

For, while the specialist equipment and training were vital for success on D-Day, the real headache was the sheer scale of the ordinary resources that had to be assembled – the men, their rifles, uniforms and basic kit. The logistical challenge of gathering the troops in southern England and supplying them for a long and growing campaign in Europe was a daunting one. Eisenhower was working on the assumption that, 'A reinforced division, in active operations, consumes from 600 to 700 tons of supplies per day.' When fighting in a fixed position, it would expend ammunition; when moving it would require petrol. Always, it would need food. Within weeks of the assault, there would be thirty-six divisions on the continent. All would require medical services, administration, engineering support, entertainment and welfare.

Churchill struggled with the sheer size of the modern army and feared that the logistical tail was too long, threatening the army's freedom of manoeuvre. His historical idols, great commanders like Alexander the Great and Napoleon, had exploited success on the battlefield by being able to move quickly, but they lived in a simpler age when armies could live from the land. Notwithstanding that, Churchill feared being bogged down and facing another prolonged and bloody war of trench stalemate. In this his views were similar to those of Hobart and Liddell Hart, who favoured a fast-moving mechanised campaign.

As the military plan evolved, Churchill was kept informed through regular meetings with Eisenhower. With progress in Italy slower than expected due to the difficulties encountered by the Allies in breaking out of the Anzio beachhead, the decision was taken not to proceed with Operation Anvil, the landings in the south of France, until after the Normandy assault. It was a decision that Churchill welcomed. He knew Anvil would pull further resources away from Italy. Montgomery wanted Anvil cancelled altogether, but Eisenhower felt that it still had a vital role to play in opening up another route for bringing Allied men and supplies into France. The issue would resurface again after D-Day and provoke a major row between the Supreme Commander and the British Prime Minister. But, for now, Churchill seemed broadly accepting of the reworked Overlord plan. His Private Secretary, Jock Colville, noted in his diary for 4 April that 'The prospect of the 2nd Front worries him, though he says he is "hardening to it".'

Three days later on Good Friday, Churchill addressed a gathering of all the military leaders at St Paul's School, Montgomery's headquarters, writing afterwards to Roosevelt that 'I do not agree with the loose talk which has been going on on both sides of the Atlantic about the unduly heavy casualties which we will sustain. In my view it is the Germans who will suffer very heavy casualties when our band of brothers gets among them.'

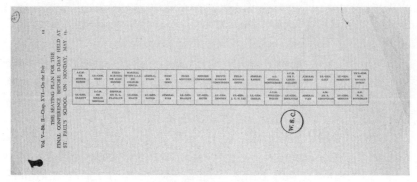

Seating plan for OVERLORD conference
at St Paul's School, 15 May 1944

He was back at St Paul's on 15 May to attend the final conference on D-Day preparations. The Chiefs of Staff and all the main military commanders were present. Churchill spoke after the King. Harry Butcher was not present but, from speaking to those who were, he gathered that 'the Prime Minister let go with a slow-starting but fast-ending stemwinder. He preached bravery, ingenuity, and persistence as human qualities of greater value than equipment.' Eisenhower described it as 'one of his [Churchill's] typical fighting speeches' but pointed out that the Americans were struck 'with peculiar force' by one of his expressions. Churchill had repeated his earlier remark to Colville, telling the gathering that he was 'hardening' toward the operation. To General Ismay, this simply meant that the more his boss thought about it, the more certain he was of its success. But to Eisenhower – and Americans then and since – this meant that, 'though he had long doubted its feasibility and had previously advocated its further postponement in favour of operations elsewhere, he had finally, at this late date, come to believe with the

Churchill where he loved to be: surrounded by the Allied commanders in North Africa, 1943. From left to right: Foreign Secretary Anthony Eden, General Sir Alan Brooke, Air Chief Marshal Tedder, Winston Churchill, Admiral Cunningham, General Alexander, General Marshall, General Eisenhower and General Montgomery.

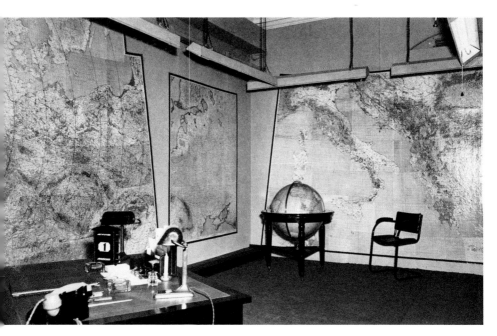

The next best thing to being at the front: Churchill's map room.

Churchill with US paratroop
March 1944.

Watching invasion training in Yorkshire, March 1944.

With Monty in France, 1944.

Supreme Commanders: with Eisenhower, c. March 1945.

Mastery of the seas and skies, June 1944.

Breaking Hitler's Atlantic Wall, June 1944.

Ready to go ashore,
June 1944.

Flak and obstacles
on the beaches,
June 1944.

Storming ashore, June 1944.

Commandos on the beach, 7 June 1944. The scene experienced by Tony Hugill.

General O'Connor, Churchill, Smuts, Montgomery and Brooke, 12 June 1944.

Churchill talking to British and Canadian troops in Normandy, 22 July 1944.

General de Gaulle
speaking in France, 1944.

Joan Bright Astley at
the Yalta Conference,
February 1945.

Roland MacKenzie DFC.

Christian Oldham (later Lamb) as a young Wren.

Company Sergeant Major Stanley Hollis, on parade, wearing medal ribbons including the Victoria Cross and two wound stripes on his sleeve, c. late 1944–1945.

T. L. Rodgers with his fellow Pathfinders, June 1944. T. L. Rodgers is third from the left, top row – his face has been blacked out for the night jump.

rest of us that this was the true course of action in order to achieve the victory'. Writing later, Churchill was adamant that he used this phrase 'in the sense of wishing to strike if humanly possible, even if the limiting conditions we laid down are not exactly fulfilled'. However good his speech, he had unwittingly provided ammunition for those seeking evidence that he was a latecomer to this party.

In the final months before D-Day, Churchill had time to brood on the impending operation. The apparent imbalance between frontline fighting forces and the huge numbers of vehicles and other personnel required to support them was one that he repeatedly returned to. On 17 May he summoned Brooke to his bedside and berated him on the fact that the invasion plan comprised '1000 clerks of the 3rd echelon' and 'catered for one lorry for every 5 men'. Two days later he dined with Montgomery and his staff. Churchill's recollection of this meeting differs from Monty's, but it seems that the Prime Minister had wanted to speak with the General's staff to interrogate them in detail on some of the numbers. According to Montgomery, he took Churchill aside, told him it was too late for changes to be made, that he had given the final decision and that he would not let him argue with his staff, who had 'a terrific job preparing the invasion'. Moreover, if Churchill thought Montgomery's plan was wrong, 'that can only mean you have lost confidence in me'. There was an awkward silence, but then tears came into Churchill's eyes. After composing himself, he moved into the next room and, addressing Monty's team, 'With a twinkle in his eye he said: "I wasn't allowed to have any discussion with you gentlemen."' This was a tilt between these two great wartime leaders. Churchill's moods could change quickly and his frustration gave way to a recognition of the burden Montgomery was bearing and an understanding of the need to back him in front of his team.

In his memoirs, Churchill confirmed this story but disputed that Montgomery had threatened to resign. He also refused to let the matter of numbers go, writing: 'I may add however that I still consider that the proportion of transport vehicles to fighting men in the early phase of the cross–Channel invasion was too high and that the operation suffered both in risk and execution from this fact.'

Churchill may not have developed the D-Day plan, but he was aware of the main problems and used his powers of patronage to advance and support those working to overcome them. Once he focused on the June date, with six months to go, he homed in on the detail, though some of his interventions were clearly more welcome to the commanders than others. He was particularly interested in the military aspects, having studied them since the First World War, but he could not escape the fact that the operation would have huge consequences for the civilian population – parts of the country were about to go into lockdown. Churchill may have been hardening on the enterprise, but the truth was that he still had plenty to worry about.

Mulberries and Gooseberries: A Layman's Guide

The artificial harbours used to support Overlord were the product of a huge construction programme, carried out around the United Kingdom and involving enormous quantities of steel and concrete. This was the Allied equivalent to Hitler's heavily fortified Atlantic Wall. The two Mulberry harbours comprised the following main elements.

Blockships: old merchant and naval ships that could sail across the Channel and then scuttle themselves to form part of the harbour wall. They provided an initial breakwater while other elements were being towed across the Channel and assembled.

Bombardons: huge cruciform steel constructions, each weighing 1,000 tons and being 200 feet in length, designed to form interlocking structures and create foundations for Mulberry harbours.

Gooseberries: artificial breakwaters assembled close to the beaches to provide protection from rough seas for landing craft and smaller ships.

Lilos: pipelines of compressed air that, when released, would create a breakwater through a curtain of rising air. These did not prove technically feasible and were not developed.

Phoenixes: large hollow concrete units, each weighing thousands of tons and being 200 feet in length, which could be manoeuvred into place by tugs and then sunk to form part of the Mulberry harbour or Gooseberry breakwater.

Tentacles: plans for floating artificial runways that could be used to provide constant air cover over the beaches. In the end these were not used as it was possible to maintain air cover from the UK.

Whales: pontoon pierheads and floating roadways designed to offload supplies from the deep-water Mulberry harbour.

Operation Overlord: The Landing Beaches and the Landing Zones

Once Supreme Commander General Dwight Eisenhower had approved the land forces Commander General Bernard Montgomery's revised plan for an assault on a wider frontage than the original COSSAC plan had proposed, the detailed selection of the landing beaches and landing zones could be confirmed. Where possible, and consistent with one of Monty's principles, each beach should be assaulted by the leading formation of each separate corps axis of advance, thus reducing the likelihood of logistic confusion. The airborne forces would protect the flanks of the beach assaults.

From west to east, the assault beaches were confirmed as:

UTAH: Between Saint-Martin-de-Varreville and Poup-peville on the east coast of the Cotentin Peninsula, Utah beach was to be assaulted by the 8 and 22 Infantry Regiments of the US 4th Infantry Division, the leading formation of the US VII Corps under the command of Major General J. (Lightning Joe) Lawton Collins.

Pointe du Hoc: This was not a landing beach, but the US 2nd Ranger Battalion was tasked to scale the cliffs of Pointe du Hoc and capture the battery of heavy guns that could be brought to bear on the Utah or Omaha beaches.

OMAHA: Between Vierville-sur-Mer and Colleville-sur-Mer, Omaha beach was to be assaulted by the 16 Infantry Regiment of the 1st US Infantry Division (the Big Red One) and by the 116 Infantry Regiment of the 29th Infantry Division, which was placed under the command of the US 1st Infantry Division for the initial assault. The 1st Infantry Division was the leading formation of the US V Corps under the command of Major General Leonard T. (Gee) Gerow.

GOLD: Between Arromanches-les-Bains and La Rivière, Gold beach was to be assaulted by 69 Brigade (including Stan Hollis's 6th Green Howards) and 231 Brigade of the British 50th (Tyne-Tees) Division, the leading formation of the British XXX Corps under the command of Lieutenant General Gerald Bucknall. The 47 Commando Royal Marines were also to land on the western end of Gold beach.

JUNO: Between La Rivière and Saint-Aubin-sur-Mer, Juno beach was to be assaulted by 7 Brigade and 8 Brigade of the Canadian 3rd Infantry Division, one of the two leading formations of the British 1 Corps under the command of Lieutenant General John Crocker.

SWORD: Between Saint-Aubin-sur-Mer and the River Orne, Sword beach was to be assaulted by 8 Brigade of the British 3rd Infantry Division, by 41 Commando and 48

Commando Royal Marines of the 4th Special Service Brigade in the west and by the 4 Commando Royal Marines of the 1st Special Service Brigade in the east. The 3rd Infantry Division was the second leading formation of the British 1 Corps.

With the proposed landings on both Juno and Sword beaches, the British 1 Corps had the most units under command of any major formation on D-Day. This had been the chief focus of the former COSSAC plan, and perhaps remained so, with the hope of capturing Caen on the first day.

The flank protection for the beach assault forces would be provided by:

In the West: The US 82nd and 101st Airborne Divisions, centred on Sainte-Mère-Église. Their mission was to protect the western flank of Utah beach and offer the opportunity for US forces to seize the port of Cherbourg as early in the campaign as possible.

In the East: The British 6th Airborne Division was tasked to capture and hold the crossings over the River Orne and Orne Canal in order to prevent German counter-attack forces threatening the eastern flank of the amphibious operation. They were also tasked to capture the battery of heavy guns at Merville that could threaten the eastern end of Sword beach.

Analysis of the landings on all the beaches and landing zones will be described in Chapter 10.

PART TWO
Execution

COPY

34

FROZEN No. 1087.

TOO 041220Z.
TOR 041620z.

IMMEDIATE

From:- Sextant.

To:- Air Ministry.

_____

FROZEN No. 1087.   4th January, 1944.

Prime Minister to General Ismay.

Your minute of January 1 about security
arrangements for OVERLORD.

1.. I do not think it will be possible to conceal
from the enemy that large preparations are being made
along our coasts. It may, however, be possible to
prevent his guessing when, where or in what strength
our forces will be used.

2. I am not in favour of such sweeping restrictions
as you now propose, particularly the visitors ban, nor
of so early a date as February 1. We must beware of
handing out irksome for irksome's sake. The question may
be brought before the War Cabinet, but Sir Edward Bridges
is to make the members acquainted with this expression
of my opinion.

3. I entirely agree with para 5 of your minute. In
this connection see a disgraceful article in the Sunday
Times of January 2 by Scrutator, para. 1. in which a
specific month is clearly indicated. No doubt many of
these considerations are present in the minds of military
correspondents and others, but none the less harm may be
done. In this case I read in the local news that the
Sunday Times "has stated that the operation will not
take place until the month mentioned" and this no doubt
is sent all over the world. You should ask the Minister
of Information to consider whether any action can be taken
against the Sunday Times and also that the strictest
injunctions must be given to all the newspapers, and
especially to their military correspondents, against
discussing and speculation upon the prospects and
possibilities of OVERLORD.

T.O.O. 041220z.

Telegram from Churchill to Ismay, 4 January 1944

7

Lockdown

'We must beware of handing out irksome for irksome's sake.'

C HURCHILL WAS WORRIED. Britain was now an armed camp. However good the deception plan, it was impossible to hide the scale of the Overlord preparations. By the beginning of 1944 it was clear that huge forces were being assembled throughout the United Kingdom with the intention of crossing the Channel.

By June 1944 there would be over 1,600,000 US service men and women in the country. They were joining Canadian naval, air and army units, as well as other forces, some drawn from the British Empire and Commonwealth, some from occupied European countries.

The whole length of the British south and east coasts was now covered in bases and training grounds. Airfields had sprung up all over the countryside. This at least helped to confuse the enemy as to exactly where the blow would fall, as it kept open possibilities for an attack from Scotland into Scandinavia, or from the east of England towards Belgium or the Pas-de-Calais, but the longer the period of waiting, the greater the risk of a security breach.

Concerned by mounting speculation in the newspapers about the nature and timing of the return to France, Churchill wrote to Eisenhower on 28 January informing him that a notice had been issued to the press telling them that there must be no attempt to forecast dates even by month or season; that discussion must be avoided of the desirability or likelihood of landings on particular places, sections of coastline or territory; and above all that there must be no estimates of the scale on which attacks would be conducted either in men or material.

The Prime Minister was particularly anxious that Eisenhower apply the same 'stringent attitude' to those press correspondents accredited to his headquarters. The fear was that reporters might be able to gather and exchange small pieces of information and so build up and publish an accurate picture of planned events. Eisenhower's natural instincts were to trust correspondents and to build positive relationships with them, but it was agreed that discretion would be used and that no reporters would be accredited to his headquarters until just before the operation.

Such speculation was not surprising, especially in the British papers. The large military presence on UK soil imposed an ever-increasing strain on the British people and their already creaking infrastructure and economy. By 1944, the civilian population had endured four years of wartime curfews, rationing and blackouts. The fact that victory was now in sight only made additional restrictions to freedom of speech or movement harder to bear. Yet this is what the military now demanded in order to protect the security of their operation.

Churchill was caught in the middle. As Prime Minister and Minister of Defence, it fell upon him to steer the difficult course between helping the military operation and preserving civil liberties and a semblance of normal life. It was not just the military implications of the Overlord plan that he began to ponder while recovering in Marrakech. On 4 January, in a minute to General Ismay, he expressed his reservations about the proposed restrictions on the Home Front and of 'handing out irksome for irksome's sake'.

Once back in London, he proposed a weekly meeting, to be held in Downing Street at 18.00 hours every Wednesday (a slot that had previously been used for his now redundant Anti-U-boat Committee), in order to deal with the civil rather than the military questions. Membership was limited to those ministers most directly concerned. And so the Overlord Preparations Committee came into being.

The first meeting took place on 2 February and heard from the Minister of Production, Oliver Lyttelton, about the potential impact of Overlord on the inland transportation system. There was a fear that the wholesale movement of troops and materials would impose a huge additional strain on the railways that might bring everything to a halt. Additional operational traffic was estimated at 900,000 tons but that would also require the carriage of an extra 400,000 tons of coal to keep the trains moving. Meanwhile, 9,000 extra men would be required to help with the faster loading of a greater number of wagons. Normal 'coastwise' traffic would need to be cut to make way for the special military requirements. More use would have to be made of roads and canals. Supplies to troops abroad would be impacted, and Lyttelton recommended that the civilian population at home should be exposed to a publicity campaign 'to bring home to every inhabitant in these Islands the absolute necessity of economizing in transport in every form'.

By spring, the ability to meet such production targets was being further hit by industrial unrest. The miners of Yorkshire were on strike, as were apprentices from the shipyards in Tyneside, the Clyde and Yorkshire (protesting against enforced conscription into the mines). If unresolved, this had the potential to become what Churchill called 'a situation of utmost gravity' and to require 'exceptional measures'.

It was a grim picture, and one that was only going to get more difficult. General Morgan, who was now working for Eisenhower on the Overlord preparations, had written to the Chiefs of Staff stating that the ban on visitors to coastal towns in the south and east was vital to the success of the operation and needed to be in place by 15 March. It was suggested that the Prime Minister should announce it. Several arguments were being made in support of the military position. The ban would reduce the non-resident population, making it easier to detect enemy agents. The leakage of vital information was felt to be more likely through visitors than residents. The strain on transport would be reduced. Enemy bombing would cause less disruption if visitors were absent, while the introduction of these measures would show the public and the United States Army the seriousness with which the British government was taking the operation. The issue pitched the military against the civilian authorities, in the form of the Home Office (responsible for domestic law and order), the Ministry for Home Security and the Scottish Office, who were not convinced that a sufficient case had been made. They questioned whether the absence of non-residents would really make it easier to detect enemy agents or reduce the danger of security breaches, and felt that the police would only be able to make a partial enforcement of the ban through snap checks. They did, however, support giving the police in these areas greater discretionary powers to arrest persons without identity cards, and to close places of public gathering, control refugee movements and introduce stricter censorship of communications.

Both sides were looking to the Prime Minister to adjudicate. At this stage, he remained unconvinced by the military case. In a minute to General Ismay and Edward Bridges, the Cabinet Secretary, ahead of the next Overlord Preparations Committee meeting, he made it clear that he was 'not in favour of the sweeping recommendations now proposed'. He was in no mood to be bossed around on his home soil by the Americans, writing, 'We do not wish to knock our people about in order to impress the United States.' The matter should be considered on security grounds alone, and here he remained sceptical. The idea that the absence of visitors would relieve the roads from panic congestion caused by enemy bombing seemed 'rather an echo from 1940' and he thought it just as likely that security breaches would come from residents as visitors.

In particular I deprecate the wholesale character of these orders. Let me have on one sheet of paper a list of the kind of things that you do not wish visitors, as apart from residents, to see and where they are primarily located. I propose shortly to go and make a tour myself of some of these districts.

At the meeting on 9 February, it was decided that further information was needed before a decision about the ban could be taken, but the police were given their extra powers. On balance, the Overlord Preparations Committee took the view, supported by Churchill, that disruption of civilian life should be minimised for as long as possible, but it was already clear that the emphasis was shifting in support of the military as the days counted down towards D-Day. There was, though, also a security argument for delay, as the announcement of any ban would indicate to the enemy that major operations were afoot.

A very similar debate took place around the question of introducing a travel ban between the United Kingdom and Ireland. The Irish Free State, comprising the counties of southern Ireland or Eire, had won its independence from Britain in 1922 and – much to Churchill's annoyance – had opted for neutrality during the Second World War. Meanwhile, the six counties of Northern Ireland had remained part of the United Kingdom, and the border between north and south had remained open. When Christian Oldham had been based in Belfast in 1943, she and her fellow Wrens escaped British wartime austerity and rationing by undertaking regular raiding parties to Dublin in order to eat as much food as possible and to buy clothes, which they smuggled back past the customs inspectors. As women in their twenties, they were not deemed a security risk, but both the Germans and the Japanese maintained a diplomatic presence in Dublin, and travel between the UK and Ireland provided an obvious channel for the escape of information about the build-up and movement of troops for D-Day.

Yet, once again, the arguments were finely balanced. Eisenhower, backed by the British Chiefs of Staff, regarded the closure of the border as 'vital to the success' of his operation and wanted it imposed as quickly as possible, and certainly no later than 15 March. In contrast, the civil ministries wanted it as late as possible and were concerned about its impact on Irish labour. They estimated that about a hundred thousand Irish workers were employed in the United Kingdom, many on vital war work, and they knew that they needed more to help meet the construction and transportation deadlines for D-Day. They feared that a ban – or the fear of a ban – would lead to many downing tools and going home. To mitigate this, they suggested that any restrictions should be imposed with only twenty-four hours' notice and emphasised as temporary.

The committee resolved to press ahead with the preparations. Roosevelt unsuccessfully urged the Irish government to break off diplomatic relations with the Axis powers, which then provided the perfect cover for the British action. The ban was subsequently announced on 12 March, coming into effect on the following day. Defending it in the House of Commons on 14 March, Churchill was keen to link it to Dublin's continued refusal to withdraw Axis representation and to separate his criticism of Irish government policy from his praise for: 'the large number of Irishmen who are fighting so bravely in our armed forces and the deeds of personal heroism by which they have kept alive the martial honour of the Irish race'. He was adamant that, 'No-one I think, can reproach us with precipitancy. No nation in the world would have been so patient.' On the advice of his colleagues in the War Cabinet, his statement had been altered to make it clear that this action had not been taken unilaterally, but rather at the instigation of the United States and in response to the need to protect American forces. Some of his more inflammatory language had also been removed to make sure that the emphasis remained on security rather than Churchill's ongoing objections to reopening discussions about the partition of Ireland (with which there might be considerable American sympathy). This did not prevent the Scottish communist MP Willie Gallacher from linking the issues in Parliament:

Mr. Gallacher: I would not like to say anything that would make more difficult a very difficult situation, but I would like to ask if it is not possible, in any further approaches to Eire, to suggest that the question of partition will be a subject for discussion when peace is being decided.

The Prime Minister: I could hardly think of a more ill-conceived approach to the unity of Ireland.

Churchill was braced for opposition to this measure, especially from Ireland and the United States. On 19 March, he sent a pre-emptive telegram to Roosevelt confirming his intention to stop Irish ships and aeroplanes heading for foreign countries. He was at pains to emphasise that these measures were not being taken out of spite, but rather to preserve the lives of British and American soldiers and to stop 'our plans being betrayed by emissaries sent by sea or air from the German minister in Dublin'. Churchill was clear that he had no intention of stopping trade between Britain and Ireland, but neither did he want to make things easy for de Valera, the Irish Taoiseach (head of government). He was firmly against giving too much reassurance to Dublin about the measures, suggesting that 'There is not much sense in a doctor telling a patient that the procedure he has just prescribed for his nerve troubles is only coloured water' and arguing that 'we should let fear work its healthy process'.

One door may have been closed against security breaches, but there were still many others by which information might leave the United Kingdom. Foreign diplomats based in Britain, including those of neutral powers, had the right to send communications through uncensored diplomatic channels, often called the 'diplomatic bag'. Should that be suspended? What about ships and aircraft leaving the country? Could these be stopped? If so, for how long, without further damaging the economy?

Churchill's son-in-law, the Conservative politician Duncan Sandys, was one of the authors of a comprehensive report on 'Security Preparations for Overlord' that sought to address these issues and identify the measures that might be taken prior to the military operation. It advocated sweeping restrictions to communications. All neutral governments should be denied the use of their diplomatic bags and secret cyphers (encoded telegrams). Their communications ought to be censored and their representatives forbidden from leaving the country. The report recognised that Ireland was a weak link between Britain and the outside world and recommended that all mail to Northern Ireland should be censored.

More generally, the report suggested various measures for further tightening censorship of mail and controlling the export of local newspapers, which might reveal the precise location of military bases (while recognising that the national papers had an important propaganda role, although there was a danger that enemy agents would use the small ads columns for messages). Greater controls were proposed for shipping, including the exclusion of fishing vessels from the English south coast, while the number of nationals from allied nations entering the UK should be kept to a minimum. The tiny British enclave at Gibraltar, bordering Franco's Spain, was identified as a specific weak spot, where the security services might play a role in vetting crews sailing to and from Britain.

Crucially, the report supported the idea of a visitors ban, advocating the introduction of restrictions in a coastal belt from the Wash (the estuary in East Anglia separating Norfolk and Lincolnshire) to Cornwall and including the area in Scotland adjacent to the Firth of Forth. Still Churchill resisted. At the Overlord Committee meeting on 1 March, he remained 'most reluctant to impose additional inconveniences on the public unless he was sure that there would be a real gain in security' and the sub-committee on security was instructed to see if the ban could be limited to certain parts of the coast without denying all access. While this may have been popular with any holidaymakers, there was an obvious flaw in the logic and, a week later, the sub-committee pointed out that a more precise definition of the areas to be excluded from any ban would 'pin-point the places where preparations were concentrated and give clues to the enemy as to the direction of the assault'. When this was reported back to the Overlord Preparations Committee on 8 March, the issue was referred upwards. It came before the War Cabinet, two days later, where Churchill grudgingly conceded and agreed to its imposition. He still doubted whether the ban would improve security, but 'it was most important to give the Forces who were to be engaged in "Overlord" the assurance that everything possible was being done for the success of the operation'. By then, he knew that Eisenhower had written to the Chiefs of Staff pressing for the ban. After more than a month of prevarication, it was introduced with effect from 1 April.

The issue of limiting diplomatic communications was particularly sensitive. It went against a long-standing convention in international relations that protected the right of diplomats to communicate freely with their home governments. To be effective, it was felt necessary to apply it to allies as well as neutrals. The only exceptions were to be the United States and the Soviet Union, where a diplomatic row could not be risked. De Gaulle and his French Committee of National Liberation were to be included. There was a justified fear of reprisals by impacted countries, who might respond by censoring the communications of British representatives abroad. While it was felt this could be circumvented by the British diplomats using the secure facilities of their American allies, there was also an unexpected security objection. On 7 March, the Cabinet Secretary Edward Bridges sent a deliberately brief note to Churchill suggesting that he meet the next day – before the Overlord Preparations Committee – with the Foreign Secretary (Anthony Eden), the Lord President of the Council (Clement Attlee), 'C' (the head of the Secret Intelligence Service MI6, Stewart Menzies) and perhaps the Chiefs of Staff to deal 'with the points of special secrecy which are vital to consideration of the ban on diplomatic communications'. Churchill's briefing notes for the ensuing Preparations Committee meeting give a further glimpse of the intelligence community lobbying behind the scenes, noting that the Foreign Office and MI6 were suggesting that a ban on uncensored diplomatic communications would be against

> our interests because it would leave us in the dark as to what information was leaking out of the country and reaching the enemy. (The extent of our knowledge of what leaks through diplomatic channels will be explained orally); and because a good deal of wrong information – including our cover plan material – reaches the enemy through diplomatic communications.

Here was proof that Britain was not only illicitly intercepting supposedly secure diplomatic communications by neutral powers to gain intelligence but was also actively using these channels as part of the Overlord deception plan. Unsurprisingly, the matter was referred by the Preparations Committee to the War Cabinet, who decided against imposing the ban at the current time. It was finally introduced at midnight on 17 April. Churchill sent a telegram to President Roosevelt defending the action (see telegram on p. 183).

Gradually, inexorably, the screw was being tightened. The Preparations Committee meeting of 15 March approved many of the measures outlined in the earlier security report: confirming 100 per cent censorship of mail to Eire, foreign countries and Gibraltar and introducing the same for Northern Ireland. It also allowed 'artificial' delays to the overseas post, guaranteeing a month's delay between the sending and receipt of most letters to foreign countries. The export of local newspapers was restricted to the Empire and United States and banned to foreign countries, Gibraltar, Eire and Northern Ireland. Overseas telegrams were subject to paraphrase and delay. Air services to Ireland were heavily restricted and those remaining were run from airports outside the Overlord area, while air services between Aberdeen and Sweden were suspended. Fishing vessels were excluded from the south coast ports and departures of all ships were controlled in an attempt to delay their arrival at foreign ports. Immigration controls

35

PRIME MINISTER'S
PERSONAL TELEGRAM
SERIAL No___ T.830/4.

PRIME MINISTER TO PRESIDENT ROOSEVELT   No. 646.
     Personal and Top Secret   15.4.44.

     To safeguard the security of "OVERLORD" we have
decided to prohibit foreign representatives in this
country from sending or receiving uncensored communications,
whether cypher telegrams or diplomatic bags. We shall
also forbid couriers or other members of diplomatic staffs
from leaving the country. The ban will come into force
from midnight Monday, April 17, and continue until after
the launching of the operation. It will not, of course,
apply to your representatives or to the Soviet representative but it will cover both neutral representatives and
representatives of other Allied Governments, including
representatives of the French Committee of Liberation and
exiled Governments in this country.

     We are imposing this bar because of our desire to
leave nothing undone which might promote the success of
"OVERLORD" and we have been much influenced by the view
of General Eisenhower who pressed strongly for it.

     We shall explain to the foreign Governments that the
ban is being imposed for compelling military reasons and
that many other restrictions are being imposed on our own
people in the interests of security.

     We hope that no foreign Government will be tempted to
retaliate by forbidding our diplomatic representatives to
send uncensored communications. If, however, any were to
do so, may we count on the help of your representative
in the country concerned to enable us to continue to send
and receive uncensored communications?

     So much information about military plans is constantly
passing between here and Washington that valuable
information might well reach the enemy through cypher
telegrams sent by representatives of foreign Governments
in the United States.

     I have no doubt that you will be ready to consider
whether some corresponding action should be taken to
prevent leakages through diplomatic representatives in the
United States.

Distribution: For Information:
The King   War Cabinet
Foreign Secretary   Secretary of State for Dominions
Sir E. Bridges   Lord Privy Seal
General Ismay   Minister of Aircraft Production
                         Minister of Information
                         Service Ministers

Telegram from Churchill to Roosevelt, 15 April 1944

were further tightened and even Allied nationals hoping to enlist were now kept to a minimum.

The increase in security occurred in an atmosphere of mounting tension: one that was undoubtedly made worse by security lapses. For obvious reasons, few people were aware of them, but Churchill certainly was, and they clearly contributed to his worries in the run-up to D-Day.

On 23 March, the Americans feared that Overlord had been compromised. A package containing essential facts about the operation had been intercepted in Chicago, en route to a private address in a part of the city with a high German population. On investigation, it emerged that it had been sent in error by a US soldier who had absent-mindedly written his sister's address on the envelope rather than that of the intended War Department recipient. The error was compounded by the fact that the plans were poorly packaged and so had been opened and seen by a number of unauthorised persons; all of which took time to ascertain.

At around the same time, the British were wrestling with a very different type of security breach. On 10 March Duncan Sandys lunched at London's exclusive Park Lane Hotel with Captain Basil Liddell Hart, the eminent historian and military strategist who had been influential in developing theories of modern mechanised warfare. After enjoying their meal, they retired to Captain Hart's private sitting room within the hotel, where, according to Sandys, 'In the course of a general conversation about military matters of a non-secret character he mentioned that he had strong doubts about the wisdom of our plan for the invasion of the continent.' This set Sandys' ears twitching. Though well connected in military circles, Captain Liddell Hart had no official reason to know about the Overlord plans. Yet in the course of his subsequent remarks, he stated that the plan was to land on the coast of Normandy, on beaches he had known well as a child, possibly mentioned Caen, and 'said that Montgomery had made a number of minor improvements to the plan since he had taken over'. Sandys 'formed the impression that Captain

Liddell Hart was in possession of precise information about future military operations'. Alarmed, he informed General Ismay and Anthony Eden.

Ismay brought the matter to the Prime Minister's attention, who ordered an investigation. Churchill decided not to tell Eisenhower at this stage, as he wanted to find out exactly who had been talking to Liddell Hart and whether it was just British officers who were implicated.

Ismay quickly established that Liddell Hart had also met with Sir Stafford Cripps, the Labour politician and Minister for Aircraft Production, at a weekend country house party on 4 March, where he had told Cripps 'that it was pretty clear that we would not undertake operations against Europe outside fighter cover, that this limited the point of attack to the North of France, whereas his opinion was that we would do better to strike in the bay of Biscay'. He then handed Cripps a paper, which Cripps subsequently forwarded to Deputy Prime Minister Clement Attlee, entitled 'Some Reflections on the Problem of Invading the Continent'. Written at the end of January, the paper speculated on a likely assault in northern France and suggested that Allied tactics would be governed by 'the time and space conventions of the past'; the danger was that if we succeeded in getting ashore we would only achieve the formation of 'a shallow and narrow bridgehead, expanded so slowly that the Germans will be allowed time to concentrate against it'.

There was much here to annoy Churchill: the attack on British tactics, the lobbying of senior members of his government (of both main political parties) and the suggestion that Liddell Hart may have been getting insider information on the forthcoming landings. There was also surely a fear, tied into Churchill's own reservations, that Captain Liddell Hart might be right. There was certainly enough for an interview and Liddell Hart was summoned to an uncomfortable meeting with General Ismay and Brigadier Jacob at quarter past five on the evening of 19 March. He admitted having given copies of his paper to Lord Beaverbrook, Stafford Cripps, Duncan Sandys and to two or three American generals, including Patton and Gerow, but denied receiving classified information about the plan, and said that 'the Generals had talked to him as a responsible person fairly freely on the general conception'.

Churchill was furious and wanted to press the matter to a prosecution, telling Ismay that 'If this man were kept worrying about the matter for some weeks it would be a lesson to him, even if we did not carry through to the end.' But the grounds for such a course of action were not really there. The Prime Minister briefed Eisenhower and was incensed to learn that Liddell Hart had still been visiting American headquarters. It led to a final angry outburst to Ismay on the matter:

> I think he should be frightened out of his wits, and have his name put on the gate of all the Armed Forces in this country. We are to blame as it is one of our black sheep and you should reconsider the letter to General Eisenhower from this point of view, making it clear that it is our fault.

Liddell Hart, who was not in good health, was encouraged to return to his home in Westmorland for a prolonged period (where the security services kept an eye on him).

Ironically, years later in 1969, he would get the last word by contributing an essay to a controversial book entitled *Churchill: Four Faces and the Man*. In his essay on Churchill, 'The Military Strategist', Liddell Hart would conclude that 'from the time the Normandy landing was achieved' Churchill ceased 'to have any important influence on the course of the war – or on its sequel'.

At the end of May, with D-Day imminent, Churchill took a similarly dim view of the presence in Britain of Mr J. Loy Maloney, the editor of the *Chicago Tribune*, well known as a fierce critic of British policy in the American press. Mr Maloney had been blocked from leaving the country. Brendan Bracken, the Minister for Information, was incensed that Maloney had been allowed into the UK in the first place at a time when most travel was being restricted, including for diplomats, writing that he would 'rather see an invitation issued to Himmler to come to England than to Maloney'. The episode occurred just as Eisenhower was asking for the diplomatic travel ban to be extended for a period after D-Day. It prompted a testy response from Churchill to Ike on 31 May:

> You probably have no idea of the enormous inconvenience and friction which this system [the diplomatic travel ban] has caused. The Free French Committee is only one instance; but in every case the Foreign Office is gravely hampered.
>
> ... I must confess that I had not realised that unofficial Americans would be free to go and come between here and the United States during all the time we are putting this ban on all the Embassies. Among those recently put to us was the case of the Editor of the 'Chicago Tribune'.
>
> Here is a real foe, serving in a paper which announced that the Americans had broken the Japanese cypher, and a paper which the President has described as "United States Fifth Column".

Add to this, the lapse of a senior American officer while under the influence and the strange (and apparently entirely coincidental) appearance of several Overlord codewords in the *Daily Telegraph* crossword and you can see why this was a nervous time. Ordinary soldiers making accidental errors; experts making guesses about plans that were too close to the truth. And all the time, constant speculation in the press. No one was immune. Even the reliable Joan Bright later confessed to an anxious moment when she suddenly realised she had just left a briefcase containing official papers in a Post Office. Thankfully, when she hastily returned, it was still there.

The longer the wait for operations to start, the greater the risk of more incidents. Churchill liked being at the centre of momentous events and taking decisions, but this was a different kind of pressure – a prolonged period of waiting for the decisive moment to arrive. It was taking a toll on his health.

Churchill was sixty-nine years old and still recovering from the pneumonia that had nearly killed him before Christmas. He had been Prime Minister for nearly four years and perhaps inevitably the strain was starting to show. There was no stroke or heart attack, but those around him were aware that things were not quite right.

His daughter Mary was with him at the beginning of February. They went together to watch the play *There Shall Be No Night*, set in Finland between 1938 and 1940:

> The first scene was 1938 – back to Munich. In the interval I said 'It takes one back a bit – we've come such a long way since then.' Papa said 'I knew what would happen then – and I don't now – that is the difference.'
>
> The last few times I've seen Papa I've been struck with his anxious preoccupation with the future – his uncertainty. I know he foresees so much more trouble and grief and struggling ahead of us than we can imagine.

Alexander Cadogan, the country's senior diplomat as Under-Secretary of State, had watched Churchill operate at close quarters since the outbreak of war, attending Cabinet meetings and travelling with the Prime Minister. But in the spring of 1944, several of his diary entries record his concerns about Churchill's physical and mental health.

> Mon 20 March – P.M. looked flushed and was very woolly. Hope he's not unwell.

> Tue 21 March – P.M. this morning confessed he was tired – he's almost done in.

> Wed 19 April – P.M., I fear, is breaking down. He rambles without a pause, and we really got nowhere by 7.40 . . . I really am fussed about the P.M. He is not the man he was 12 months ago, and I really don't know whether he can carry on.

On 7 May, with the Overlord operation only a month away, Churchill made a rare admission of weakness to General Brooke. After watching a film at Chequers, they retired to a little study where Churchill sat by the fire, drank some soup, and – looking very old and tired – said that he was no longer the man he had been:

> He said he could still always sleep well, eat well and especially drink well! but that he no longer jumped out of bed the way he used to, and felt as if he would be quite content to spend the whole day in bed. I have never yet heard him admit that he was beginning to fail.

Harry Butcher noticed that Churchill's broadcast of 26 March 'lacked his usual inspirational vigour', while Jock Colville considered it indifferent. The language used certainly hints at weariness and frustration. Churchill opened by thanking his audience for all the kindness with which they had treated him 'in spite of my many shortcomings'. He admitted that 'Our progress has not been as rapid or decisive as we had hoped', mentioning the delays to the advance in Italy and referring to his disappointment over Allied failure to dominate the Aegean Islands. An earlier draft even contained a deleted passage in which he had complained about what a full-time job it was 'keeping things sweet between us and all the other powers, great and small'. Although he concluded with the confident assertion that 'Britain can take it. She has never flinched or failed', this was not quite 'fight on the beaches'.

At times, his anger surfaced. Eisenhower recounted how the Prime Minister launched into an impassioned tirade against a British staff officer who inadvertently referred to British soldiers as 'bodies' in his presentation; 'he said it was inhuman to talk of soldiers in such cold-blooded fashion, and that it sounded as if they were merely freight – or, worse, corpses!'

There is no suggestion that Churchill was like this all the time. There were clearly lighter moments. Joan Bright loved to tell the story of how General Leslie Hollis was on duty for Churchill's office one Saturday morning when Overlord was being planned. The three British Chiefs of Staff – Brooke, Cunningham and Portal – had all gone fishing in the country and, faced with a potentially quiet day, General Ismay had gone home. Inevitably, the phone rang. It was Churchill, from Chequers: could the Chief of the Imperial General Staff come down and see him as there were one or two things he would like to discuss. Hollis had to explain that he was out of London. The Prime Minister then asked about the Chief of the Air Staff and, with sinking heart, Hollis had to give the same answer. He knew what was coming next. Churchill asked for the First Sea Lord. Same answer.

> So there was a pregnant silence . . . 'and what might they all be doing?' And Hollis, after a lot of thought, he said 'Prime Minister they are fishing.' 'Fishing' he said, the wires fused, 'fishing' and then there was a long thing about there was this great war going on with one of the greatest build-ups going on for the greatest invasion in history, they go fishing! And he went on saying 'fishing' and 'fishing' and then he asked if he could see General Ismay and was told that he was in the country. So in desperation the Prime Minister said 'Well Hollis' he said 'perhaps you could come down.'

A wonderful story, probably embellished with the retelling, and one that also appears in Hollis's own memoirs. It captures the spirit of Churchill's restlessness at this time. He was keen to maintain an overview of the preparations. As winter 1943 merged into summer 1944, the intensity of personal, unit and formation preparation for the invasion of Europe intensified. The success of the largest multi-national amphibious operation ever conceived would only be achieved by rigorous training and realistic rehearsal of all the naval, land and air force units assigned to the Overlord order of battle. The armed camp that was southern England was the setting for some of the final exercises before the operation was launched. Slapton Sands on the south coast of Devon was identified as being similar in topography to Utah beach on the Cotentin Peninsula where the 4th US Infantry Division was to make its assault.

With the surrounding villages evacuated and some 3,000 local residents required to leave their homes, training on Slapton Sands began in late 1943, but on 27 and 28 April 1944, disaster struck twice. Exercise Tiger was scheduled to last from 22 to 28 April, culminating in practice landings by 30,000 American troops from the 4th Infantry Division. To add realism, the rehearsal landings were to be conducted with naval gunfire support screaming from sea to shore over the heads of the young troops as part of their battle inoculation, as they assaulted the beach. The first of the landings was scheduled for 07.30 hours on 27 April; however, a number of the landing craft had been delayed by difficult sea conditions and the US naval commander ordered a delay to H-Hour for the exercise until 08.30 hours. The naval gunfire support was due to be provided by the British HMS *Hawkins*. Unfortunately, there were communication failures between the British and American exercising troops. Although the exercise plan had included a thirty-minute pause between the end of the shelling of the beach and the assault landings, the new timings were not received by all units. The tragic result was that US soldiers began landing on Slapton Sands while the British warship was still bringing down lethal fire onto the beach. It is not known to this day how many Americans lost their lives that morning, but worse was to follow.

The final phase of Exercise Tiger was to be an even larger landing on Slapton Sands the following morning. It remains remarkable after the initial tragedy that the exercise was not paused, but nevertheless it went ahead. Although operational security and deception were overriding considerations in the preparations for D-Day, information about Exercise Tiger became known to the German *Kriegsmarine*. Although most German capital ships had been either sunk or neutralised, flotillas of torpedo-armed E-boats (known as S, or *Schnellboote* to the Germans) were based in Cherbourg and the Channel Islands. As the exercising fleet of tank- and infantry-landing craft formed up and sailed out of Lyme Bay on the night of 27/28 April towards Slapton Sands, nine German E-boats tracked them and got ready to pounce. Convoy T-4 should have been protected by two British warships, but one of them, HMS *Scimitar*, had suffered collision damage and was withdrawn from the exercise. Although British radar picked up the approach of the E/S-boats, it was assumed that they were part of the exercise. The remaining escort ship, HMS *Azalea*, took no action. 'We sailed along in fatal ignorance', wrote Lieutenant Eugene E. Eckstam, a medical officer aboard the first of two Landing Ship Tanks (LSTs) to be attacked.

Shortly after 01.30 hours on 28 April, the *Kriegsmarine* S-boats launched their attack. Over the next chaotic hour, two of the LSTs were sunk with huge loss of life. Other vessels were badly damaged. Vehicles and men had been embarked with full loads of live ammunition and fuel to simulate the real landings, but this merely added to the intensity of the fires on the stricken ships. Extraordinarily, the soldiers had not been trained how to wear their lifejackets properly. Many drowned as their lifejackets, incorrectly tied around their waist, caused them to turn upside down in the water. At a sea temperature of only 42 degrees Fahrenheit, many more were to die of hypothermia before they could be rescued. The confusion of the night was further exacerbated by the exercise being conducted in radio silence and the subsequent realisation that the British escort ships and the American landing craft were on different radio frequencies.

With dawn came the appalling knowledge that there had been a major tragedy. In total, some 749 US soldiers and sailors lost their lives that night, two LSTs were sunk and two others badly damaged. Although the S-boats escaped with no casualties, Supreme Headquarters Allied Expeditionary Force (SHAEF) ordered RAF Lancaster bombers with 12,000-pound 'Tallboy' bombs to eliminate the S-boat bases in early June (finally having bombs that could destroy the concrete defences). Other lessons were learnt from the Convoy T-4 tragedy. Ships were to zig-zag, not steam in straight lines, radio frequencies were to be common across the fleet, rescue boats would be among the landing craft to pluck struggling soldiers from the sea and all ranks were to be trained in how to wear their life-jackets properly. After the disasters of 27 and 28 April, the supreme irony was that the 4th Infantry Division landed success-fully on Utah beach on 6 June 1944 with the loss of only 197 soldiers killed or wounded. Their success had come from the awful price paid during Exercise Tiger, the truth about which was suppressed at the time as classified information. Later, the losses during Exercise Tiger were not reported by SHAEF until August 1944 and were then absorbed within the reported casu-alties of the actual D-Day landings. There is now a memorial on Utah beach commemorating the 946 American servicemen known to have died in the two tragedies off the coast of Slapton Sands during Exercise Tiger. Their sacrifice was not in vain. Rehearsal was essential to ultimate success, but such losses did nothing to lessen Churchill's anxiety about the actual landings. Here was an illustration of why preparation, deception, security and lockdown were so important.

Yet despite being only too aware of the need for security, the Prime Minister allowed his twenty-nine-year-old Private Secretary Jock Colville to re-join the RAF and undertake a short period of operational flying around D-Day. He admired bravery and remem-bered his own youthful military adventures with fondness and nostalgia. In granting permission, he spoke of his own desire to see action, telling Colville that he [Churchill] 'would be among the first on the bridgehead . . . if he possibly could – and what fun it would be to get there before Monty'. An idea had been sown to which he would return. But even releasing his Private Secretary carried risk. Colville had been photographed alongside the Prime Minister. If shot down and captured, he knew many secrets, including the likely date and place for Overlord. It was agreed that he would not fly over France until after D-Day. When Colville joined his squadron, he found that speculation about the date for the operation was rife, and also dangerously accurate. When his new colleagues correctly guessed the likely date and place of the assault, he 'could only hope the Germans were less intelligent in their deductions'.

It was in Churchill's character to show his emotions and in the months leading up to D-Day the dominant ones were increasing impatience and frustration. He was able to oversee and to influence the civil preparations, but he longed to play a bigger role in the military operations. Eisenhower kept Churchill informed but also at arm's length, working from his headquarters outside London at Bushy Park, near Hampton Court Palace, and through the Combined Chiefs of Staff. The British Prime Minister was not yet ready to give up all influence. The political could not always be so easily disentangled from the military. Questions remained over the control and use of air power. The stage was set for one last prime ministerial foray into the strategy for Overlord.

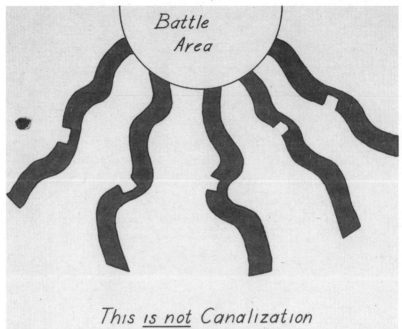

This is not Canalization

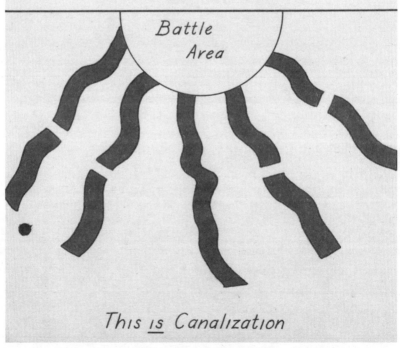

This is Canalization

Diagram from papers of Air Vice-Marshal Bufton illustrating the type
of damage to railway lines needed to disrupt the enemy, c. 1944

8

The Last Ounce of Available Force

'There was a limit to the slaughter and the resulting
anger and resentment which it would arouse among
Frenchmen beyond which we could not go.'

IT WAS NOT just lockdown that Churchill was wrestling with.
He was also brooding on the nature that the Allied offensive
would take. Air superiority over France had been one of the
preconditions for Overlord and by early 1944 the Allies had huge
air forces assembled in Britain. But this does not mean that there
was full agreement on how to deploy them.

The command structure was complicated. Eisenhower's Deputy
Commander was the British Air Chief Marshal, Arthur Tedder,
and their Allied Expeditionary Force had its own air force, which
was under the command of Air Marshal Trafford Leigh-Mallory.
This comprised fighter aircraft, light and medium bombers that
could be used in support of the ground troops, and specialist
reconnaissance, transport and glider-towing craft.

Control of the American heavy bombers, part of the United
States Eighth Army Air Force, lay with Lieutenant General
James Doolittle. He reported to Lieutenant General Carl
Spaatz, as Commander of the US Strategic Forces in Europe,
who in turn reported to Eisenhower as the overall American
theatre commander. Yet the British heavy bombers were
controlled separately by Bomber Command, run by Air Marshal
Arthur Harris, reporting to the Chief of the Air Staff, Charles

Portal. RAF Coastal Command was also independent, under Air Chief Marshal Sholto Douglas. Above it all, sat the Combined Chiefs of Staff, Churchill and his Defence Committee, the War Cabinet and Roosevelt, as American Commander-in-Chief. This would not have been a problem if they had all agreed on a clear strategy for use of air power, but they did not. (For more information on the different usages of air power by the Allies, see pp. 219–20.)

Eisenhower believed that all Allied air forces operating in the Western European theatre should be subordinated to his command for the period immediately preceding and following the D-Day operation, arguing that 'when a battle needs the last ounce of available force, the commander must not be in the position of depending upon request and negotiation to get it'. Spaatz and Harris argued that the best use of their strategic heavy bomber forces was to continue what they were doing already, and that their ongoing large-scale bombing of German cities and industry would cripple the German economy and destroy the enemy's morale, thereby weakening resistance to Overlord. Spaatz, in particular, was strongly of the view that hitting German oil supplies was the best way of bringing the enemy to a standstill. They did not believe that it was right to use the huge – but often inaccurate – destructive power of their forces in support of ground troops or on specific military objectives, such as railways, roads and bridges, that might be pinpointed more accurately by smaller aircraft or sabotage. Harris was characteristically blunt:

> the only efficient support which Bomber Command can give to OVERLORD is the intensification of attacks on suitable industrial centres in Germany as and when the opportunity offers. If we attempt to substitute for this process attacks on gun emplacements, beach defences, communications or dumps in occupied territory we shall commit the irremediable error of diverting our best weapons from the military function, for which it has been equipped and trained, to tasks which it cannot effectively carry out. Though this might give a specious appearance of 'supporting' the Army, in

reality it would be the gravest disservice we could do them. It would lead directly to disaster.

Eisenhower was not to be moved. He maintained that he needed an all-out bombing offensive against German fortifications and infrastructure to support an assault on this scale and that the bombers were needed as far more than 'a mere adjunct to the Tactical Air Command'. He got his way. Bomber Command and the Eighth Army Air Force were brought under his overall control for the period immediately surrounding Overlord.

For Churchill this raised several questions. Was it right to divert so many resources from the bombing of Germany? What was the best way of using the bomber forces to support operations in France? And what would be the impact on the French population of a bombing campaign on the scale now proposed by Eisenhower? Churchill had expressed concerns as early as November 1943 that the Germans 'will gain a very sensible relief from Air Attack in consequence of the opening of Overlord' but had also recognised that it would be very difficult to resist a claim from the Commander-in-Chief 'to control all the strategic bomber forces during the actual period of OVERLORD as they are an integral and vital part of his operation'. In practice, control was always going to pass to Eisenhower for the period around D-Day; a question of when, not if. But this did not mean the Prime Minister lost interest in how the bomber forces would be deployed.

Churchill had already enjoyed a long relationship with the development and use of air power. As Secretary of State for War and Air in the immediate aftermath of the First World War, he had presided over the early growth of the RAF, and as the minister in charge of the colonies he had sought to harness that new power for political ends, using planes instead of troops to police the deserts of Mesopotamia and Transjordan (Iraq and Jordan). During the 1930s he had argued passionately for rearmament and in particular the development of a modern bomber force. On becoming Prime Minister in 1940, one of his first actions had been to sanction bombing raids against the enemy and he had continued to advocate these as a means of taking the offensive, wearing Germany down in an attempt to break her economic capacity; destroying her morale and easing pressure on the Russian and Mediterranean fronts. In his celebrated speech at the height of the Battle of Britain, praising the bravery of the fighter pilots – 'Never in the field of human conflict has so much been owed by so many to so few' – he had gone on to pay tribute to the bomber crews:

> but we must never forget that all the time, night after night, month after month, our bomber squadrons travel far into Germany, find their targets in the darkness by the highest navigational skill, aim their attacks, often under the heaviest fire, often with serious loss, with deliberate careful discrimination, and inflict shattering blows upon the whole of the technical and war-making structure of the Nazi power.

At the Casablanca Conference he had supported the directive intensifying the Combined Air Offensive against Germany and he had consistently presented the ever-increasing raids against German cities as a means of offering support to the Soviets. He supported Operation Pointblank, the strategic campaign to bomb Germany by night and day in order to cripple the country's military, industrial and economic system.

He saw the bombing campaign as both a prerequisite for, and an accompaniment to, Overlord. Having watched Britain endure the Blitz, he had few qualms about the impact of the bombs on the German civilian population and was influenced by his scientific adviser, Lord Cherwell, who argued that it would help to break the spirit of the German people. Understandably, however, he was not so keen on breaking the spirit of the French people. Indeed, ever since 1940, he had actively encouraged their resistance and continued to believe that they could and would play an important role in their own liberation, rising up against their Nazi occupiers. But could he expect them to do so, while suffering from an escalating Allied bombing campaign?

Britain and her Allies had been bombing German targets in France since 1940, and the scale and intensity of these actions had gradually increased as more resources had become available. Richard Overy, in his excellent book *The Bombing War*, has documented the process. In July 1940, the War Cabinet had agreed that any *military* target could be bombed in the occupied parts of France, extended a year later to the bombing of factories – albeit only in daylight to ensure better accuracy and so minimise civilian casualties. Then, in early 1942, the rules were relaxed again, and Churchill consented to the general bombing of European targets. Shortly afterwards, a huge bombing raid, the largest yet undertaken by the Allies, dropped 419 tons of bombs on the Renault motor works and surrounding workers' housing on the outskirts of Paris, killing almost four hundred people. Thereafter, Britain's desperate situation in the Battle of the Atlantic led to devastating raids on the port city of Lorient in early 1943, with Allied bombs destroying almost everything – except their target, the seemingly indestructible concrete U-boat pens.

By the beginning of 1944, there were already signs of growing French hostility to the bombing. Churchill's fear was that this would now get much worse. The air plan favoured by Eisenhower advocated using bombers to maximise disruption to the transportation infrastructure before, during and after D-Day. The aim was to buy the Allied troops crucial time to secure their positions by preventing the Germans from moving vital reinforcements and supplies towards the Normandy beachheads. This plan put a particular emphasis on the bombing of railway hubs and marshalling yards, where troops and equipment were likely to assemble. Unfortunately, these also tended to be located in densely populated urban areas.

By the end of February, Churchill was aware that the Allied air staffs were divided. Support for the transportation plan was balanced by those who argued strongly for the bombing of sites connected with the German Air Force or enemy oil supplies. There was criticism of the 'transportation plan'. It would divert resources from other targets, it would be ineffective unless all rail facilities were destroyed and 'Attacks on the scale proposed would have an adverse effect on the French.'

The War Cabinet, concerned to minimise the loss of civilian life, had initially imposed operational restrictions on the targets that could be attacked from Britain. This meant that only thirteen of the seventy-four French and Belgian railway centres identified by Eisenhower as critical to the success of his plan could be bombed. Eisenhower wanted them all attacked 'by day or night without any operational restrictions'. As Chief of the Air Staff, Portal wrote to Churchill on 29 March confirming that it had been agreed that 'the so-called "Transportation Plan" was the best way for the strategic bombers to pave the way for a successful OVERLORD' while also warning that 'In the execution of this plan very heavy casualties among the civilians living near the main railway centres in occupied territory will be unavoidable, however careful we may be over the actual bombing.' The Ministry of Home Security were estimating that, without evacuation, the number of civilian casualties would be between eighty thousand and a hundred and sixty thousand, 'of which a quarter would be killed'. The Chiefs of Staff felt such action needed the Prime Minister's approval and argued that the French civilian population and especially the railway workers should be warned. Portal brought Eisenhower's request before the War Cabinet on 3 April. Churchill immediately expressed 'some doubts as to the wisdom of this policy'. He referred the matter to the Defence Committee and wrote to Eisenhower expressing his concerns in no uncertain terms:

> The Cabinet today took rather a grave and on the whole an adverse view on the proposal to bomb so many French railway centres, in view of the fact that scores of thousands of French civilians, men, women and children, would lose their lives or be injured. Considering that they are all our friends, this might be held to be an act of very great severity, bringing much hatred on the Allied Air Forces.

He worried that the plan would provide a gift to enemy propaganda and suggested that General de Gaulle be notified. Eisenhower was uncompromising in his reply, arguing that 'we must not fail to make such preliminary employment of this [air] force as will later help us in our moment of crisis'. He believed that the probable casualties had been exaggerated and argued that ultimately, 'The French people are now slaves. Only a successful OVERLORD can now free them.'

The British Defence Committee met late on 5 April with Churchill in the chair. It brought together the leading politicians with the Chiefs of Staff and was attended by a number of the relevant air experts, including Tedder, Norman Bottomley (Deputy Chief of the Air Staff) and Sydney Bufton (Director of Bombing Operations). The scientists were represented by Lord Cherwell and Solly Zuckerman (Scientific Director of the British Bombing Survey Unit). The meeting exposed deep divisions, not just between the military and the politicians, but also within the military and scientific ranks over whether the 'Transportation Plan' was going to be the most effective bombing strategy.

The Prime Minister set the scene by announcing his fear that 'even if the casualties were not so great as was estimated, they might well be sufficient to cause an unhealable breach between France and Great Britain & USA'. He also questioned whether

the effect which would be achieved by bombing attacks on railway centres, would justify the slaughter of masses of friendly French allies, who were burning to help us when the day came, and who showed their friendly feelings by giving unstinted help to any of our airmen forced down among them. It was one thing to launch attacks which would result in heavy loss of civilian life during the hot blood of battle; it was quite another to begin, when no fighting was going on, a policy which was bound to result in the butchering of large numbers of helpless French people.

These were strong words and were most likely even stronger in the meeting itself, where Churchill's draft of the minutes shows his deletion of the phrase 'in cold blood'.

The Prime Minister questioned whether bombing the railway lines was the right strategy. He felt that it would be just as easy for the enemy to move troops and materials by road. The issue divided the room. The two scientists took opposing views. Cherwell felt that the attacks were unlikely to do sufficient damage to disrupt enemy transportation and that other alternatives had not been adequately explored. Zuckerman, on the other hand, defended the study he had undertaken on the Tunisian and Sicilian campaigns, which had shown that the greatest effect on disrupting enemy communications had been achieved by systematic attacks on the railway centres. The airmen present were similarly divided: Portal, Tedder and Leigh-Mallory spoke in favour of the plan while Commodore Bufton argued for more direct attacks on the aerodromes, repair facilities and factories of the German Air Force, as well as the bombing of military training centres. Among the politicians, Attlee was worried about the antagonism that would be aroused in the French, while Eden felt that the attacks might drive the French and Belgians away from the British and Americans and into the arms of the Soviets. 'After the war we would have to live in a Europe which was already looking more to Russia than he would wish.' When Churchill suggested bombing the Romanian oilfields as an alternative, thereby depriving the Germans of much-needed fuel, Portal countered by pointing out that it would not impact on Overlord, as the Germans already had sufficient fuel stocks in France to sustain operations for several months.

An impasse was reached. It was decided to continue with experimental attacks against three railway centres where there was a reduced risk of civilian casualties. Brooke's diary records his frustration at being kept up until 12:45 a.m. by this discussion. He would endure a similar fate on the 13 and 19 April as the matter was returned to the Defence Committee for consideration on a weekly basis. At each meeting, similar arguments were made, and, on each occasion, Churchill deferred a final decision while allowing the bombing to continue on a temporary basis. He would not

let his concerns drop and returned repeatedly to his main worry.
On 13 April, he complained that

> This slaughter was likely to put the French against us and he was
> doubtful if the results achieved by the plan would justify this.
> There was a limit to the slaughter and the resulting anger and
> resentment which it would arouse among Frenchmen beyond
> which we could not go.

By 26 April, he was concerned that

> by continuing the attacks over a long period we should build up a
> volume of dull hatred in France which would affect our relations
> with that country for many years to come and would lead to the
> Royal Air Force, which had hitherto been regarded with admira-
> tion, being looked upon with odium and accused of killing our
> friends by blind night bombing attacks.

At the War Cabinet meeting on the following afternoon, it was
agreed that the plan for bombing targets in enemy-occupied territory should be limited to attacks on those railway centres with low
estimated casualties and that consideration should be given again
to attacking ammunition dumps, military camps and vehicle parks.
Churchill now accepted that the total casualties from the
programme would be much lower than originally envisaged,
perhaps twelve thousand people, but he still felt that it was offering an advantage to German-controlled Vichy propaganda. The
task of bombing French targets was falling disproportionately on
the RAF, who, bombing at night, had dropped twelve times the
weight of bombs of their American counterparts and Churchill
feared the loss of life would 'be blamed on blind night bombing
carried out by the British'. On balance, he felt that the bombing
'might well do more evil than good' and he undertook to discuss
the matter with Eisenhower and to prepare a telegram for the
President. The Chiefs of Staff disagreed and appended their own
paper to the official minutes endorsing the bombing as the only

effective plan for supporting the troops and preventing a German counter-offensive.

By this time the bombing had started, and Churchill was getting daily intelligence updates on its impact. These only reinforced his anxiety. The report on reactions to bombing in the twenty-four hours up to 13.30 hours on 29 April 1944 confirmed that 'the raids in the Paris area have not been satisfactory, as there were too many civilian casualties. Those on Rouen, Lille and Villeneuve-St-Georges have been "Catastrophic" for French morale.' The underlining was Churchill's and was accompanied by his handwritten note: 'General Eisenhower to see'.

He got short shrift from Ike, who wrote to Churchill on 2 May pointing out that 'casualties to civilian personnel are inherent in any plan for the full use of Air power to prepare for our assault'. The Supreme Commander argued that 'Railway centres have always been recognized as legitimate military targets, and attack on them is clearly obvious to the general population as a strictly military operation.' In his view, and that of the Chief of the Air Staff, there was 'no effective alternative plan', and if operations were limited in the way now being suggested, it 'would emasculate the whole plan'.

On the same day, Churchill received a note from Brendan Bracken, his close friend and Minister of Information, warning him that

> we are shouldering a grim responsibility in consenting to constant raids on a town like Malines which, as a centre of Belgian religious and educational life, has great spiritual significance for the Belgian people. There can be no doubt that the odium which we are incurring will be intense and lasting.

Churchill was caught between the operational needs of Overlord and a possible political breach with France and Belgium, which might lead to those countries emerging from the conflict with hostility towards Britain. Their workers might be driven towards communism.

That evening at the War Cabinet, Churchill reported on Eisenhower's strong response. While recognising that 'Very great consequences might follow from interference with his [Eisenhower's] plan on political grounds', he ruefully remarked that he had not 'fully realized that our use of air power before OVERLORD would assume so cruel and remorseless a form' and he suggested that 'these air operations should be governed by some laws of war laid down by the War Cabinet and accompanied by an immense programme of leaflet dropping, to warn the inhabitants of the threatened areas, even if this involved some additional risk to our airmen.'

The Defence Committee reconvened the next day. There was now about a month to go before D-Day. Churchill wanted to look again at the level of bombing against railway targets as a proportion of the total bombing effort between then and three months after the invasion. Faced with his rebuff from Eisenhower, he was keen to use the meeting to gather views for a communication to President Roosevelt. He also wanted to ensure that the Americans 'accepted their share of responsibility for the heavy casualties that would be inflicted on the friendly civilian population of the occupied countries'.

Portal and Leigh-Mallory set out the plans for the air campaign. It would evolve over four phases. First the attacks on railway targets, then strikes on tactical targets – enemy units and fortifications – starting about three weeks before the assault, then supporting operations for the landings themselves and finally tactical support for the ensuing campaign. In the run-up to the invasion about 35 to 40 per cent of bomber effort would be directed against the railway targets, with 30 per cent against airfields and 15 per cent focused against batteries dominating the assault area. To preserve secrecy over which beaches were to be used, and to reinforce the deception plans, attacks would also be mounted against batteries in other coastal areas.

Other targets scheduled for attack included ammunition dumps, military transport hubs and radar stations. Those most likely to involve heavy civilian casualties were the telephone exchanges, transport hubs, ports and headquarters. Churchill said that, with the exception of the railway centres, no one could reasonably object to the other targets being attacked, as they were clearly of a military nature. But he feared that enemy and foreign propaganda would contrast the German and Russian armies, fighting 'bravely despite the lack of air superiority', with the 'ruthless employment of air power' by the British and Americans 'regardless of the cost in civilian casualties'. He remained particularly worried that the British would be singled out as the 'greatest offenders' for their bombing by night, which was less accurate and scattered the bombs over a wide area, 'whereas the Americans carried out precision bombing in daylight'. He called for a special study of the case for and against using delayed-action bombs and for special attention to be paid to warning the French civilians 'which areas were dangerous'.

Returning to his concern over the bombing of railway centres, Churchill once again tried to put a limit on the civilian casualties, asking Tedder if he would approve a plan that would restrict them to ten thousand. Cherwell jumped in, pushing for alternative attacks on ammunition dumps and bridges. Tedder refused to be drawn on casualties, estimating the number killed to date at between three and four thousand. He defended the railway plan. In attacks on bridges, a large number of bombs missed and were completely wasted; in attacks on railway centres, 'every bomb which fell within the area of the centre did some damage of military value'.

The politicians present, Clement Attlee, Anthony Eden and Oliver Lyttelton, all shared Churchill's reservations. Attlee was worried that the railway plan would 'spoil our political future in Europe'. 'He felt that the political disadvantages of the plan outweighed its military advantages.' This was a point that the Prime Minister was particularly keen to emphasise, and it was agreed that he would draft a letter for the American State Department, to be communicated to the President. One more appeal would also be made to Eisenhower to try and limit civilian casualties to under ten thousand.

By this point, the bombing campaign had been running for weeks and it was probably too late to reverse it. In any event, the air offensive would shortly be switching to its tactical phase, which included hitting the railways alongside other targets.

The Prime Minister was running out of time and options. On 7 May, he wrote to Roosevelt informing him of the divisions within air circles over the 'Railway Plan'. He was at pains to point out that these cut across national divisions and that his concerns were shared by some Americans, before confirming that he was 'personally by no means convinced that this is the best way to use our Air Forces in the preliminary period and still think that the G.A.F. [German Air Force], should be the main target'. He feared that by pursuing their existing plan the Allies might 'leave a legacy of hate behind them' and that 'It must be remembered on the one hand that this slaughter is among a friendly people who have committed no crime against us, and not among the German foe with all their record of cruelty and ruthlessness.' However, aware perhaps of growing American concerns about his own level of commitment to Overlord, he ended with a note of reassurance: 'On the other hand we naturally feel the hazardous nature of Operation OVERLORD and are in deadly earnest about making it a success.'

Roosevelt's reply came on 11 May and was unambiguous in its support for Eisenhower:

> However regrettable the attendant loss of civilian lives is, I am not prepared to impose from this distance any restriction on military action by the responsible commanders that in their opinion might militate against the success of OVERLORD or cause additional loss of life to our Allied Forces of invasion.

This effectively brought the political debate to an end. The episode shows the limits of Churchill's power to influence the military strategy. On the eve of the largest Allied operation yet undertaken, when faced with a determined Supreme Commander who ultimately had the backing of the Combined

Chiefs of Staff and the President of the United States, Churchill had no option but to approve the military plans, whatever the level of his personal reservations. His intervention had ensured that the matter had been thoroughly debated and may have played a small role in reducing French casualties by limiting the initial onset of the bombing and by his insistence throughout that appropriate warnings be issued. On the other hand, the delay in making a firm decision and the amount of debate occupied the key commanders – Eisenhower, Tedder and Leigh-Mallory – at a time when they were already very busy finalising their preparations.

Unfortunately, bombing in early 1944 was not all one way. Faced with the obvious build-up of Allied forces, Hitler unleashed a mini-Blitz on Britain, which clearly added to Churchill's concerns. Between January and May 1944, German bombers returned to the skies above the United Kingdom, and particularly London, though not in the same numbers as in 1940. Harry Butcher recorded a 1,000-kilo bomb hitting St James's Square in central London and damaging the windows at Norfolk House, where some of the Overlord planning staff were still based. He was responsible for finding a suitable air-raid shelter for Eisenhower near his London headquarters. His choice of a basement in a house owned by the Oxford Group, who preached Christian fellowship, proved somewhat controversial. It quickly led to an offer of alternative accommodation from Churchill when Eisenhower pointed out to the Prime Minister that 'it seemed a bit incongruous for him as a military leader to seek safety in an air raid shelter run by pacifists'. This was not quite fair to the Oxford Group, many of whom had taken up arms against fascism.

With hindsight, the German campaign achieved little, though there must have been initial fears about the vulnerability of some of the Allied invasion forces being assembled on the south coast. Fortunately, the Luftwaffe was not the force it had been and disruption to Overlord preparations was minimal. But the bombing was a further trial for the civilian population and impacted negatively on morale. Ultimately, it helped to wear down German air forces ahead of the cross-Channel operation, as every bomber lost over Britain would not be available to counter-attack in France. But that was only apparent with hindsight; at the time, the threat was made worse by a growing fear that this renewed German air attack was a precursor for Hitler's release of his new secret weapons.

From late 1942, the Allies started to receive intelligence that the Germans were trialling long-range rockets (later to be known as V2s). These were quickly linked with a research centre at Peenemünde, on the German Baltic coast. By April of the following year, the Prime Minister had been notified and a special investigating committee established under the chairmanship of Duncan Sandys. Intelligence was gathered from photographic reconnaissance, interrogation of prisoners and analysis by British scientists, but details of the weapon remained elusive. In June, the Ministry of Home Security estimated that a rocket containing ten tons of explosive might devastate a radius of 850 feet and Churchill was subsequently informed that 'if one such rocket fell in the London area every hour for thirty days the cumulative casualties might be 108,000 killed and as many seriously injured'. Churchill turned to Cherwell, who was sceptical, correctly questioning whether such weapons could be produced in sufficient numbers and even wondering if this might be an elaborate hoax. But the government could not afford to ignore a potential threat on this scale. Peenemünde was the target for a massive raid on the night of 17 August 1943, RAF Bomber Command using 597 aircraft to drop 1,937 tons of bombs. Rocket production was disrupted and slowed but not halted.

Then came news of a second possible weapon. By September 1943, it was known that the Germans were also developing pilotless aircraft (V1s), though there remained significant confusion as to exactly what was being produced. The Defence Committee met on 25 October. Scientists were galvanised, photographic reconnaissance was increased (Sarah Churchill was among those analysing the photographs) and bombing raids against possible production sites were intensified. The pressure was mounting. Construction sites now began to appear in northern France, including 'ski sites' with ramps pointing at London. By the end of 1943, eighty-eight had been identified and at least fifty more were suspected. Photographic reconnaissance and other intelligence sources soon linked them to the pilotless flying bombs, which now replaced the rockets as the most immediate threat. The new German weapons were given the codename Crossbow and bombing operations were commenced against the launch sites, but they were not easy to pinpoint and destroy.

All of this added to the Prime Minister's burdens during this crucial period. If the flying bombs and rockets could be unleashed in significant numbers, they might lead to huge dislocation in London or the southern ports; displacing large numbers of the population, further disrupting production and transportation (which were already stretched by the Overlord requirements) and threatening the required concentration of ground troops and naval forces. In his broadcast to the nation of 26 March, Churchill warned that Britain might become 'the object of new forms of attack from the enemy'. Here was an additional threat that had to be watched on a daily basis. It also resulted in the diversion of some strategic bomber forces away from other targets.

It was against this backdrop that Roland MacKenzie was assigned to 166 Squadron and arrived at RAF Kirmington on 2 April 1944. From then until 6 June, he undertook eighteen sorties in his Lancaster Mark III. They illustrate the range of hazardous missions being required of the strategic bomber forces in the run-up to Overlord. On the nights of 9, 10 and 18 April he bombed French marshalling yards at Villeneuve-Saint-Georges outside Paris, Aulnoye and then Rouen. These raids were conducted as part of Zuckerman's railway plan ahead of the Normandy landings. Then, on 20, 22, 24 and 27 April, he was hitting targets in Germany at – respectively – Cologne, Düsseldorf, Karlsruhe and Friedrichshafen. These were part of Bomber Command's strategic air campaign against German industry, with some of the targets linked to probable production centres for the V-weapons. The risks were high. Roland's logbook entry for Cologne noted that, 'The Kitchen Sink Came Up But Missed Us'. Then it was back to France to provide tactical support for the impending invasion by attacking an ammunition dump near Rouen (30 April), the German Panzer military camp at Mailly (night of 3 May) – at which forty-two Lancasters, including three from his squadron, were lost – the ammunition dump at Rennes (7 May), and the coastal defences at Dieppe (10 May). May the 12th found him laying mines in the North Sea, while on the 19th he attacked the marshalling yards in Orléans. His next three missions were in Germany, but on 2 June he was attacking defences in Calais as part of the Overlord deception plan, before flying over the invasion fleet en route to Cherbourg on D-Day itself.

Tedder sent a report on the operation against Mailly to the Prime Minister, prompting a note from Cherwell on 25 May that, despite the heavy losses, it had been an outstanding success. Even now, Cherwell refused to let go of his arguments against the railway plan, arguing that 'Such direct results are surely much to be preferred to the individual and debatable consequences of the attacks on marshalling yards, particularly as few, if any, French casualties are involved.' Churchill clearly agreed, replying to Tedder on 29 May:

> It would seem right as we urged to give a high priority to operations of this sort which contribute directly towards the disorganisation of the German armies and involve no French casualties. You are piling up an awful load of hatred. I do not agree that the best targets were chosen. Have you exceeded the 10,000 limit?

While French civilian casualties from the bombing campaign never approached the levels of Churchill's worst fears, losses still ran into the thousands. Churchill did not know it in May 1944, but the worst was still to come. He probably took small comfort from the note he received back from Tedder on 13 July: 'I don't believe the figure of 10,000 which you gave was greatly exceeded. I am afraid, however, that those casualties are being dwarfed by the casualties involved in the liberation of Caen and other Normandy towns and villages.' It was a small piece of a grim picture. The total figures for civilians killed by Allied bombs in German-occupied countries during the war would ultimately reach 75,000.

Churchill was exhausted by the waiting. He had been fighting hard and often unsuccessfully to make his voice heard on the military plan. He was worried about the ratio of frontline troops to vehicles and support services, concerned about the political and ethical implications of aspects of the bombing policy, and troubled by last-minute security breaches. The country was in a state of semi-lockdown, its transportation and production capacity stretched to their limit, with normal communications and diplomatic relations suspended and facing the risk of direct attack from new weapons of unknown proportions. The weather also remained an unpredictable variant, and one that Churchill was watching closely. From the end of May, he demanded daily updates from the Admiralty. Everything now hung on the next move, which lay with Eisenhower as Supreme Commander. Small wonder then that he sought a temporary escape from Whitehall.

Churchill was already planning to visit the troops on the south coast prior to D-Day. He knew that his presence was important for morale and that the frontline troops would want to see their commanders before embarking. King George VI, Eisenhower and Montgomery were all doing the same. Now he decided that he wanted to take this a step further, and actually accompany the Allied forces across the Channel and see the battle for himself, writing: 'I thought it would not be wrong for me to watch the preliminary bombardment in this historic battle from one of our cruiser squadrons.' It was probably at the final conference at St Paul's School that he asked Ramsay to draw up a plan. The naval commander did so, producing a schedule that would have seen Churchill embark on HMS *Belfast* on D-1, before later transferring to a destroyer to make a tour of the beaches on D-Day itself.

THE LAST OUNCE OF AVAILABLE FORCE

TOP SECRET AND PERSONAL.

THE
CHARTWELL
TRUST

Office of Allied Naval Commander-in-
Chief, Expeditionary Force,
c/o Admiralty,
London, S.W.1.

16th May, 1944.

My dear Prime Minister,

   I did not have a further opportunity yesterday to
discuss the plan you asked me to make, so I though it advisable
to give you an outline of it by letter.

   Briefly the plan is that you should embark in H.M.S.
"Belfast", Flagship of Rear-Admiral F. Dalrymple Hamilton, in
Weymouth Bay in the late afternoon of D - 1, the ship being
called in on her passage from the Clyde for the purpose, and
rejoining her squadron at full speed.

   I consider that nothing smaller than a cruiser is
suitable for you during the night and the approach. She is
one of the bombarding ships attached to the centre British Force.
Next day, it should be possible to transfer you to a destroyer
which has completed her bombardment and which is due to return
to England to re-ammunition. You could make a short tour of
the beaches, with due regard to the unswept mine areas, before
returning in her.

   I shall not make any detailed arrangements until I
know that the above arrangements are satisfactory to you. You
told me not to mention this plan to the First Sea Lord and I
have not done so, but you will appreciate that, as Supreme
Commander, it was essential that General Eisenhower should know
of what was in the air, and I must tell you that he is very
averse to your going. You mean so much to the Nation at this

          /stage in.........

Letter from Admiral Ramsay to Churchill, 16 May 1944

It is clear from the text that both Churchill and Ramsay knew
how controversial this request was. Churchill specifically
instructed Ramsay not to tell Admiral Cunningham, the First Sea
Lord, whom he knew would oppose it. Ramsay did not do so,
but he felt compelled to tell General Eisenhower as the Supreme
Commander with ultimate responsibility for all military aspects

of Overlord, including the naval operation. Unsurprisingly, Eisenhower was against it. While recognising that Churchill's request 'was undoubtedly inspired as much by his natural instincts as a warrior as by his impatience at the prospect of sitting quietly back in London to await reports', the Supreme Commander could not risk the British Prime Minister becoming an accidental casualty, nor did he want others distracted from the operation at hand by the need to protect him. Churchill was not to be so easily put off, pointing out that Eisenhower did not have administrative control over the composition of any British ship's company and that if he made himself a 'bona fide member of a ship's complement it would be beyond your authority to prevent my going'.

Eisenhower had to concede, and there the matter rested until Tuesday 30 May, when Churchill went for his weekly luncheon with the King. In his diary, George VI recorded what happened next. He asked Winston

> where he would be on D-day or rather the night before & he told me glibly he hoped to see the initial attack from one of the bombarding ships . . . I was not surprised & when I suggested that I should go as well (the idea had been in my mind for some time) he reacted well, & he and I are going to talk it over with Ad[miral] Ramsay on Thursday . . . W[inston] cannot say no, if he goes himself, & I don't want to have to tell him he cannot. So?
>
> . . . I told E [Queen Elizabeth] who was wonderful & encouraged me. A.F.L. [Sir Alan Lascelles] was more reticent.

Perhaps Churchill felt he had no choice but to go along with the King's wishes, they being identical to his own. Perhaps he realised that, constitutionally, the monarch was the only person who could order him not to go. In his own memoirs, he said he would submit the request to the Cabinet after they had discussed the matter with Ramsay.

For Sir Alan Lascelles, the King's Private Secretary, this would never do, and his diary entry describes his response:

I think I shook the King by asking him whether he thought the project would be quite fair to the Queen; and whether he was prepared to face the possibility of having to advise Princess Elizabeth on the choice of her first Prime Minister, in the event of her father and Winston being sent to the bottom of the English Channel. Another point, of course, is the paralysing effect which the presence on board of either the Sovereign or the PM, or both, would inevitably have on the unfortunate captain trying to fight his ship in the middle of what can only be an inferno.

By the following day, Lascelles had talked the King down and persuaded him of the necessity of restraining his Prime Minister. George VI sent a handwritten letter to Churchill urging him to reconsider his plan, lest 'a chance bomb, torpedo or even a mine should remove you from the scene'.

Churchill and the King met with Ramsay, Lascelles and Ismay in the map room at Churchill's Treasury Annexe at quarter past three on the afternoon of 1 June. The Admiral outlined his plan for the Prime Minister but 'reacted violently' when informed that the King might want to go too. Churchill now said that this would require the approval of the Cabinet but refused to apply such restrictions to himself. Lascelles tried to convince Churchill of the risks, warning of the difficulty of changing Prime Minister in the middle of the largest military operation of the war, and arguing that he would need the Sovereign's consent to leave the country. Churchill brushed these objections aside. Arrangements were in hand for his successor (presumably Anthony Eden, the Foreign Secretary) and he would be on board a British ship. For all of his persistence, it was clear that he was now in a minority of one – that the King, Lascelles, Ramsay and even Ismay were against his going. But still he insisted. Lascelles felt that 'Winston knows perfectly well that he oughtn't to do this, but when he gets these puckish notions, he is just like a naughty child.' He felt it could be self-defeating. If the Prime Minister was killed in the early stages of Overlord 'the news of his death might easily have such an effect on the troops as to turn victory into defeat'.

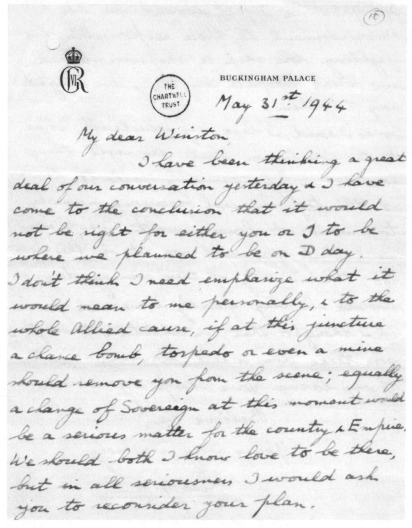

BUCKINGHAM PALACE

May 31st 1944

My dear Winston,

I have been thinking a great deal of our conversation yesterday & I have come to the conclusion that it would not be right for either you or I to be where we planned to be on D day. I don't think I need emphasize what it would mean to me personally, & to the whole Allied cause, if at this juncture a chance bomb, torpedo or even a mine should remove you from the scene; equally a change of Sovereign at this moment would be a serious matter for the country & Empire. We should both I know love to be there, but in all seriousness I would ask you to reconsider your plan.

Letter from King George VI to Churchill, 31 May 1944

One of those troops preparing to go was the young naval officer, Tony Hugill. He had been recruited by naval intelligence, and specifically by Ian Fleming, into a special unit (30 Assault Unit) that would go into Normandy on D-Day with the role of seeking out and securing German military technology. His camp for 3,500 men near Felixstowe, which he nicknamed the cage, brought back memories of his Officer Training Camp: 'same smell of grass trodden down, same toughness in the meat, same latrines'. He sought to distract himself from impending events, throwing himself into the routine of camp life, organising his small group of marines, and trying not to dwell on the dire warnings of casualty levels as high as 60 per cent.

D-Day was now imminent. The King left for Windsor. Churchill headed for the south coast. Whether he would get further still hung in the balance.

Types of Air Power

Tactical air power involves the use of air forces in support of units on the ground or at sea. Tactical forces can be called upon to provide fighter protection in the air above the battle-field and to bomb enemy positions, fortifications, vehicles or vessels threatening Allied troops. They also provide specialist functions such as photographic reconnaissance and air trans-port, bringing troops and supplies to the battlefield. The aircraft protecting the D-Day assault on 6 June were operat-ing tactically.

Operational air power involves the use of air forces to obtain specific operational objectives, such as the preliminary bombardment of a shoreline or the destruction of specific targets. The famous 'Dambusters' raid by 617 Squadron RAF against the Möhne and Edersee dams in Germany on the night of 16 May 1943 is an example of operational air power.

Strategic air power involves the large-scale use of air power, bypassing the battlefield on the ground, to obtain a specific strategic or political aim. Operation Pointblank, the combined Allied bomber offensive aimed at crippling German fighter production and conducted over a sustained period between summer 1943 and spring 1944, is an example of strategic air power.

In 1944, the Allied Expeditionary Force had its own

tactical air force under Leigh-Mallory that was also capable of conducting operations essential to the success of Overlord. The US Eighth Army Air Force and British Bomber Command were operating as independent strategic forces, engaged in a wholesale bombing campaign against Germany in north-western Europe, but were now called upon to offer operational and even tactical support for the operation.

June 5th 1944
?

10, Downing Street,
Whitehall.

Monday Morning

My Darling.
          I feel so much for
you at this agonising
moment — So full of Suspense,
which prevents me from resting over Rome.
I look forward to seeing
you at dinner — Write
write a nice letter to
the poor King —
                    Tender Love from
I've sent such to
to Margaret?
Alexander
                    Clemmie

Just off to her Hospital

Clementine to Winston Churchill, 5 June 1944

9

This Agonising Moment

'Do you realize that by the time you wake up in the
morning 20,000 men may have been killed?'

FRIDAY 2 JUNE. D minus 3. Just forty-eight hours to go
before the launch of the proposed liberation of France, now
scheduled for Monday 5 June. The United Kingdom was in a
state of virtual lockdown. But where was the Prime Minister? He
was not to be found in 10 Downing Street or his offices in
Parliament or even in the Treasury Annexe. At a time when travel
around England was being severely restricted, Churchill had
made his way to the south coast in his private train. He could not
bear to be away from the centre of events and still harboured
fading hopes of being allowed to accompany the assault force
across the Channel.

Accompanied by his friend, the South African Prime Minister,
Field Marshal Smuts, and by the Minister for Labour, Ernest
Bevin, he then transferred from train to car and spent some time
on Friday trying to see some of that force for himself before dropping in on Eisenhower's headquarters at Southwick House, located
about five miles north of Portsmouth. It did not prove easy to
locate the action. According to Eisenhower's naval aide Harry
Butcher, the Prime Minister's motorcade 'had bad luck hitting the
right loading places at the wrong time' and, as a result, Churchill's
naval aide Commander Thompson told Butcher his boss was
'peevish'.

Churchill was a man of action who liked to be at the centre of events. He was aware that there was a high chance that many of the troops he was about to see boarding would not return. He still felt compelled to try and share some of their risks and had not yet responded to the King's handwritten letter. We can assume, therefore, that he had not been best pleased on receiving a second communication from his sovereign just before leaving London on Friday. In it, George VI made 'one more appeal to you not to go to sea on D-Day', pointing out that

> You will see very little, you will run a considerable risk, you will be inaccessible at a critical time when vital decisions might have to be taken, and however unobtrusive you may be, your mere presence on board is bound to be a very heavy additional responsibility to the Admiral and Captain.

So nervous was the King that Churchill might still go that Lascelles then followed up with a late-night telephone call to Churchill's carriage. The conversation was apparently friendly, and Churchill finally and grudgingly deferred to the King's wishes, admitting to Lascelles that 'if that poor ship should go to the bottom, you will all say, "I told you so"'. His written reply, dictated in the early hours of that Saturday morning and taken back to London by a motorcycle despatch rider, was more revealing of his mental state. Though couched in suitably deferential language, in which he reluctantly deferred to 'Your Majesty's wishes and indeed commands', the Prime Minister made it clear that

> . . . as Prime Minister and Minister of Defence, I ought to be allowed to go where I consider it necessary to the discharge of my duty and I do not admit that the Cabinet have any right to put restrictions on my freedom of movement. I rely on my own judgement, invoked in many serious matters, as to what are the proper limits of risk which a person who discharges my duties is entitled to run.

His strong words hinted at his irritation. Churchill was now as close to the frontline as he was going to get, at least for the time being. His office and bedroom were a railway carriage; his hotel a secluded wooded siding outside the sleepy Hampshire village of Droxford. Today the tracks have disappeared and become a footpath, the line a victim of Dr Beeching's cuts to the British railway network in the 1960s. The station is now a private house; the wartime role of the site marked only by a small round plaque beneath a postbox. At first glance, it seems an incongruous location for the Prime Minister's headquarters at such a time, but in fact it had been carefully chosen precisely because its location combined both isolation, and therefore security, with close proximity to the main D-Day embarkation points. To Churchill, this was his 'advance headquarters', but the Prime Minister's desire to get close to the action imposed huge practical difficulties on his staff and did not make things easy for himself.

On Saturday morning, General Ismay awoke to find himself faced with a Prime Minister who wanted to speak to everyone – 'to the President in the White House, to Eden at the Foreign Office, and to the Chiefs of Staff in Whitehall' – from a train in a remote siding that was only connected to the outside world by a single line through the local exchange. He complained to Joan Bright back in London that

> It's hell here – impossible to get a moment to oneself, and ONE telephone, very inefficiently staffed, in a room four feet by three feet occupied by three people . . . No bath, except for a very poor shower – damned stuffy; and no privacy . . . We are hopelessly out of touch here; and there are vital decisions to take which can only be properly taken if we get around a table and assemble all the relevant facts and arguments. How I've hated the last forty-eight hours.

When Duff Cooper visited with General de Gaulle on the following day, he described the Prime Minister's temporary accommodation as a 'perfectly absurd scheme', noting in his diary that one of Churchill's team had told him 'that he intended to lead a reformed life in future because he now knew what hell was like'. The gravity of the moment, combined with the chaos of the new surroundings, meant that everybody was on edge. Churchill was clearly at his worst, complaining about the delays, but when Ismay suggested 'in desperation that it might be better to get back to civilisation', his 'head was bitten off. Were we not next-door to Eisenhower and at the very centre of affairs?'

During the day, Churchill travelled from Droxford to the port city of Southampton. There, with Smuts and Bevin still in tow, he witnessed the huge armada assembled in the Solent, ships of all sizes and functions filling the narrow stretch of water between the mainland and the Isle of Wight and stretching away as far as the eye could see. He watched the embarkation of Tyneside troops, part of the 50th Northumbrian Division, shortly to land on Gold beach. He was there to lift their morale, but their cheers must have been equally helpful in lifting his troubled spirits. His bodyguard Inspector Walter Thompson (not to be confused with his naval aide) recalled one soldier asking Churchill if he had his ticket. When Churchill asked what ticket, the man held up a piece of paper claiming it entitled him to a free trip to France. 'I wish I had. If only I were a few years younger . . .' replied Churchill. The soldier did not realise how hard Churchill had tried to gain just such a ticket. The prime ministerial party then took to the water, travelling by motor launch to Portsmouth to view the assembly of landing craft, before once again visiting the Supreme Commander at Southwick House. Winston arrived back at Droxford anxious but amiable.

For Tony Hugill, embarkation was also taking place and was proving a slow process. It had all begun on the Friday. The troops had made their way to the landing craft, waved off by the local population. Hugill had sought to grasp comfort from 'a final familiar sight – an early 19th century house with roses on it. Magnolia by the road, a mother holding her children's shoulders . . .' Sixty-six men and extra vehicles had then crammed onto a landing craft, which had been shoved off by two bulldozers. The troops had bedded down wherever they could find space, with a can of self-heating soup to help send them to sleep. They had spent Saturday waiting in harbour, expecting to sail early on the Sunday. But during the day, the weather outlook steadily worsened.

By the time Churchill and his party sat down for dinner on board his train on that Saturday evening, the hour was late, and the storm clouds were already gathering. The latest news from Eisenhower's headquarters was not good. The weather forecast for the following night was for high winds, rough seas and low cloud. Halfway through the meal Ismay took the call confirming that a postponement seemed very likely and that a final decision would be taken by Eisenhower in the early hours of Sunday morning. Some ships were already at sea, many troops were already embarked and waiting to go. You would expect the mood to have darkened, but this is where Churchill and his choice of travelling companions came into their own. Eden had now joined Bevin and Smuts. They dined with 1926 champagne and brandy while Smuts reminisced about the two most difficult moments of his life: urging that the Boers surrender to the British in 1902 and then convincing the South Africans to fight alongside Britain in 1939. His choice of subject was clearly designed to distract Churchill. Talk of the Boer War must surely have led Winston to recall his own escape from Boer captivity in 1899. There had been a train then, too; an armoured troop carrier. Churchill, aged just twenty-four and in South Africa as a war correspondent, had been captured when it had been ambushed. He had not remained a prisoner for long, escaping over his prison wall and making his way to safety through a series of adventures, coincidentally involving two further trains. No doubt, the conversation was a chance to briefly escape into the past from the pressures of the day. Revived by alcohol and conversation, the Prime Minister even indicated that he would be happy to relinquish office to either Bevin or Eden. Though presumably not quite yet. The party broke up after midnight and when asked if he wanted to be woken with the news of Eisenhower's decision, Churchill replied: 'Of course not . . . What can I do about it?'

Churchill needed the refreshment of action and the consolation of sharing some of the risks faced by those he was sending into danger. It is the same spirit, the same impulsive side of his character, that saw him want to escape Boer captivity in 1899, personally supervise the siege of anarchists within a house in London's Sidney Street when Home Secretary in 1911, take command of the defences in Antwerp while still First Lord of the Admiralty in 1914, and resign from the government and command a battalion on the Western Front in 1916. He hated waiting on events. The truth was that there was no longer anything he could do to influence the final stages of the D-Day operation. The decision to go rested with its Supreme Commander. Churchill's Droxford excursion was about maintaining his visibility, impressing his presence on the military commanders, and staving off his personal frustrations.

The provisional postponement by twenty-four hours was confirmed in the early hours of Sunday morning. Perhaps predictably, Churchill summoned and berated Ismay for not waking him: 'I suppose it never occurred to you to let me know at once. I suppose you think you are running this war?' The anxiety was back. Those ships already at sea were being recalled, while troops previously embarked (like Tony Hugill and his comrades) faced a long and unpleasant day of rolling in the waves while waiting anxiously on board for further news. What was worse was the continuing uncertainty. There seemed little hope that the weather would get better sufficiently quickly. The window of opportunity provided by a full moon and low tide might be lost. This had huge implications for Churchill. How long could effective security measures and deception plans be maintained? What would happen if the operation were undertaken at a later date in sub-optimal conditions? Was there now an increased risk of failure? To make matters worse, there followed the news that a female typist working for the Associated

Press, while practising, had accidentally placed a statement on the live tape that the Allies were invading France. The story had been quickly cancelled, but not before it had gone around the world. But this was not the worst thing facing the Prime Minister on that uncertain morning. Churchill's mood, by all accounts already 'peevish' and frustrated, was about to be further tested by the arrival of General Charles de Gaulle.

De Gaulle had flown in 'bristling' from his headquarters in Algiers, then part of French North Africa, at Churchill's personal request and on board the Prime Minister's luxury Avro York aircraft. As leader of the Free French forces, he clearly had to be briefed on the liberation of French soil, especially as the Ministry of Economic Warfare and Special Operations Executive felt that a personal broadcast by the General on D-Day would have an 'immense psychological effect' on the resistance movements in France, telling the Prime Minister that, 'There is no getting away from the fact that his personal influence with the fighting elements among the French is of the highest importance.' But there were huge difficulties and the conversation had been left to the last possible moment. While the British and Americans feared that Free French communication channels were not secure, and that their headquarters in Algiers leaked like a sieve, the real tensions were political. President Roosevelt still remained firmly opposed to any formal recognition of de Gaulle's Committee of National Liberation as the Provisional Government of France and continued to advocate free elections after the restoration of France. All of which made de Gaulle extremely reluctant to assist the Anglo-American Allies with the post-liberation civil administration of Normandy.

Churchill was caught between his American and French allies. Roosevelt was adamant that his US representatives in Britain could not talk to de Gaulle about any future political arrangements for France. Nor was the President prepared to issue an invitation to the French General to visit Washington DC, as de Gaulle was only the head of a committee, not a head of state. His one concession was that he was prepared to extend 'an immediate and cordial affirmative' should de Gaulle request such a visit to America. That seemed unlikely. It would de facto involve de Gaulle in recognising that he was not the leader of France, something that he would clearly see as an affront to his position, especially as his Committee of National Liberation had pointedly decided just before his departure to adopt the title of Provisional Government of France. De Gaulle's visit had hung in the balance until the last moment, with telegrams flying backwards and forwards between Churchill and Duff Cooper, the British representative to the Free French Committee in Algiers. Aware of the lockdown in Britain, de Gaulle was insisting on complete freedom to communicate with his African headquarters in cypher and to leave Britain whenever he wished. He had also made it clear that he wanted to talk with the British and Americans about the government of France.

Valentine Lawford, Eden's Private Secretary, got up early to collect de Gaulle and his party from Northolt airport. Their convoy of cars swept into Carlton Gardens, the Free French headquarters in London, before heading off in search of Churchill's carriage in the Hampshire countryside. To Lawford the English landscape looked 'green and wonderfully beautiful' but, like Hugill, he became sentimental as they raced past lorries carrying soldiers towards the coast: 'Their features were young and plebeian, but there was a strained, set impression upon them, the result of knowing what they were in for in the next few days.'

An awkward Sunday lunch on the train inevitably ensued. Duff Cooper, Smuts, Bevin, Anthony Eden and Pierre Viénot (Free French Ambassador to the United Kingdom) were all in attendance, along with French Generals Béthouart, Billotte and Koenig. Despite the dire weather predictions for the forthcoming night, it was a hot summer's day, and the carriage must have been crowded.

The two leaders exchanged greetings and got down to business. De Gaulle, tall and taciturn; Churchill, short, voluble. Both men under pressure. Churchill aware that the operation had been delayed by at least twenty-four hours, perhaps longer, and fearful that any information supplied to the French party might leak out from Algiers; de Gaulle determined to ensure that the Free French would not be ignored. Refusing to rely on Lawford's interpretation, and insisting on speaking in his best pidgin French, Churchill made some attempt to be conciliatory. He drank to the health of France, but as Lawford noted: 'Luncheon was long and not genial . . . De Gaulle has no small talk . . . and declined to respond to W[inston]'s badinage . . . Those two will never be happy together.'

The official Cabinet record of the conversations is revealing. The contemporary diaries of Lawford and Duff Cooper suggest it conflates into one document talks that took place before and after lunch. It certainly captures Churchill's concerns. He emphasised the scale of the military operation in terms of ships, assault troops and follow-up divisions, and talked at length about the reasons for the postponement, which he felt might be as long as ten to twelve days, in which case he feared the Allies might lose 'the advantages of moon, tide, weather and wind'. 'As he had recognised General de Gaulle as the head of a Great Empire, he felt it would be impossible for him not to have free right of communication', but this did not stop him repeatedly requesting an assurance that 'no military details of the operation should be imparted by the General to any of his colleagues except those at the meeting'. De Gaulle in turn expressed his gratitude to the Prime Minister for inviting him, stressing that 'It was important for the future of both our countries that we should be together when the operation began.'

So far so good, but thereafter things went downhill. When Churchill urged de Gaulle to go to Washington and seek recognition from Roosevelt, de Gaulle replied that the French government already existed and that 'I have nothing to ask, in this respect, of the United States of America nor of Great Britain.' According to de Gaulle's later account, his subsequent refusal to recognise the 'so-called French currency' being issued to the British and American troops prompted an outburst from Churchill in which the British leader declared:

We are going to liberate Europe, but it is because the Americans are in agreement with us that we do so. This is something you ought to know: each time we have to choose between Europe and the open sea, we shall always choose the open sea. Each time I have to choose between you and Roosevelt, I shall always choose Roosevelt.

The British official version records slightly different words but with the same meaning. While de Gaulle professed himself 'quite content with the battle, which he felt showed that the United States, Great Britain and France were all together . . . on the practical question of administration of territories he had difficulties'. To which Churchill responded by stating:

> the United States and Great Britain were two great nations who were willing to risk the loss of scores of thousands of their men in an operation designed to liberate France . . . He must tell him [de Gaulle] bluntly that, if after every effort had been exhausted the President was on one side and the French National Committee of Liberation on the other, he, Mr Churchill, would almost certainly side with the President and that anyhow no quarrel would ever arise between Britain and the United States on account of France.

Moreover, he was certain that this view would be endorsed by the House of Commons. In this, he may well have been wrong. It is clear that not all of Churchill's colleagues shared such a binary, pro-American and anti-French line. Anthony Eden later wrote: 'I did not like this pronouncement nor did Mr Bevin, who said so in a booming aside. The meeting was a failure.' The two leaders went together to see Eisenhower after lunch, which must have been an awkward meeting, but damage had been done and they dined separately; de Gaulle refusing to travel back to London in the prime ministerial train that evening, leaving the Prime Minister brooding and nursing ill feeling towards his erstwhile ally. The hot weather deteriorated into a howling gale.

Churchill's departure from the coast was clearly welcomed by Ismay and the beleaguered Private Office team. It must have also taken pressure off Eisenhower and his staff, who had been subject to Churchill's repeated visits over the course of that long weekend. The Prime Minister's place was in London, with the War Cabinet and Parliament. The collapse of his plan to accompany the troops and the delay of the operation effectively forced him back to the capital. Once there, he worked continuously until almost 4 a.m. on 5 June.

When Churchill awoke, one of the documents waiting for him was this short and simple manuscript note written by his wife Clementine. Like many couples, they had pet names for one another. She would sign off her personal letters to him with a drawing of a cat; he would often reply with a hastily scrawled pug or pig. Her letter read:

June 5th 1944

> 10 Downing Street
> Whitehall
> Monday morning

My Darling,
I feel so much for you at this agonising moment – so full of suspense, which prevents me from rejoicing over Rome.
I look forward to seeing you at dinner – write a nice letter to the poor King-
I've sent enclosed to Margaret Alexander

Tender Love from
Clemmie

[Cat drawing]

Just off to her Hospital.

Clementine was heading off for a routine committee meeting at the Fulmer Chase Maternity Home, a hospital facility for the wives of officers of all three services and one of several wartime charities she supported. They were both aware that momentous events were imminent, and, after nearly thirty-six years of marriage, Clementine understood better than anyone what her husband was going through. She also knew from long experience that he was much more likely to take notice of something that she put in writing.

The British Prime Minister was wrestling with his usual large in-tray, delivered to him by his Private Secretaries in his official despatch boxes. His responses to the many minutes, telegrams, reports and papers were dictated to his personal secretary, who sat patiently at the end of the bed. We must imagine him propped up on his pillows, resplendent in his favourite red, green and gold dressing gown and occasionally puffing on his cigar; his flow of dictation interspersed with moments of deep concentration or interrupted by his barking of sudden orders. One contemporary account from around this period, by his personal secretary Elizabeth Layton, has him reaching for the little white telephone by his bed and, upon being connected to the duty Private Secretary (the civil servant John Peck), gruffly demanding, 'Gimme the moon.' What he wanted was the chart depicting the moon's phases, vital for predicting the all-important tides that would dictate the timing of the D-Day landings on the beaches of Normandy. He sent a telegram to Stalin noting that 'the difficulties of getting proper weather conditions are very great'.

This was a global war and, as always, he was dealing with a range of issues: among them the future political government of Greece, the retreat of Tito and his communist Yugoslav partisans to the island of Vis, and improvements to aerial photography techniques. The previous night before retiring late he had received the news of the liberation of Rome by the Allied forces under General (soon-to-be Field Marshal) Alexander. On any other day this would have been a cause for significant rejoicing. But on this morning Churchill was clearly distracted.

He now knew that Eisenhower's momentous decision had been taken. At a further meeting at Southwick House on the evening of Sunday 4 June, British meteorologist Group Captain Dr James Stagg had predicted a potential break in the inclement weather on the morning of Tuesday 6 June and identified a narrow window for the landings. General Eisenhower had seized the opportunity and authorised Operation Overlord. Had he been right to do so? This was the question that inevitably dominated Churchill's waking thoughts upon that Monday morning.

Eisenhower's decision had set in train events that could not now be reversed, and that would see the British, American and Canadian forces and their allies begin their attempt to liberate France the following day, Tuesday 6 June. As Churchill sat trying to focus on his papers, he was aware that the airborne troops were getting ready to embark in their gliders to seize key bridges and that the vast armada was now preparing to set sail from the British south coast. The clock was ticking; the countdown had begun. This was the 'agonising moment – so full of suspense' referred to in Clementine's letter.

Tony Hugill's landing craft was finally underway. The journey was not pleasant. 'This old cow of a craft is chucking herself about a good deal.' There would be much vomiting.

By lunchtime Churchill was in bullish mood. His dining companions were the British Chiefs of Staff: Cunningham, Brooke and Portal. All three were feeling the weight of the pending operation on their shoulders, but they could not refuse Churchill's summons. Cunningham recorded a 'good lunch' at 10 Downing Street with 'as usual lots of wine. PM very worked up about "Overlord" and really in about a hysterical state. Much conversation. He really is an incorrigible optimist.' Field Marshal Sir Alan Brooke, the Chief of the Imperial General Staff (military head of the British Army), noted the same, confiding to his diary that he found Churchill 'over optimistic as regards prospects of the Cross-Channel invasion'.

Perhaps Churchill was just putting on a brave face in front of his most senior commanders. Those around him often noted that he was at his best in a crisis. Maybe he was being swept along by the excitement of the moment and the possibilities that were now opening up. He liked nothing more than discussing military operations while eating, and we can imagine him moving the plates and cutlery to represent the military units. It was also surely a manifestation of a palpable sense of relief. A decision had been taken. The period of waiting was over. The difficulties and dangers associated with delay had at least been lifted, even if plenty of other dangers remained.

As Hugill looked around him and saw a sea with convoys stretching all the way to the horizon, the larger landing craft looking like Roman triremes, he reflected: 'There must be a lot of people in the Whitehall area walking around with their fingers crossed.'

The War Cabinet met at 18.30 hours. Leo Amery, the Secretary of State for India, had known Churchill since their school-days at Harrow. He thought that 'Winston was evidently greatly stirred and also at the end of his tether nervously, and no wonder. It is the most anxious moment of the whole war.' Churchill began by briefing his colleagues on the postponement. The formal agenda then started with the liberation of Rome and there was agreement that Churchill should send a message of congratulation to General Alexander and make a statement in the House of Commons. There followed a report of naval, military and air operations over the course of the last six days. In the home theatre (meaning north-western Europe), Bomber Command had flown 2,550 sorties, the United States bombers 4,900 and the Allied Expeditionary Force and the Tactical Air Force 13,000. Between them they had dropped over 22,000 tons of bombs, largely on the occupied territories (meaning France and Belgium). Churchill still entertained huge anxieties about the impact on the morale and support of the French civilians.

He also remained worried about German reprisals against the British mainland and must therefore have been gratified to learn that the V-Weapon or Crossbow targets had once again been attacked. Equally pleasing would have been the news that there had been no shipping losses in June to enemy action – at least thus far.

But the main discussion that evening clearly raised his blood pressure. De Gaulle was now refusing to broadcast after Eisenhower on D-Day unless the Free French were given control over re-establishing civil government in France. Arguing that the 'effective civil administration of France must be provided by Frenchmen', he refused to send liaison officers to work alongside the Anglo-American forces. Even the diplomatic language of the official minutes fails to disguise Churchill's angry response:

> The PRIME MINISTER said that if General de Gaulle refused to agree to the liaison officers proceeding with Operation "Overlord" it would not be possible for us to have any further discussions with General de Gaulle on civil or military matters. It might even be necessary to indicate that an aeroplane would be ready to take him back to Algiers forthwith.

According to Sir Alexander Cadogan, Under-Secretary of State at the Foreign Office (the country's most senior diplomat) and another inveterate diary keeper, 'We endured the usual passionate anti-de G[aulle] harangue from P.M. On this subject, we get away from politics, diplomacy and even common sense.' Churchill certainly liked to have someone to rail against. At different points in the war, it was a role that would be filled by the Indian nationalist leader, Mohandas Gandhi, or by the Labour politician and government critic, Aneurin Bevan. In June 1944, the intransigence of General de Gaulle provided an outlet for his pent-up anger and frustration.

In a letter to de Gaulle that he drafted but ultimately did not send, Churchill let off steam. He complained that he had 'tried very hard on many occasions during four years, to establish some reasonable basis for friendly comradeship with you. Your action at this juncture convinces me that this hope has no further existence.' He railed against the 'heinous character' of the General's actions and concluded: 'I can conceive no useful purpose in your staying longer, and that the aeroplanes will be at your disposal to-morrow night, weather permitting.' Ultimately, de Gaulle did broadcast, and some French liaison officers joined the assault force, but Churchill's personal relationship with the French leader was at a low point.

Fortunately, the rest of the agenda was less controversial and probably seemed less relevant in light of the huge operation that was about to unfold. Preventing the export of wolfram (the metal tungsten) from Portugal to Germany, determining the composition of the British delegation to the international economic conference at Bretton Woods in the United States, creating a refugee camp in Tripolitania (Libya) and recognising the constituent Republics of the Soviet Union. These were all no doubt important issues, but in the minds of those gathered around the Cabinet table they must have paled into insignificance beside the imminence of Overlord. It was clearly a long Cabinet meeting, but not yet the end of a long day.

Later that evening, Churchill dined alone with Clementine. Afterwards, she joined him in his map room before retiring. Here, laid out before them both in great detail, were the beaches. There may even have been a three-dimensional papier mâché model provided by the Americans. Breaking off from his study of the final dispositions for D-Day, Winston turned to Clementine and said, 'Do you realize that by the time you wake up in the morning 20,000 men may have been killed?'

As we have seen, his worries were not limited to the military casualties. For weeks he had been exercised by the impact of Allied bombing on French and Belgian civilians. Southern England had been turned into an armed camp and areas of the coast completely sealed off. The levels of restriction in place could not be maintained for long. All this, and there were signs that the Germans were preparing to unleash deadly new weapons on the United Kingdom.

An often-overlooked fact is that Churchill also had an additional and very personal worry. His only son Randolph was serving as part of a British military mission to the headquarters of Marshal Tito, the leader of the Yugoslav partisans. But, as Churchill knew only too well from his daily telegrams, Tito's mountainous hideout in Bosnia had been stormed by German paratroopers and the Yugoslav guerrilla leader was now on the run and being relentlessly pursued by the Germans. Randolph's exact whereabouts were unknown and his safety in doubt.

The 2017 film *Churchill* depicts the British Prime Minister in these hours as a lonely leader plagued by doubts and haunted by the ghosts of the Dardanelles operation. Much has been written about Churchill's 'black dog' of depression, a term that only appears in one of his letters. It is an aspect of his health that will no doubt continue to be debated by historians. The latest research by two eminent medical consultants has concluded that 'Churchill suffered no major psychiatric disorder' and that 'Churchill's despair – always in response to events – was quickly followed by recovery'. There is no doubt that he struggled with periods of enforced inactivity and that he hated this period of waiting prior to D-Day, his mood probably exacerbated by his fragile physical health, but his instinctive reaction was to visit the troops, to seek the solace of action and to lash out against those he deemed to be obstructing him. On the eve of the landings, we can see him running a range of emotions; from over-optimism to anger with de Gaulle to anxiety over potential casualties. They are all surely symptoms of his overarching worry about the price of failure.

Was Churchill wrong to be worried? The consequences of failure were surely immense. If the Allies were unable to gain a foothold on the beaches, the war in the West would certainly be prolonged. The casualties would be high and the blow to morale huge. Would the public in Britain and the United States have the appetite to try again? Would Churchill and Roosevelt remain in office? Would pressure re-emerge for some form of settlement, leaving Hitler in charge of swathes of Western Europe? Would America abandon the continent and turn east against Japan? These were all imponderables, but they were very real concerns to Churchill on Monday 5 June.

It is clear from the contemporary diaries and letters of all those around Churchill, both in his Private Office and among the ranks of the senior military commanders, that the success of the operation could not be taken for granted. Admiral Ramsay worried about 'the critical period around H-Hour when, if initial flights are held up, success will be in the balance'.

General Brooke wished 'to God it were safely over' and later reflected that

> I knew too well all the weak points in the plan of operations. First of all, the weather, on which we were entirely dependent; a sudden storm might wreck it all. Then the complexity of an amphibious operation of this kind, when confusion may degenerate into chaos in such a short time. The difficulty of controlling the operation once launched, lack of elasticity in the handling of reserves, danger of leakage of information with consequent loss of that essential secrecy.

Even General Eisenhower, the Supreme Commander, wrote out and sealed a letter accepting responsibility in the event of failure:

> Our landings in the Cherbourg-Havre area have failed to gain a satisfactory foothold and I have withdrawn the troops. My decision to attack at this time and place was based upon the best information available. The troops, the air and the Navy did all that Bravery and devotion to duty could do. If any blame or fault attaches to the attempt, it is mine alone.

It was a long day for all concerned and a long night too. Sir Hari Singh, the forty-eight-year-old Maharaja of Jammu and Kashmir, was in London as a representative of the Imperial Government in India. In this capacity, he had been invited to attend the evening's Cabinet meeting and so had learnt of the imminence of the D-Day invasion. According to Churchill's Principal Private Secretary, John Martin, 'such was the immediate effect upon his mind that he was unable to sleep and had to call for sleeping draughts'. It seems unlikely Sir Hari slept for long. Joan Bright recorded hearing a deep throbbing in the dark hours that at 6 a.m. changed to a thunder. The planes were in the air. 'It was on.' Valentine Lawford heard them too, knelt by his bed and prayed that 'all this sacrifice and longing should not be in vain'. It is difficult to imagine that anyone got much sleep thereafter.

COPY

PRIME MINISTER'S
PERSONAL TELEGRAM
SERIAL No. *T. 1203/4.*

④

PRIME MINISTER TO MARSHAL STALIN
Personal and Top Secret

Everything has started well.   The
mines, obstacles and land batteries have been
largely overcome.   The Air landings were very
successful and on a large scale.   Infantry
landings are proceeding rapidly and many tanks
and self-propelled guns are already ashore.
Weather outlook moderate to good.

W.S.C.

6.6.44.

Telegram from Churchill to Stalin, 6 June 1944

10

We'll Start the War from Here

'As it was in the beginning so may it continue to the end.'

CONVINCED THAT THE weather was too poor for the Allies to mount their attack on mainland Europe over the period of 5/6 June, German commanders made various decisions that were to have catastrophic consequences for them. Field Marshal Erwin Rommel, the commander of German Army Group B, defending the Atlantic Wall, decided to go home to Germany to celebrate his wife's birthday. General Friedrich Dollman, the Commander-in-Chief of the German Seventh Army in northern France, decided to gather his divisional commanders together in Rennes for a command-post anti-invasion exercise. Major General Edgar Feuchtinger, the commander of 21st Panzer Division, whose tanks were closest to the Normandy coast, decided to spend the night with his mistress in Paris. Senior commanders were not at their posts at a critical moment. Decisions have consequences.

As they crossed the French coast, the singing inside the Horsa glider piloted by Staff Sergeant Jim Wallwork died away. The 139 soldiers of the Oxfordshire and Buckinghamshire Light Infantry under the command of Major John Howard realised that the moment for which they had been training was upon them. The silence intensified as their glider, along with the other five gliders carrying their regimental comrades, parted company with their tug aircraft and began the silent descent towards their objectives – the two bridges over the River Orne and the Caen Canal.

Capturing these bridges intact was a key part of the overall Operation Overlord plan and would help defend against a German counter-attack into the left flank of the Allied invasion. The sky was clear and the moon bright as Jim Wallwork spotted the tiny strip of land between the two bridges and steered his heavily laden glider towards his landing site – one so small that the German defenders had not bothered to erect anti-glider poles. In a feat of flying by the army's Glider Pilot Regiment that Air Chief Marshal Sir Trafford Leigh-Mallory later declared to be one of the 'most outstanding flying achievements of the war', Jim Wallwork crash-landed his glider just yards from the bridge to be secured. He, and his co-pilot Johnny Ainsworth, were knocked unconscious by the impact of the landing but the Ox and Bucks soldiers stormed across the bridge – known thereafter as Pegasus Bridge – and secured it within ten minutes. Lieutenant Den Brotheridge, leading the assault, was fatally wounded but the first ground objective of the Allied assault was a complete success. Moments later, the first French house to be liberated, the Café Gondrée, was entered, much to the delight of its owner, Georges Gondrée, who at once dug up a bottle of champagne from his garden, hidden years before from the Germans, to celebrate with the British soldiers. To this day his daughter, Arlette, then just five years old, opens champagne for British soldiers every year at midnight on the 5/6 June. But in 1944, the battle had just begun.

From airfields across southern England, paratroopers from the British 6th Airborne Division and the US 82nd and 101st Airborne Divisions flew through the night skies towards their objectives in Normandy as Allied minesweepers cleared pathways for the troop-carrying ships to approach the invasion beaches. The ships rolled and heaved, many of the soldiers were violently sick, regretting their early breakfast, but as dawn began to break the stage was set for the largest amphibious operation that history has ever seen and may never see again. Aircraft roared overhead as targets on the coast and inland were struck and the Allied Fleet belched forth its enormous firepower ahead of the landing craft and amphibious tanks as they made their way towards Sword, Juno, Gold, Omaha and Utah beaches. The overture reached a crescendo as the first assaults from the sea heralded the opening acts of the deadly adventure. Back in England, Churchill, Eisenhower and Montgomery held their breath. Stan Hollis clambered down into his landing craft. The die was cast. There would be no second chance.

While the British 6th Airborne Division secured objectives on the left flank of the Allied invasion, the US 82nd and 101st Airborne Divisions dropped inland of Utah beach to secure the right flank and begin to threaten the German defenders of the Cotentin Peninsula and the key port of Cherbourg. The poor weather and intense anti-aircraft fire caused many of the para-trooper's transport and glider-tug aircraft to take evasive action, with the result that many of the American airborne troops were scattered very widely over their objective areas, many tragically drowning in deliberately flooded marshes. Amid the darkness and dispersion, the soldiers struggled to marry up with their own units; nevertheless, a strong attack was mounted by various units of the 82nd Airborne Division on the key village of Sainte-Mère-Église. In among the real soldiers, dummy paratroopers with simulated gunfire devices were also dropped, which increased the confusion in the minds of local German commanders struggling to identify the strength and objectives of the airborne landings. As dawn broke, the amphibious assaults began.

Spearheaded by the heavy cruiser USS *Augusta*, a naval flotilla of some twenty Allied warships began their preliminary bombard-ment on the German positions of the 709th and 243rd Infanterie-Divisions and the 91st Luftlande-Division defending Utah beach. The assault wave of the 8th Infantry Regiment of the US 4th Infantry Division, supported by thirty-two special amphibious DD Sherman tanks, was scheduled to hit the beaches a half-hour after dawn at 06.30 hours. Strong currents took the landing craft nearly a mile and a half further east than intended, the navigation problem exacerbated by the loss of three of the four control vessels that were intended to act as guides. Fortune favoured the 8th Infantry Regiment as the beach on which they landed was less strongly defended than their original objective. Sensing some topographical confusion and doubt, Assistant Division Commander Brigadier General Theodore Roosevelt made his famously reassuring remark: 'We'll start the war from here!' By 12 noon, the forward troops had contacted the paratroopers of the 101st Airborne Division and by the end of the day the 4th Division had pushed inland by about four miles. The westernmost units were within a mile of linking up with the 82nd Airborne Division in Sainte-Mère-Église. The 4th Infantry Division suffered only 197 killed or wounded on D-Day itself (lessons having been learnt on Slapton Sands), though the two airborne divisions lost around two and a half thousand of their men, killed, wounded or missing in the first twenty-four hours of Overlord.

Although the 4th Division had got ashore with very limited casualties, the picture on Omaha beach for the US 1st and 29th Infantry Divisions was very different. While a battalion of US Rangers heroically scaled the cliffs of Point du Hoc four miles to the west to silence a German gun battery, the first assault waves approached the beach to also land at 06.30 hours. From their landing craft, with the heavy shells of the naval bombardment screaming overhead from 05.50 hours, the waiting soldiers witnessed over three hundred Fortress and Liberator bombers of the US 8th Air Force drop more than a thousand bombs from 06.05 hours. But the heavy bombers, more used to bombing large industrial targets in Germany, were incapable of the pinpoint accuracy required and their bombs fell not on the beach defences of the German 716th Infanterie-Division and forward elements of the more experienced 352nd Infanterie-Division, but further inland. The complaint on the landing craft was that all the bombing had done was wake up the Germans. Worse still, despite the very choppy sea conditions, some of the tank-landing-craft commanders stuck rigidly to their original orders and paused over two miles from the shore to launch the thirty-two amphibious DD Sherman tanks of the 741st Tank Battalion. Of the thirty-two tanks, twenty-seven foundered with the loss of their crews and only two of that battalion landed successfully. In contrast, the officers controlling the launching of the tanks of the 743rd Tank Battalion decided to take their thirty-two amphibious tanks right onto the beach. Caught up in the subsequent mayhem of the infantry landings, nine members of the 743rd were to be awarded the Distinguished Service Cross for their actions on D-Day.

From the original beach reconnaissance, it was always known that the fight on Omaha would be tough, with only five possible exits off the beach through gaps in the cliffs. For most of D-Day, the outcome on this beach hung in the balance. Some three hours after the initial landings, General Leonard T. Gerow, commanding the US V Corps, painted such a bleak picture to US 1st Army Commander, General Omar Bradley, anxiously awaiting reports on the command ship USS *Augusta*, that Bradley began to consider suspending further landings on Omaha. Eventually, by nightfall, through heroic leadership and selfless determination amid the bloodshed and chaos, the beach was secured, and the forward troops began to move inland. The beach itself remained under German artillery fire while demolition teams continued to destroy the vicious beach obstacles and clear the battlefield debris to allow reinforcements and supplies to get ashore. Casualties on Omaha beach on D-Day were initially reported at around 2,300 of which 1,465 were killed. At ten times the casualty rate at Utah, it is not surprising that the US government later decided to place its national memorial in Normandy on the high ground above Omaha beach.

Further east, it was the comparative success of the British 50th (Northumbrian) Division landing on Gold beach that took some of the pressure off US forces on Omaha. Brigadier Dietrich Kraiss, commanding 352nd Infanterie-Division, felt obliged to order one of his reserve battalions to block the British at Crépon, some six miles inland, rather than counter-attack towards Omaha. Landing an hour later than the Americans due to tidal differences, the assault brigades of the 50th Division began to land at 07.30 hours. The 231st Brigade landed at Le Hamel supported by two squadrons of DD Sherman tanks of the Sherwood Rangers Yeomanry, which had also ignored the five-thousand-yard launch order and took to the water only a thousand yards offshore. However, even that shorter run-in meant delay and the 1st Royal Hampshires had a tough fight around Arromanches-les-Bains. Supported by the 1st Dorsets and 2nd Devons, they eventually secured their objectives by the end of the day. Also landing on Gold beach were the Royal Marines of No. 47 Commando, who pushed west towards Port-en-Bessin and would be the first British troops to join up with the American 1st Infantry Division from Omaha. Further east, it was Stan Hollis's 6th Green Howards alongside the 5th East Yorks that approached La Rivière supported by the tanks of the 4th/7th Dragoon Guards, again launching only yards offshore. Lieutenant Colonel Robin Hastings of the 6th Green Howards knew that his battalion was landing exactly in the right place, as a house with a prominent circular drive, which had featured in all the briefing photographs, was immediately inland from where his landing craft hit the beach. Unlike enduring the intense machine-gun fire that wrought such havoc as the landing-craft ramps came down on Omaha, the experience on Hastings' vessel was different. The landing craft's ramp jammed. It took a huge shove from two burly Royal Marines to open it. Not sure how deep the water was in front of the craft, Hastings dangled his feet over the edge. The water only came up to his knees so he, and his command group, took off up the beach. The fighting intensified inland and in the course of the day CSM Stan Hollis carried out the two actions that were to win him the only Victoria Cross awarded on D-Day. By nightfall the 2nd Essex and the tanks of the Sherwood Rangers were just short of Bayeux. The 50th Division suffered around 1,100 casualties on D-Day, of which 350 were killed.

Further east still, the Canadian 3rd Division was determined to put the ghosts of the failed Dieppe raid behind them as they prepared to come ashore on Juno beach. At 05.30 hours, the cruiser HMS *Belfast*, and an international flotilla of British, French, Norwegian and Canadian warships, began their bombardment. In the first wave, the Canadian 7th Brigade headed towards Courseulles-sur-Mer and the 8th Brigade towards Saint-Aubin-sur-Mer, supported by the swimming tanks of the 1st Hussars and the Fort Garry Horse (a Canadian armoured regiment). Despite the overwhelming weight of incoming fire, the German defenders of two battalions of the 716 Infanterie-Division held their fire until the ramps of the landing craft came down. As the troops rushed ashore the machine-gun and artillery fire was intense. The Canadians suffered 961 casualties of which 340 were killed. The shoreline was largely a built-up area of houses and commercial buildings, which afforded the Germans considerable protection. Tanks were needed to blast exits inland off the beaches. Although the beaches were cleared only slowly, nevertheless the reinforcement waves and logistic supplies kept coming forward. This produced considerable confusion on the beaches, which slowed the move inland. By the end of the day, however, the Canadians were some seven miles inland at Le Fresne-Camilly and Villons-les Buissons – the furthest inland of any Allied troops – but were short of their objective to cut the Caen–Bayeux road and to capture Carpiquet Airfield. Whether this degree of exploitation inland on the first day was ever achievable has remained an open question. It would be another month of fierce fighting against the 12th SS Panzer Division Hitlerjugend before Carpiquet Airfield was taken.

Furthest to the east were the landings of the British 3rd Division, the division that Bernard Montgomery had commanded in France and at Dunkirk in 1940. To this division he gave the most ambitious task of D-Day – to capture Caen. Unlike the 50th Division landing on Gold beach, which had fought with Montgomery across the North African desert, into Sicily and Italy, the 3rd Division had been out of combat, in England, and training for future operations. Their moment came on 6 June 1944.

As with the other assault divisions, Major General Tom Rennie's 3rd Infantry Division was supported by a huge naval bombardment led by the British battleships, HMS *Warspite* and *Ramillies*, and eighteen other warships, including one from Poland. They fired not only over the heads of the soldiers of the 8th Infantry Brigade and Royal Marine Commando units in the assault wave, but also in support of the swimming DD tanks of the 13th/18th

Hussars and the Staffordshire Yeomanry. Common sense was applied to the launching into the sea of the tanks, with the majority surviving the five-foot-high waves during their run-in, a few arriving ahead of the assaulting infantry. With the capture of Caen as the prize objective of D-Day, doubt has lingered over whether enough planning was given as to how to exploit the initial successful landings by the 3rd Division. Strongpoints, code-named as Morris and Hillman, held by the German 736th Grenadier Regiment, had to be seized by 8 Brigade before 185 Brigade could pass through them on the Périers ridge to launch their attack on Caen itself. Congestion on the beach delayed the tanks of the Staffordshire Yeomanry getting ahead to support the 1st Suffolks' battle to secure Hillman. Worse still, the naval gunfire support officer had been killed, the initial bombardment had left Hillman intact, and intelligence had failed to identify this position as the strongly held headquarters of the defending regiment. Despite individual acts of heroism, including that of Private 'Tich' Hunter, later awarded the Distinguished Conduct Medal, Hillman was not subdued until late afternoon. The 1st Norfolks of 185 Brigade, eager to press the attack on Caen, bypassed Hillman too soon and took over a hundred and fifty casualties from unsuppressed German positions. By nightfall the 3rd Division, despite having suffered over a thousand casualties during the day, had not been able to attack Caen and fulfil that part of Montgomery's Overlord plan. It would take another six weeks and huge Allied and French loss of life before Caen was liberated on 19 July.

Reports and news about the landings in Normandy filtered back slowly during the morning and afternoon of 6 June. Public announcements needed to be cautious, as Operation Fortitude was still running to persuade the Germans that Normandy was not the main Allied landing and that they should keep their eyes firmly on the Pas-de-Calais. Nevertheless, the peoples of Europe and North America needed to know what was happening.

Churchill spent the morning of Tuesday 6 June in his map room trying to interpret the latest information about the landings ahead of his midday statement in the Commons. Everything was still shrouded in uncertainty, but the initial reports seemed good. The Germans had failed to correctly interpret the increased signals traffic coming from the Allied Fleet and had missed an early warning when some advance ships had been called back after Eisenhower's initial postponement in the early hours of Sunday morning. Their own meteorological services had failed to spot the gap in the weather. Tactical surprise had been achieved.

Bletchley Park was reading the German naval communications in almost real time, though not quite quickly enough to prevent the loss of the Norwegian destroyer *Svenner*, which was sunk by E-boats operating out of Le Havre. The American destroyer USS *Corry* was also lost to enemy action, most probably hit by fire from a shore battery, but the fleet had got across the Channel almost unscathed. Air superiority seemed absolute. News was filtering back about the difficulties of the Americans on Omaha, but landings on the other beaches appeared to be progressing well. The casualties were still unclear, but they were far lower than the twenty thousand that Churchill had feared.

The Prime Minister took lunch with George VI at Buckingham Palace. Sir Alan Lascelles felt the full force of Winston's glare on first meeting. He concluded he had not yet been forgiven for his role in preventing Churchill's trip to France. Thereafter, the Prime Minister accompanied the King to Leigh-Mallory's headquarters at Stanmore and then to Eisenhower's at Bushy Park, where the two men could follow the action on the large maps and charts on which progress was being plotted. There were no satellite communications, no real-time images, but the intelligence was continuing to flow in. A picture was emerging. The weather had caught the Germans off guard, but it had also created some difficulties for the Allies. The overcast sky had limited the effectiveness of the huge naval and air bombardment preceding the assault, while the onshore wind had created a higher-than-expected tide, making the approach to the beaches more difficult, especially for the swimming tanks, and hiding some of the deadly obstacles that now became real death-traps. And yet the Allied troops were clearly getting ashore. There were also encouraging signs that their enemy was confused. Key Panzer divisions had not yet been released for the battle.

For his part, Lascelles noted with wry amusement that 'Though they [the King and Churchill] had lunched together, and driven a number of miles in the same car, neither of them, apparently, made any allusion to their recent exchange of letters!'

While Churchill toured the headquarters, his Private Secretary Jock Colville, now serving with his RAF squadron and finally allowed to fly over France, was taking part in two reconnaissance flights, looking down on 'a sea boiling with ships of all kinds heading for the landing beaches' and part of 'a vast aerial armada, bombers and fighters thick as starlings at nesting-time'. For once, he probably had a better overview than his boss.

On the military front at least, there seems to have been a palpable sense of relief. The Allies were ashore. The worst-case scenario had not come to pass, and Lascelles observed that 'all those who have been entrusted with the very well kept secret, look ten years younger'. Churchill received a note from Montgomery on 6 June, sent before the General crossed over to France, admitting that, 'The past 5 months have not been an easy time for any of us. But I have always felt that you would see that all was well, and that your support was available at all times.' Of course, that support may have sometimes bordered on interference.

A sense of relief can certainly be seen in the telegram that Churchill fired off to Marshal Stalin. Finally, after years of delay and changes to strategy, he was able to deliver on his promise of a Second Front in north-west Europe. Finally, he was able to hold his head up and report an Allied operation on a scale comparable to the great battles of the Eastern Front.

PRIME MINISTER TO MARSHAL STALIN
Personal and Top Secret
Everything has started well. The
mines, obstacles and land batteries have been
largely overcome. The Air landings were very
successful and on a large scale. Infantry

landings are proceeding rapidly and many tanks
and self-propelled guns are already ashore.
Weather outlook moderate to good.
W.S.C.

6.6.44.

The Prime Minister had promised to report back to the British
Parliament before the end of the daily session. He did so on his
return to central London, addressing the House of Commons at
18.15 hours, just before it adjourned:

I promised to report to the House later on in the Sitting. I have
been at the centres where the latest information is received, and I
can state to the House that this operation is proceeding in thoroughly satisfactory manner. Many dangers and difficulties which
at this time last night appeared extremely formidable are behind
us. The passage of the sea has been made with far less loss than we
apprehended. The resistance of the batteries has been greatly
weakened by the bombing of the Air Force, and the superior
bombardment of our ships quickly reduced their fire to dimensions which did not affect the problem. The landing of the troops
on a broad front, both British and American—Allied troops, I will
not give lists of all the different nationalities they represent or the
States they represent—but the landings along the whole front have
been effective, and our troops have penetrated, in some cases,
several miles inland. Lodgements exist on a broad front.

The outstanding feature has been the landings of the airborne
troops, which were on a scale far larger than anything that has
been seen so far in the world. These landings took place with
extremely little loss and with great accuracy. Particular anxiety
attached to them, because the conditions of light prevailing in the
very limited period of the dawn—just before the dawn—the
conditions of visibility, made all the difference. Indeed, there
might have been something happening at the last minute which
would not have enabled airborne troops to play their part. A very
great degree of risk had to be taken in respect of the weather.

But General Eisenhower's courage is equal to all the necessary decisions that have to be taken in these extremely difficult and uncontrollable matters. The airborne troops are well established, and the landings and the follow-ups are all proceeding with much less loss—very much less—than we expected. Fighting is proceeding at various points. We have captured various bridges which were of importance, and which were not blown up. There is even fighting proceeding in the town of Caen, inland. But all this, although a very valuable first step—a vital and essential first step— gives no indication of what may be the course of the battle in the next days and weeks, because the enemy will now probably endeavour to concentrate on this area and in that event heavy fighting will soon begin and will continue without end, as we can push troops in and he can bring other troops up. It is, therefore, a most serious time that we enter upon. Thank God, we enter upon it with our great Allies all in good heart and all in good friendship.

Churchill may have been relieved on the military front, but his anger towards de Gaulle had not abated. If anything, it seemed to have intensified. The General was still refusing to cooperate over the civilian administration of France and the bitter row continued to rage over whether he would broadcast to the French people. The Allies felt this to be essential for mobilising the resistance and encouraging French support for the operation, but they also sought to retain control over the symbolism and content of the moment. De Gaulle would only be allowed to speak after Eisenhower and not as Head of the French State.

To make matters worse, Eisenhower had shown de Gaulle the content of his broadcast. It ordered the French people to follow Allied military instructions. De Gaulle was not mentioned by name. Existing French officials were to be kept in place for the time being, and it repeated Roosevelt's line that the French would choose their own government after the liberation. In short, it made no recognition of de Gaulle's authority or the legitimacy of his newly self-declared Provisional Government of France. His reaction was not surprising: 'By speaking immediately after Eisenhower, I should appear to sanction what he said – of which I disapproved – and assume a place in the succession unsuitable to the dignity of France. If I were to make a speech, it could only be at a different hour . . .'

To Churchill, concerned to minimise Allied casualties and maximise French support, this seemed a betrayal of their alliance. In the early hours of 6 June, as the operation began, the angry Prime Minister berated Pierre Viénot, de Gaulle's Free French Ambassador to the British government, for his leader's intransigence. In the end, de Gaulle got his way and broadcast individually at 18.00 hours on D-Day, stating that 'The orders given by the French Government and by the leaders which it has recognized must be followed precisely.' Here was a very different emphasis. De Gaulle was deliberately giving the impression that Eisenhower derived his authority from the French Provisional Government. For Churchill, this was a red rag to a bull. De Gaulle had no great forces in the battle, the liberation was being led by the Anglo-Americans, and the French General's authority was entirely dependent on British and American patronage and support. Moreover, the President had been clear about not recognising de Gaulle's Provisional Government.

As Foreign Secretary, Anthony Eden had seen the text of de Gaulle's broadcast before delivery. He had considerably more sympathy for the General's position than his Prime Minister and was actively trying to engineer a compromise that would allow the Americans to sit in on British discussions about civil affairs with representatives of de Gaulle's committee. It prompted two angry phone calls from Churchill, working from his bed: the first just after de Gaulle's radio message and the second, lasting a full forty-five minutes, after midnight. Unable to influence military events in France, Churchill was clearly brooding on the political row and accused Eden of trying to turn the Cabinet against him: 'He [Churchill] said that nothing would induce him to give way, that de Gaulle must go. Said I had no right to "bully" him at a time like this and much more.' When Eden refused to budge,

Churchill vented his wrath on Brendan Bracken. It was becoming increasingly clear to Churchill that his hard-line position against de Gaulle did not command the agreement of a majority of his Cabinet colleagues. Attlee, Bevin and Eden were all sympathetic to the position of the General and in favour of trying to talk de Gaulle round.

It was at this point that two telegrams arrived from Roosevelt. The first, dated 4 June, but delayed in the sending until D-Day, wished Churchill 'all good luck in your talks with Prima Donna [de Gaulle]' and, referring to Churchill's previous communications on the matter, added, 'Please for the love of Heaven do not tell de Gaulle that I am sending him a "friendly message to come over to see me". The whole point of it is that I decline absolutely as Head of State to invite him to come over here.' This was a reiteration of the President's earlier line.

Fortunately, things had changed, and de Gaulle had grudgingly reached out to Roosevelt. The 4 June message was immediately superseded – indeed, due to the delay possibly preceded – by a further communication from the President announcing that 'I have sent word to de Gaulle that in view of his expression of hope that I will see him over here, I shall be very glad to do so . . .' Here was the prospect of a softening in the relationship between Roosevelt and de Gaulle that might take the pressure off Churchill, who remained caught in the middle. The President's first message of 4 June also referred to his pleasure on hearing that 'Randolph got out of the cave safely', referring to Tito's dramatic escape from the Germans in Bosnia. The Yugoslav leader had had to scale a cliff after German paratroopers had surrounded his forest hideout. The President knew that Randolph had been with Tito. Here at least, for Churchill, were some positives at the end of a long day.

It had also been a long day for Tony Hugill, waiting on board his cramped landing craft. Disembarkation did not come until the morning of 7 June after four days on board. The crowded scene that greeted him, with boats of all sizes trying to get on and off the beach, was an 'absolute skipper's nightmare' but the actual coming ashore was an anti-climax. There were British and German bodies and burnt-out equipment, but the battle had already moved inland.

For Churchill, any respite was short-lived. By the time the War Cabinet met at 18.00 hours on 7 June, a new complication had arisen. In addition to withholding his liaison officers and refusing to discuss civil affairs, de Gaulle was refusing to recognise the special French currency that Eisenhower was proposing to issue to enable the Allies to pay for goods and services in liberated France. Churchill was not impressed by these new notes, which he thought 'singularly silly' because of their poor design, which made it hard to differentiate between amounts, but his bigger concern was that de Gaulle was attempting to use the issue to get himself recognised as the head of the French Provisional Government. There was also a related question of financial liability. Would the British and American governments be liable for redeeming these notes if they were not officially recognised in France? Churchill spoke about the deterioration of relations with de Gaulle and accused him of 'a most non co-operative attitude' and being 'primarily concerned with his personal position'. His Cabinet colleagues, while sympathising with Churchill's difficulties, encouraged the more conciliatory Eden to reach out to de Gaulle and persuade him to send commissioners to discuss these civil issues. They perhaps wisely sensed that their Prime Minister was still too emotive on this issue.

Churchill wrote to Roosevelt on 8 June summarising the position as he saw it and concluding that if de Gaulle refused 'to send for the commissioners, we shall suggest he had better go back to Algiers . . . I have repeatedly told de Gaulle and he acknowledged it without irritation that failing an agreement, I stand with you.' At the end, he added, probably only half in jest, 'I think it would be a great pity if you and he did not meet. I do not see why I should have all the luck.' Under increasing pressure from his own Cabinet members for a clearer American policy towards de Gaulle, he followed this up with further telegrams to the President on 9 and 10 June pressing him for an early answer on the currency issue. It finally came on 13 June, when Roosevelt replied that

> If for any reason the supplementary currency is not acceptable to the French Public, General Eisenhower has full authority to use yellow seal dollars [specially produced dollars for military operations overseas] and British Military Authority notes . . . It seems clear that Prima Donnas do not change their spots.

This did not allay all British worries about their liabilities, but Churchill refused to take the matter further with the President. The issue was a source of internal tension within the British Cabinet and took up a significant amount of the Prime Minister's time in the crucial first days of Overlord. He faced questions from the Australian government and murmurings in Parliament about the lack of recognition for the Free French and their leader. When de Gaulle gave an interview with a news agency on 10 June, criticising the absence of French authority and officials in the liberated area and openly denying the value of the Allied currency, Churchill minuted to Bracken that it would 'be well for you to warn the press that there are two sides to this story, and that a Government statement may easily be forthcoming when the time is ripe. One tale is good till another is told.' Churchill's pro-American stance had been made very obvious to everyone, including de Gaulle and those around him. This would inevitably impact on longer-term Anglo-French relations.

It is ironic that just as Churchill's relationship with de Gaulle reached its lowest point, his hitherto uneasy correspondence with Stalin suddenly became extremely friendly, at least superficially. The Soviet leader responded immediately to Churchill's D-Day message, writing that 'It gives joy to us all and hope of further successes', while confirming that the simultaneous offensive by Soviet forces, which he had promised to deliver at the Tehran Conference, would begin towards the middle of the month. Keen to exploit the opportunities provided by this friendly overture, and to use it to find out more about Soviet intentions, Churchill despatched a minute to Ismay on 7 June asking for further information that he could send to Stalin. He explained that he was trying to 'extract a voluntary statement from the Bear [Stalin] of what he is going to do. Thus we must give something which is real and novel to him.'

What Churchill gave, in a long telegram to Stalin dictated later on 7 June, was detailed figures on the initial success of the Overlord operation. Twenty thousand airborne troops had been safely landed behind the flanks of the enemy's lines, overall losses had been small and, by the end of the day, the Allies hoped to have the best part of a quarter of a million men ashore. Winston gave news of the special tanks that had swum onto the beaches by themselves, though admitted there had been 'a good many casualties' as a result of them being overturned by the waves, especially in the American sector. He proudly reported on the success of British armour in a tank battle with the 21st Panzer-Grenadier Division 'late last night near Caen' and announced that, 'All the Commanders are satisfied that in the actual landing things have gone better than we expected.' The novel element, which he reserved until last, was the news that two large synthetic harbours were about to be constructed on the wide sandy bay of the Seine estuary. 'Nothing like these have ever been seen before. Great ocean liners will be able to discharge and run by numerous piers supplies to the fighting troops.' He confirmed that the Allies expected to have twenty-five divisions deployed by D+30 (5 July) and to have captured the port of Cherbourg: 'But all this waits on the hazards of war which, Marshal Stalin, you know so well.'

The correspondence between the two leaders continued in a similar vein over the course of the next few days. On 9 June, Stalin confirmed that the Soviet summer offensive would open the following day on the Leningrad front. The next day, Churchill reported that 'By to-night, 10th, we ought to have landed nearly 400,000, together with a large superiority in tanks and a rapidly growing mass of artillery and lorries.' Suddenly, the Prime Minister seemed more positive about the number of vehicles accompanying the assault. From the British Ambassador in

Moscow came the news that Churchill had been presented with a sketch of Stalin inscribed to him with the message, 'In memory of the day of the invasion of Northern France by Allied British and American troops from his friend Joseph V. Stalin'. What Churchill clearly liked more, and proudly shared with President Roosevelt, was the telegram he now received from the Soviet leader. It had evidently been specially crafted by Stalin and his advisers to appeal to Churchill's love of history and sense of destiny, and read:

> My colleagues and I cannot but admit that the history of warfare knows no other like undertaking from the point of view of its scale, its vast conception and its masterly execution. As is well known, Napoleon in his time failed ignominiously in his plan to force the Channel. The hysterical Hitler, who boasted for two years that he would effect a forcing of the Channel, was unable to make up his mind even to hint at attempting to carry out his threat. Only our Allies have succeeded in realising with honour the grandiose plan of forcing the Channel. History will record this deed as an achievement of the highest order.

This correspondence probably marks the high point in the wartime relationship between Churchill and Stalin. The promise to deliver the Second Front in Europe had finally been fulfilled. Behind the scenes, Churchill was pushing for the quick resumption of the Arctic convoys to Russia (which had been suspended in order to prioritise the Overlord operation). Yet the very success of Overlord, and the rapid advances of the Soviets in the east, was already threatening to create new tensions over the future of Poland, Germany, the Balkans and Greece. The seeds of discord were already there. As Churchill received these glowing telegrams from Stalin, he was worried about communist infiltration of the government in Italy, was attempting to broker a deal between communist and royalist forces in Yugoslavia, was worried about the rise of communism in Greece, and was increasingly frustrated by American opposition to his desire to negotiate spheres of influence with Stalin in the Balkans. The quicker the German collapse, the more important these issues would become.

An insight into Churchill's real mindset is provided by the American war correspondent Virginia Cowles. She was part of a small luncheon party for the Prime Minister on 7 June, a gathering that was presumably intended to take his mind off the huge pressures of the moment. Arriving in a blue siren suit (his zip-up overalls), the Prime Minister seemed 'worried and preoccupied'. Then, over food, he launched into an angry diatribe, against the 'parlour pinks' who were criticising his foreign policy in supporting the current regimes in Spain and Italy. ' "When this war is over," he growled, "England will need every ally she can get to protect herself against Russia." ' Churchill still believed that Britain could emerge from the conflict as a world power, but the country's position in the Mediterranean and influence in Europe would be threatened by Soviet expansion in south and eastern Europe.

The immediate priority was to win the battle in Normandy. Churchill could offer support through his words in public and private. He was quick to send out a message to those who had made the artificial harbours possible:

> This was a fine feat . . . The production of this novel and complicated equipment and its towing to the final erection sites and thence to the assembly areas, has been a very considerable undertaking. I feel that all Departments concerned are to be congratulated on the completion of the work.

Churchill may have been relieved by the launch of the operation, and even more so by its initial success, but he was also frustrated about not being able to do more. He could study the latest reports, monitor the casualty figures, follow the progress of the troops in his map room, and seek information from the Chiefs of Staff and the various military headquarters in the UK, but he chafed at not being able to influence events on the ground.

21 Army Group

<u>Most Immediate</u>

M1   7 June

For Chief of Staff from General Montgomery ⊙ Have seen BRADLEY and DEMPSEY ⊙ situation as follows ⊙ Para 1 ⊙ UTAH landings good and 4 DIV lodgement area about 5 miles deep with 82 and 101 DIVS further to WEST and SOUTH ⊙ Para 2 ⊙ OMAHA not so good and lodgement area about 2 miles deep ⊙ much fighting took place on the beaches and considerable casualties suffered in personnel and vehicles and craft ⊙ infantry of five regiments now on shore but short of artillery and supporting weapons ⊙ Para 3 ⊙ Second Army situation good ⊙ 50 DIV yesterday secured area ARRAMANCHES — BAZENVILLE — COULOMBS — VAUX SUR AURE — LONGUES and attacking BAYEUX today ⊙ Canadians are astride road

Handwritten telegram from General Montgomery
to Chief of Staff, 7 June 1944

By 8 June, Brooke was having to talk Churchill out of plans for additional landings on the west coast of France. By then, Churchill would have been aware of Montgomery's initial impressions of the battlefield, which – while generally good – included reference to the high casualties on Omaha beach.

This top copy of the General's telegram of 7 June survives in the papers of John Selwyn Lloyd (see telegram on p. 262), who was then serving as Deputy Chief of Staff to General Dempsey of the Second Army.

The initial assault was just that. It was clear that weeks of serious fighting in Normandy lay ahead. On Thursday 8 June, Churchill addressed the Commons ahead of the weekend, sounding a note of caution and realism:

> I earnestly hope that when Members go to their constituencies they will not only maintain morale, so far as that is necessary, but also give strong warnings against over-optimism, against the idea that these things are going to be settled with a run, and that they will remember that although great dangers lie behind us, enormous exertions lie before us.

Edgar Granville, the Liberal MP for Eye in Suffolk, responded by asking the Prime Minister whether he 'could give an assurance that the reason why he is not going to make any statement in the immediate future is not that he is going to make a visit to the coast of France'. No response is recorded. But for those who knew him well, it was obvious that it was going to be impossible to keep Churchill away from the scene of the action for long, and Brooke cannot have been surprised to get a minute from Churchill on 9 June telling him to make the necessary arrangements for a visit to the bridgeheads in France on Monday 12th (D-Day + 6). Churchill specified the wording his CIGS should use when informing Montgomery: 'We do not wish in any way to be a burden on you or your headquarters, or in any way to divert your attention from the battle. All we should require is an A.D.C. [Aide de Camp] or other staff officer to show us round. We shall bring some sandwiches with us.'

Montgomery replied to Brooke, not realising his message would be copied to the Prime Minister, stating that

Will meet you and give you full picture. Road not (repeat not) 100 per cent safe owing to enemy snipers including women. Much enemy bombing between dusk and dawn. Essential P.M. should go only where I take him and you must get away from here in early evening. Am very satisfied with progress of operations.

And so it was that the Prime Minister, accompanied by Brooke, Field Marshal Smuts and his personal assistant, Commander 'Tommy' Thompson, finally crossed the Channel on board the Royal Naval destroyer HMS *Kelvin*. The presence of Smuts is significant. Churchill trusted his judgement, particularly on military issues, and used him as a source of independent advice. The South African Premier had been sceptical about D-Day, at one point warning Hughes-Hallett that it was the only operation the Allies could undertake that might lose them the war. He was there to act as Churchill's expert adviser and to play devil's advocate.

Sailing from Portsmouth at 08.00 hours, in good weather on a calm water, the party enjoyed a panoramic view of the intense Allied activity: the culmination of so much preparation. The water was full of landing craft, minesweepers, supply ships and tugs towing steel and concrete parts for use in the artificial harbours; above them, the air was a mass of Allied planes. Arriving at a Gooseberry formed from the sunken blockships, the Prime Minister's party was met by Admiral Vian, commander of the eastern naval task force for the British and Canadian beaches, who transferred them into his barge and then into an amphibious DUKW for the drive ashore. Here, in a moment captured by the official photographer (and featured on the cover of this book), they were greeted by General Montgomery, who whisked them inland by jeep to his headquarters for a briefing and lunch.

For Churchill it was a moving experience. It was almost exactly four years since he had last set foot in France, at that fateful meeting with Reynaud at Tours on 13 June 1940. It had been a long road back. Both he and Brooke were struck by the beauty of the countryside. Churchill later described how

> We drove through our limited but fertile domain in Normandy. It was pleasant to see the prosperity of the countryside. The fields were full of lovely red and white cows basking or parading in the sunshine. The inhabitants seemed quite buoyant and well nourished and waved enthusiastically.

He turned to Brooke and told him, 'We are surrounded by fat cattle lying in luscious pastures with their paws crossed!' Brooke agreed about the cattle, but not about the attitude of the French people. To him, they 'did not seem in any way pleased to see us arrive as a victorious country to liberate France. They had been quite content as they were, and we were bringing war and desolation to the country.' This is not what Churchill wanted to see or remember.

Lunch was taken in a tent outside Montgomery's chateau looking towards the front, which was about three miles away. When Churchill asked about the risk of an incursion by German armour, Montgomery casually dismissed the threat. Yet, if one account is to be believed, the threat may have been much closer at hand than they realised. Tommy Thompson's memoirs describe a strange incident when, upon emerging from Montgomery's caravan, Smuts sniffed the air before telling the astonished ADC, 'There are some Germans still here – quite close to us.' 'Standing bareheaded in the sunshine, Smuts continued to frown in a puzzled way, staring suspiciously at the clumps of laurels and rhododendrons which almost surrounded the caravans, but he said no more, and they followed Montgomery into his Mess tent.'

Two days later, two German paratroopers, long since cut off from their unit, emerged bedraggled and exhausted but still armed from their hiding place in the very same bushes and surrendered. If the story is true, they could have killed Churchill, Brooke, Smuts and Montgomery, but it is a tale that does not appear in the

memoirs of Churchill or Montgomery and so may well be embellished or apocryphal.

What is clear is that Churchill enjoyed the stimulus of travel and
risk. Inspecting the British landing zone at Arromanches, he
caused alarm by climbing to the top of a small lighthouse, tried
unsuccessfully to board a Monitor (a small warship carrying large
guns) that was bombarding the coast, before persuading Admiral
Vian to allow HMS *Kelvin* to fire its guns in anger on the enemy
before departing for home. After which, he slept soundly on the
return trip: 'Altogether it had been a most interesting and enjoy-
able day.' The simple note he left in Montgomery's visitors' book
read: 'As it was in the beginning so may it continue to the end.'

It had also been an educational experience. Churchill had spent
time touring the British beachhead. He had seen the artificial
breakwater in operation and the ongoing preparations for
construction of the full Mulberry harbour. He had also been
pleased to learn about the three local ports of Port-en-Bessin,
Courseulles and Ouistreham, which were playing a far larger than
anticipated role in bringing in materials.

On arrival back in Portsmouth, Winston met up with the
American Chiefs of Staff – Marshall, King and Arnold, who were
visiting the UK and had also just crossed the Channel and toured
the American positions. They all dined together in Churchill's
railway carriage and Marshall wrote out a message for Admiral
Mountbatten, now Supreme Allied Commander in South-East
Asia, which they all signed, acknowledging that the 'success of the
venture, has its origin in developments effected by you and your
staff of Combined Operations'. Churchill must have retired with
a sense of things having come full circle.

The timing of Churchill's trip was carefully calculated. He
made sure that he got to Normandy before de Gaulle, who travelled across on 14 June, and King George VI, who visited troops
there on 16 June. News of the Prime Minister's visit spread rapidly
and was noted by Hugill in his diary.

De Gaulle's return to France was also symbolic and led inexorably to the recognition he wanted. By 16 June, even Churchill

was prepared to write to him in slightly more conciliatory tones, declaring: 'Ever since 1907, I have in good times and bad times, been a sincere friend of France, as my words and actions show, and it is to me an intense pain that barriers have been raised to an association which to me was very dear.'

It was now time to tie up loose ends. Back in London on 13 June, the Prime Minister chaired a Cabinet meeting that agreed to extend the ban on private diplomatic communications. Eisenhower had requested an extension until D+15 (20 June) in order to protect Overlord security. So far, the Germans had held forces back in the Pas-de-Calais area believing that further attacks might still come. The Bodyguard deception plan was working, and there remained a fear that neutral diplomats based in the UK might be able to convey information to the enemy that would undermine this. The government were unsure. Churchill and Eden had a strong desire to normalise diplomatic relations as quickly as possible. Indeed, the Prime Minister was aware that his intelligence services believed that diplomatic communications could be used to feed misinformation to the enemy and thereby enhance deception. In the end, it was agreed to lift the ban from Monday 19 June. The visitors ban to the coastal areas and the travel ban to Ireland were also to be lifted by the end of the month.

A week after the landings, Churchill could take comfort from the fact that the initial assault had succeeded. The beachheads had been established and the initial losses had been significantly less than expected. The UK had risen to the challenge of the immense dislocation. The transport system had not crashed under the additional strain, and troops and material were being successfully delivered to their disembarkation points. Production targets for the Mulberries had been met and the artificial ports were now coming on stream. Relations with Roosevelt and Stalin were good, even if de Gaulle was proving problematic.

In spite of the several near misses, security had not been compromised, deception had worked, and tactical surprise had been achieved. For more than a month after D-Day, the Germans continued to hold significant forces in the Pas-de-Calais area, expecting a second invasion. The teams of deceivers in Britain worked hard to maintain the pretence, and Churchill wrote to Eisenhower on 15 July to urge continuation, writing that 'Uncertainty is a terror to the Germans. The forces in Britain are a dominant preoccupation of the Huns.'

On the personal front, Randolph had reached the safety of Vis and subsequently returned to Britain, though Churchill had been clear that his son should not be given any special consideration. His relief may have been short-lived. By 11 July Mary Churchill's diary was recording that 'RANDOLPH – is, as usual, a bone of sorrow & contention', behaving 'with such odious unkindness, rudeness and heartlessness to Papa & Mummie.' Winston's relationship with his oldest son was always complex.

By then he had other problems. It was on 13 June that the first V1 self-propelled flying bombs fell on the country, eclipsing the success of D-Day in the public mind and replacing any relief with a visceral new threat. Today, a blue plaque in Grove Road, East London, commemorates the site of the first explosion, which killed six, injured forty-two, and destroyed a bridge on the railway line from London Liverpool Street to Stratford. Losses and damage in the coming weeks would be significant, but at least Churchill knew that Hitler's new weapon had come too late to impact on D-Day itself. If the Allies could break out in Normandy, then these firing sites in northern France and Belgium could be quickly overrun and neutralised. But worries remained. What of the other weapon, the liquid-fuel rocket that the Nazis were developing? When and where might this be deployed? And how dangerous might it prove?

And what of the Normandy breakout? When would it come? The town of Caen had been a final objective for the British and Canadian forces on 6 June. The first week of Overlord had passed, and the town was still in German hands. Churchill was once again left studying the mounting casualty figures, military and civilian, and his worries about high losses were returning.

For T. L. Rodgers it was already too late. Deployed as an elite Pathfinder, he was one of the first Americans to parachute into

Normandy, dropped into Sainte-Mère-Église behind the American beaches an hour before the main airborne assault to set up beacons to guide his comrades in. As with so many, the exact circumstances of his death are unclear. One account has him killed on landing, dropped into the courtyard of a farmhouse hosting a German garrison, another dying days later in a firefight around an orchard. His story here stands as just one tale of bravery and loss. By all accounts, he was a giant of a man, physically but also in moral stature. Sainte-Mère-Église was the first French town to be liberated.

A volume would be required to recount the story of
the crossing of the Channel and the landing of the Armies of
Liberation on the soil of France.   I have only a few minutes.
In ____April____, 1943 General Morgan of the British ~~Service~~ Army
became the head of a British and American Planning ~~Committee~~ Staff
which surveyed the whole ~~scene.~~ ~~That Committee~~ Key Staff made a plan
which I took with me last year to Quebec, where it was
submitted to the President and to the ~~American~~ Combined Chiefs of Staff.
This plan selected the beaches for the attack and presented
the ~~simple~~ outlines with a mass of detail to support them.
It received in principle complete agreement.   At Teheran we
promised Marshal Stalin we would put this plan or something
like it into operation at the end of May or the beginning of
June, and he for his part promised that the whole of the
as indeed they have been
Russian Armies would be thrown into general battle in the East.
    In January the Commanders were appointed.   We took
over the command of the Mediterranean and General Eisenhower
in Britain
assumed the command of the Expeditionary Force ~~with General~~
Montgomery in command of the invading troops.   For more than
a year past American stores, equipment and men had been

Draft for Churchill's speech to House of Commons, 2 August 1944

11

Tyranny of Overlord

'All right, if you insist on being damned fools, sooner
than falling out with you, which would be fatal, we
shall be damned fools with you, and we shall see that we
perform the role of damned fools damned well!'

WITH THE BENEFIT of hindsight, we know that D-Day led
to the liberation of France, but success was not immediate.
For the first three months, the Allied armies faced a tough battle
of consolidation and attrition.

Set against the 19,240 British fatalities on the first day of the
Somme offensive on 1 July 1916, the success of the D-Day landings came at a terrible but comparatively much lower cost. There
were just under eleven thousand Allied casualties, including
around three thousand eight hundred killed, of which slightly
over a thousand were British. By the end of 6 June 1944, over
five thousand ships had landed one hundred and thirty-three
thousand Allied troops, supported by fourteen thousand six
hundred and seventy-four air sorties and immense naval gunfire.
However, D-Day was only the first day of the extended
Normandy campaign, which continued until 30 August 1944
with the crossing of the River Seine and the liberation of Paris.
Although the fighting on D-Day was fierce, much worse was to
follow in the close bocage country of Normandy, characterised
by sunken lanes and high hedges, during the battles for Caen
and in the eventual breakout towards Paris. As Stan Hollis's

commanding officer, Lieutenant Colonel Robin Hastings of the 6th Green Howards, records:

> On the first day, we suffered about ninety casualties, a compara-
> tively low figure but one which included two company command-
> ers and several of our best NCOs. We lay down with a feeling of
> relief at having achieved a landing without excessive cost. Little
> did we know what we had to look forward to.

And there was much 'to look forward to' or, put with less British understatement, there was a tremendous amount to be done. If the Allies were successfully ashore by nightfall on 6 June, their toehold in Europe was precarious. At the final briefing presenta-tion in front of King George VI and Winston Churchill at St Paul's School on 15 May, Montgomery had set out his plans for the land campaign in Normandy. Although the tri-service plan-ning for the initial landings was meticulous, Monty set out in stark terms that the real challenge would be the rate at which the Allied forces could build up their strength compared to the Germans. Having assumed initial operational surprise, Montgomery predicted that by D+8, the Allies would have eighteen divisions ashore but would be faced by twenty-four enemy divisions of which ten would be Panzer divisions. Knowing that his old rival, Erwin Rommel, would try to defeat the landings as close to the beachheads as possible, his design for battle was to contain, absorb and reduce the German counter-attack capability before breaking out decisively to the south and east – ultimately towards Germany. Turning to a large map on the panelled wall of his old school's lecture room, Montgomery set out his intentions for the develop-ment of operations up to D+90. Although there has been much criticism subsequently that Monty revised the outline of his plan afterwards to secure his place in history, nevertheless events on the ground broadly followed the outcome that he had predicted, albeit not at the speed that he anticipated. Caen was captured on D+33 not on D-Day, Cherbourg on D+22 not on D+8 and Falaise on D+71 not on D+17.

Many factors affected the way in which the campaign unfolded. The success of Operation Fortitude continued to keep doubt in the minds of the German High Command as to whether the landings in Normandy were the Allied main effort or a feint. Although Hitler himself seemed to have a two-way bet on which location was his enemy's main focus, he nevertheless was reluctant to release the Panzer reserves, despite pressure from Rommel to do so. Even when the German armour was ordered to attack, the Allied domination of the skies confined their movement to the hours of darkness or in bad weather. Daylight moves incurred huge casualties to men and vehicles. However, the weather had a major effect on the Allies too. Having nearly caused a two-week postponement of D-Day itself, on the night of 19 June the most violent storm in forty years struck the Normandy coast, exacerbating the effects of a spring tide. Both Mulberry artificial harbours were destroyed, the one at Omaha beyond repair with the one off Arromanches-les-Bains put out of commission for many days. The storm finally blew itself out by 22 June. Although it had a major delaying effect on the manpower and logistical build-up, Eisenhower reflected that had he ordered the fortnight's postponement, the armada would have been at sea when the storm struck. In a note to Group Captain Stagg, the senior meteorological officer, he wrote: 'I thank the gods of war we went when we did.'

With a growing force ashore, Montgomery and his senior commanders were faced with how to develop their operations to maintain the momentum that the landings had achieved. The capture of Caen on D-Day had proved to be an objective too far. The hapless inhabitants of Caen were to be subjected to horrendous bombing attacks in which over the next six weeks much of the ancient city was destroyed, many citizens were killed, and others suffered at the hands of the Gestapo, keen to cover their tracks before they withdrew. As the first major French city to be liberated, the cost at three thousand citizens killed was a devastatingly high one. Through June and July, the battle ebbed and flowed around Caen. General progress by the Allied armies was severely impeded by the nature of the terrain over which they had to fight. Inland from the sandy assault beaches they found themselves in the lush cornfields and thick hedgerows of the Normandy bocage. Fields were typically about the size of a football field, separated one from another by high, thick hedges and deep ditches or sunken lanes. This was the ideal environment for the defending Germans to site anti-tank and machine guns to cover any possible path to advance. Allied casualties were heavy, and the manpower drain on the attacking infantry was becoming a significant factor. The attacking armies needed to adapt, and rapidly. Although many tanks had been adapted to swim ashore, others now needed to be given the means to bulldoze their way through the hedges and across the ditches to provide firepower support to the infantry. Field workshops quickly devised metal battering rams to be welded onto the front of tanks, some made from the metalwork of Rommel's beach defences. In the detailed study of the landing beaches, it had to be acknowledged that insufficient thought had been given to fighting in the close country inland.

As the overall commander of the Allied landings, it was Montgomery's responsibility to orchestrate the defeat of the German forces in Normandy and set up General Eisenhower to begin the liberation of Europe. Although Churchill's first fear of the landings being a failure had been removed there was, nevertheless, the nagging worry that the invasion force could be marooned as in Gallipoli in 1915/16 or at Anzio earlier in 1944. The bloody battles around Villers-Bocage between 11 and 14 June added to that fear. Montgomery resolved that he must wear down the defending Germans' strength by drawing them onto the British 2nd Army on the Allied left around Caen to provide the opportunity for Bradley's 1st US Army, and later Patton's 3rd US Army, to break out on the Allied right. Montgomery's first major attack was Operation Epsom to the west of Caen from 26 June to 1 July, but this was contained by the 1st and 2nd SS Panzer Corps after intense fighting. The concern over infantry manpower grew. General Miles Dempsey's 2nd British Army was, however, not short of tanks. Dempsey persuaded Montgomery that an attack by three armoured divisions preceded by a heavy bombing strike could achieve a breakthrough to the east of Caen. At 05.30 hours on 18 July, two and a half thousand British and US bombers began two and a half hours of aerial attack on the defending Germans, dropping nearly eight thousand tons of bombs. Despite the devasting effect of the bombing, the British armour was slow to follow up and, when it did so, it faced surprisingly stiff resistance, particularly from German anti-tank guns that had survived the onslaught from above. The so-called 'death ride' of the British armour in Operation Goodwood failed to achieve the breakout promised by Montgomery to Eisenhower.

Tensions in Downing Street by the end of June were once again running high. The initial relief on getting ashore had worn off. Everyone was tired after the stress of the last few weeks; a situation only made worse by the arrival of the V-weapons in the skies above London and the return of terror to the streets of the capital. General Brooke admired Churchill's staunch response to the flying bombs; he praised the firm way in which the Prime Minister slapped down his Home Secretary, Herbert Morrison, for expressing doubts that London could take such a renewed attack, noting at the Cabinet meeting on 19 June that 'Winston was in very good form, quite 10 years younger, all due to the fact that the flying bombs have again put us into the front line!!'

But such moments were not typical. More often, Brooke found dealing with Churchill at this time to be frustrating. When discussing strategy, he felt Winston was meandering, 'producing a lot of disconnected thoughts which had no military value', guilty of 'strategic ravings' and of 'giving one strategic lecture after another'. For the Prime Minister, it seemed that the relief at getting safely ashore, and the excitement of seeing the beachheads for himself, had given way to uncertainty about the next steps and renewed argument concerning the best way of exploiting Overlord.

The Prime Minister's thoughts kept returning to Italy. Hitler's decision to contest the Italian peninsula had served to keep German forces away from Normandy in the run-up to D-Day, effectively replacing the delayed Anvil assault on the south of

France as a diversionary campaign, but Eisenhower now wanted Alexander's operations scaled back. More troops and resources were to be diverted to France and a new version of Operation Anvil, rebranded for security reasons as Dragoon, was to take place as soon as possible. This would open up a new route into northern France from the south, thereby taking pressure off the beachheads.

Initially, Churchill seemed torn. He briefly toyed with further operations against the west coast of France, returning to the strategy of widening the assault front that he had first advocated in 1942. The problem was that he still wanted the best of both worlds. He wanted to ensure the success of the operation in France, but he also wanted to continue to fight in Italy.

On 21 June, he met with Brooke and Smuts to discuss options. Influenced by the positive reports he was receiving from General Alexander in the aftermath of the capture of Rome, Churchill was now excited by the idea of being able to strike northwards from Italy into Austria via Trieste and the Ljubljana Gap. Smuts, too, was attracted by this idea but spoke in favour of a new cross-Channel assault at Calais. To Brooke, both ideas seemed hopelessly over-optimistic. The Allies did not have the capacity to launch and sustain another major invasion of France from Britain (though they were continuing with the deception plans to try and convince the Germans they did), while Alexander was unlikely to be able to cross the Italian Alps before the onset of winter, which would then make further operations impossible until the spring. Brooke did not want to see Alexander denuded of troops – he favoured continuing to wear the Germans down in Italy – but in the course of repeated conversations about strategy over the next few days he found it hard to make Churchill 'realize that if we took the season of the year and the topography of the country in league against us we should have 3 enemies instead of one'.

Churchill's desire to continue the fight in Italy was entirely consistent with his policy prior to Overlord. He still did not want to risk everything on one throw of the dice in Normandy. It was already clear that as the campaign in France developed it would become more and more of an American show. In contrast, the Mediterranean theatre under its Supreme Commander General Wilson, and the Italian campaign, under soon-to-be Field Marshal Alexander, were British-led operations that he could present as an important counterweight to growing American and Soviet influence in Europe. With the Red Army advancing so rapidly towards Austria and Germany from the east, and the post-war settlement of Europe now in sight – a matter of when, not if – he felt it vital for Britain to end the war in a strong geopolitical position on the continent. While the soldiers were quite rightly focusing on the military defeat of the enemy, the politicians were already thinking in terms of the political aftermath. For Churchill, this meant obtaining a stable Europe (which for him meant non-communist) while protecting British imperial interests in the Mediterranean; for Stalin, it meant establishing buffer zones of client states between the Soviet Union and other powers in eastern Europe and the Balkans; while for Roosevelt, it was about the creation of the United Nations organisation and a world order based on the values of the Atlantic Charter. It was increasingly obvious that these aims would conflict and pull in different directions.

The immediate fight was with the Americans over Anvil/ Dragoon. At one of the rambling meetings about strategy, held in Churchill's map room on 22 June, the Prime Minister and his Chiefs of Staff attempted to thrash out their own position before negotiating with their allies. Churchill was very keen that any troops in the Mediterranean theatre that were surplus to the requirements of Alexander's main northern advance should be used for an amphibious assault in the Trieste area. He was proposing another operation in the style of Salerno or Anzio, speeding up progress on the peninsula by using the sea to leapfrog up the coast. He greatly preferred this to 'an "Anvil" type operation on the south coasts of France', which

was too far removed from General Eisenhower's battle-front for an Allied landing there to have any tactical effect on "Overlord" . . . The enemy would probably be more sensitive to a thrust developing from the head of the Adriatic than to an advance up the Rhone Valley.

Churchill also returned to a familiar theme, one calculated to annoy Brooke, when he made the further argument against Anvil that it would require an enormous 'tail', necessitating a new base in the south of France. For his part, Brooke spoke in favour of Alexander advancing in northern Italy but recommended using any surplus forces that could be released to support a landing in the south of France rather than in the Bay of Biscay or Loire area. No firm decision was taken but Churchill dug in. He was encouraged by Smuts, who telegraphed from Italy backing Alexander and Wilson, the British commanders on the ground, who were keen to push north.

In his war memoirs, Churchill would later present this as a straightforward clash between Eisenhower and the American Chiefs of Staff on the one hand, and himself and the British Chiefs of Staff on the other. As Brooke's more nuanced position makes clear, it was not quite that simple, but when the Prime Minister raised the issue with Roosevelt, the President once again made it very clear that he was backing Eisenhower. He wrote that the proposal 'for continued use of practically all the Mediterranean resources to advance into Northern Italy and from there to the northeast is not acceptable to me, and I really believe we should consolidate our operations and not scatter them'.

FDR then followed up with a second, much longer telegram a day later, on 29 June, in which he outlined all his reasons for prioritising operations in France that struck 'at the heart of Germany'. His 'interest and hopes' centred 'on defeating the Germans in front of Eisenhower and driving on into Germany, rather than on limiting this action for the purpose of staging a full major effort in Italy'. Alexander would still have enough forces to hold the Germans, while the Allies already exercised mastery of the air and sea in the Mediterranean. Eisenhower regarded Anvil as being of 'transcendent importance', and the plans were already well advanced and had been approved with Stalin. The President could not agree to the deployment of US troops into Istria as politically he would 'never survive even a slight setback in "Overlord" if it were known that fairly large forces had been diverted to the Balkans'. The President's message called for the immediate withdrawal of five divisions, three American and two French, from Italy for use in the south of France.

Roosevelt's view was clear. Here was Churchill up to his old tricks of trying to divert American forces away from their prime focus and into the Balkans and, just as with Rhodes and the Dodecanese Islands in 1943, the President would not countenance it. The Americans wanted Anvil and they wanted it as soon as possible and on a scale that would inevitably weaken Alexander's ability to go forward in Italy.

Churchill was left fuming. He briefly contemplated flying over to Washington to argue his case in person, but, according to Brooke:

> . . . in the end we got him to agree to our outlook which is: 'All right, if you insist on being damned fools, sooner than falling out with you, which would be fatal, we shall be damned fools with you, and we shall see that we perform the role of damned fools damned well!'

The episode is a clear illustration of the changed political dynamic within the 'special relationship'. Once Overlord was launched, its scale and significance trumped all other operations in the European theatre. For Roosevelt, Marshall and Eisenhower winning in Normandy and striking quickly and directly at Germany was the only game that mattered; Overlord and the strategic bomber offensive were their vehicles for delivering victory. Everything else was now secondary.

Rather than risk an open breach, the Prime Minister phoned Eisenhower agreeing to Anvil and informed him that General Wilson would be authorised to make the attack on the south of France using forces from the Mediterranean theatre.

But it would not be his last word on the matter. By 6 July, 'he [Churchill] was in a maudlin, bad tempered, drunken mood, ready to take offence at anything, suspicious of everybody, and in a highly vindictive mood against the Americans'. Unfortunately, events on the ground in France only served to exacerbate the Prime Minister's ill mood. Contrasts were being drawn in the Allied media between the advances of the American forces, who were now sweeping across Brittany from their western beaches, and the inertia of the British and Canadian forces, who were still stalled in front of Caen in the east. To make matters worse, it seems that Eisenhower, and perhaps Tedder and others, had begun to drop hints to Churchill that Montgomery was being too cautious.

Matters reached a head at a meeting that evening. When Churchill began to disparage Montgomery in front of the politicians present, Brooke lost his temper and accused the Prime Minister of not being able to trust his generals for five minutes and of 'continuously abusing them and belittling them'. Churchill was furious. He kept 'shoving his chin out' and protesting (perhaps too much) against the accusation.

Things then got worse when the Prime Minister decided to revisit the Normandy battlefield for himself. All hell broke loose on 19 July. Brooke was summoned to Churchill's bedside, where he found the Prime Minister in 'a new blue and gold dressing gown' and 'an unholy rage'. When Brooke finally managed to get a word in, he discovered the reason for the outburst. Eisenhower, in an apparently well-meaning but ill-thought-through conversation, had told Churchill that Montgomery did not want the distraction of visitors. Churchill assumed that this had come from Monty himself. As Minister of Defence, Winston did not consider himself an ordinary visitor and clearly felt that this was a conspiracy by his generals to stop him from exercising his rights to see what was really going on. Fortunately, it was a passing storm. After some frantic diplomacy by Eisenhower and Brooke, and an assurance by Montgomery that a visit would be welcomed, Churchill was appeased, and the trip went ahead on the following day.

Churchill flew first to the Cotentin Peninsula, where he inspected a flying-bomb launch site and saw the extensive German damage to the harbour, admiring the bravery of the divers who were charged with clearing the deliberate German sabotage. Hugill had been there just days before him and observed the controlled destruction of the underwater minefield: 'The domes of spray were lovely to watch, in the way a big underwater explosion always is . . .' But it was clear that Cherbourg was not yet a working harbour.

There then followed a rather rough sea voyage to the British Mulberry – Port Winston – at Arromanches. According to Commander Thompson, Winston was bored and seasick en route (a version contested by Churchill, who later wrote that he did not suffer and slept soundly), 'but as soon as we arrived at Mulberry Harbour he was in his element, for the port was seething with activity'. Here he stayed for three days, observing the constant loading and unloading of supplies, and the 'waddling' on shore of the amphibious DUKWs. On his last day, he visited Montgomery's headquarters before flying low over the Allied bridgehead in the General's captured German Fiesler Storch aircraft and visiting some of the air stations. Ismay and Thompson from his party made it to Caen and must have made Churchill aware of the scale of the utter devastation of the city.

As with his earlier visit, the trip seems to have had a rejuvenating effect. Back in London, Churchill had initially seemed 'supremely happy' with the military situation, but there then followed a series of further conversations with Eisenhower and a lunch on 26 July. The table talk turned on whether Montgomery was being too hesitant and whether the British Second Army could do more to take the offensive to the enemy. Churchill was highly sensitive to accusations that the British were not pulling their weight and were taking fewer casualties.

News of a plot was quick to reach Montgomery. It must have been unsettling. He knew that Churchill made a habit of dismissing generals whom he considered too cautious, most notably Montgomery's own predecessor in North Africa, General

Auchinleck. That said, Monty's position was somewhat stronger. His reputation remained high after the victory at El Alamein, making him the most famous and recognisable contemporary British figure after Churchill, and any attempt to remove him at the height of the battle would have required the support of both Eisenhower and Brooke, which would not have been forthcoming. His disappearance would have been damaging to morale and a propaganda gift to the enemy.

Even so, such rumours were hardly the support that the commander in the field needed while in the throes of a major battle. Brooke rushed in to talk Winston down. This time, perhaps acknowledging the force of Brooke's previous arguments, Churchill was more receptive to his army head and even damned Brooke with faint praise, describing the CIGS as his 'alter ego' on military matters. Ultimately, Churchill's reservations evaporated in the face of Montgomery's battlefield success. By 20 July, the capture of Caen was complete, and German eyes were firmly fixed on containing the British.

While the British and American politicians and generals were sniping about one another politely over lunch, the real plotting was taking place in Germany. Encouraged by the prospect of a British breakout in Normandy, a group of German army officers now embarked on a daring but ill-fated assassination attempt on Hitler. On 20 July, as Caen was finally being liberated, Colonel Claus von Stauffenberg flew to the Führer's secluded headquarters in East Prussia known as the Wolf's Lair (*Wolfsschanze*) to attend a military conference with Hitler. He then placed a bomb in a briefcase underneath the table in the wooden hut where the meeting was taking place, made his excuses and left. The ensuing blast narrowly failed to kill Hitler, resulting in terrible reprisals as the conspirators were rounded up, tortured and executed. News of this plot and its impact on the higher echelons of the German Army were gradually filtering back to Churchill. What he did not know at this point was that Rommel himself would soon be implicated and forced to take his own life. From a strictly military perspective, though, this had ceased to matter. Rommel had been badly injured on 17 July, when his car was strafed in Normandy by the RAF. For Germany's most famous general, the campaign and the war were over.

Field Marshal von Kluge, now commanding German forces in Normandy, remained convinced that any breakout attempt would come in the British sector. He was wrong. On 25 July the 1st US Army launched Operation Cobra, its major assault being towards St Lô and Avranches. Again, it was spearheaded by a heavy bomber attack but once more the lack of precision-bombing skills by the aircrew caused casualties to both sides. Several aircraft dropped their loads short of their targets killing US troops on the ground, including Lieutenant General Lesley McNair who had gone forward to witness the opening of the attack. Nevertheless, the 1st US Army pushed ahead and by 1 August had achieved their objectives. On that date, Patton's 3rd US Army became operational with four army corps under his command. Patton's first mission was to seize Brittany and the port of Brest in conjunction with the *Forces françaises de l'intérieur*, who had been ordered onto the offensive by their headquarters in London. Events began to move quickly. The British VIII Corps struck south and west of Caen in Operation Bluecoat, which ran until 7 August. That morning the most dominant feature in Normandy, Mount Pinçon, was in British hands and German Army Group B reported that it had taken over a hundred and fifty thousand casualties since 6 June with only twenty thousand reinforcements coming forward. There was a growing inevitability about the outcome of the campaign, but it was not seen by Hitler in the *Wolfsschanze*.

With the Allied breakout, things were now moving in the right direction. By early August, Churchill felt confident enough to give a detailed report to the House of Commons. Speaking just before the summer recess, he was finally able to tell the whole story as he saw it. Addressing the critics who had wanted an earlier Second Front, he declared:

> I do not believe myself that this vast enterprise could have been executed earlier. We had not the experience. We had not the

tackle. But, before we launched the attack in 1944 we had made five successful opposed landings in the Mediterranean, and a mass of wonderful craft of all kinds had been devised by our services and by our United States colleagues on the other side of the ocean.

He then went on to describe some of the extraordinary equipment that he had seen in action during his trips to Normandy, the landing craft with drawbridges that could unload directly onto the beaches, the American amphibious DUKW, 'a heavy lorry which goes at between 40 and 50 miles an hour along the road, and can plunge into the water and swim out for miles to sea', and the harbours which 'had been created compared with which Dover seems small'. His glowing tribute to the ability of these artificial ports to supply 'the entire elaborate equipment of modern armies', which required one vehicle to four or five men, must have prompted raised eyebrows from Brooke, Montgomery and those planning staff who had faced his previous harangues on the subject of there being too much transport.

He was drawing lines in the sand. What had been contentious issues were now part of the operation's successful history. At the request of the Air Ministry, he praised the 'strategic bombing by the combined British and American Bomber Forces, and the use of the medium bomber and fighter forces' for providing 'the essential prelude to our landing in Normandy'. Prompted by the Foreign Office, he also sought to build bridges with the Free French, admitting his many differences with de Gaulle but recognising him as 'the first eminent Frenchman to face the common foe in what seemed to be the hour of ruin of his country, and possibly, of ours'.

He even used the occasion to restate his credentials as a lifelong friend of France.

... all my life I have been grateful for the contribution France has made to the culture and glory of Europe, and above all for the sense of personal liberty and the rights of man which has radiated from the soul of France. But these are not matters of sentiment or personal feeling. It is one of the main interests of Great Britain that a friendly France should regain and hold her place among the major powers of Europe. Show me a moment when I swerved from this conception, and you will show me a moment when I have been wrong.

Finally, he took the opportunity to emphasise that the British and Canadian troops were holding their own, and that 'the losses of the British and Canada forces together are about equal to those of the larger United States Army in proportion to their relative strength'. He was basing this on casualty figures supplied to him for the period up to 23 July. These showed British and Canadian losses at one in thirteen or 8 per cent and American losses at one in eleven and a half, or 8.7 per cent.

There was praise for the long-suffering General Brooke and even for the War Office, though Churchill did point out that 'To say this is by no means inconsistent with any criticisms that it may be necessary to put forward from time to time.' Towards the end, there was even a brief mention of the Stauffenberg plot, with a passing reference to 'The highest personalities in the German Reich . . . murdering one another.'

There was more he would have liked to say and could not. He had wanted to include more about the logistical planning and mounting of the operation, but it was felt that this might prejudice Fortitude, as the deception operation was still running, and Eisenhower wanted the Germans to be kept guessing about forces that might still be in Britain. Winston had wanted to celebrate the bravery of the divers he had seen clearing the harbour at Cherbourg, but it was felt that this might react to their disadvantage by causing the Germans to lay booby traps in future.

The speech brought Churchill's D-Day campaign to an end, but there was still one battle left for him to fight. The recent success in Normandy meant that he now felt confident enough to return to the charge against Dragoon. For him, the tactical moment for an invasion of the south of France had passed. As he later wrote: 'once we joined battle in Normandy "Anvil's" value

CASUALTIES.
NORMANDY.

1st August, 1944.

Dear Martin,

At last night's Cabinet the Prime Minister
stated that he proposed to refer to the Allied
casualties in Normandy and in this connection asked
my Secretary of State to furnish him with certain
information.

In this connection My Secretary of State has
asks me to send you the following figures which
are from the published casualty returns up to 23rd July
last.

	Total Forces Landed	Casualties	Ratio
British and Canadian	653,950	49,280	1 in 13, or 8 per cent
American	809,440	70,300	1 in 11.5, or 8.7 per cent.

The ratio to total strength at a certain
date is perhaps slightly misleading as the average
strength is different; the British build-up started
quicker and the Americans have a rather larger tail.

/The

J.M. Martin, Esq., C.V.O.

*Material on casualties compiled for Prime
Minister's speech, 1 August 1944*

was much reduced, because Hitler was not likely to detach troops
from the main struggle in the north for the sake of keeping his
hold on Provence'.

It was not just about Italy, though Churchill still favoured operations there; it was also about the potential difficulty of opening a
new front in the south of France, especially one that was so far

removed from the main Overlord battlefield. Arguing that Eisenhower no longer needed reinforcements from the south of France, as these could now come directly into Brittany and Normandy and other French ports, he lost no opportunity to lobby the Supreme Commander.

Eisenhower described it as 'one of the longest sustained arguments that I had with Prime Minister Churchill throughout the period of the war'. It reached a head on Saturday 5 August when Churchill used an aborted trip to France, cancelled due to bad weather, to divert to Eisenhower's forward headquarters near Portsmouth and hold an impromptu conference. Accepting that forces would still have to be transferred from the Mediterranean theatre, he advocated changing the plan to sail them through the Straits of Gibraltar and land them in western France. According to Harry Butcher, 'Ike said no, continued saying no all afternoon, and ended saying no in every form of the English language at his command'. The Supreme Commander was clear that he needed another port of entry into France (as many of those in the west were not yet fully operational or were already at capacity), was keen to open up a new flank that would further stretch the enemy and relieve pressure on those fighting in Normandy, and – unlike Churchill – believed that results could be achieved quickly by an assault in the south.

Both men would later dwell on this row in their memoirs. Eisenhower would claim that he had recognised that Churchill's real concern was political; a desire to establish an Allied presence in the Balkans ahead of the Russians. Churchill would later deny it was about moving armies into the Balkans but would write of the lost strategic and political positions in Istria [now Croatia, Slovenia and Italy] and Trieste that 'might exercise profound and widespread reactions, especially after the Russian advances'. In both cases, of course, they were writing with the benefit of hindsight, as leaders in the Cold War, but in the summer of 1944, they were both astute enough operators to see the political as well as the military arguments. Their analysis with regard to the likely extent of Soviet expansion was probably similar, but their immediate priorities and solutions were very different. For Eisenhower, the protégé of Marshall, the surest route to victory was still Germany via France, and he was not prepared to be diverted.

Churchill appealed to Washington DC, but Marshall and Roosevelt also continued to say no. Grudgingly, the British Prime Minister conceded and afterwards reflected: 'It is worth noting that we had now passed the day in July when for the first time in the war the movement of the great American armies into Europe and their growth in the Far East made their numbers in action greater than our own.' At the time, he vented to his doctor, Lord Moran, complaining that the Russians were 'spreading across Europe like a tide' and describing the impending landings in the south of France as 'Sheer folly . . . If only those ten divisions could have been landed in the Balkans' (a sentiment which – if true – confirmed American suspicions and gave the lie to his denials about wanting to dominate south-eastern Europe).

Yet his response was typically Churchillian. Rather than sit at home and brood on his failure to influence his allies, he took himself off to the Mediterranean to see the situation in the British theatre at first hand and to meet 'the commanders and the troops from whom so much was being demanded, after so much had been taken'. For a man approaching his seventieth birthday, whose last bout of long-distance travelling had brought him close to death, this was another epic trip. He flew first to Algiers and then on to Naples, where he met with Marshal Tito and urged him to form a combined front with the Yugoslav King against the Germans. In rare moments of relaxation, he enjoyed the sunshine, swam and visited the islands of Ischia and Capri. But Churchill was never off duty for long. When his barge encountered a large convoy of US troops sailing towards the French Riviera to take part in the Dragoon operation, he passed between the ships flashing his famous V for Victory salute and receiving their cheers while thinking to himself that 'They did not know that if I had had my way they would be sailing in a different direction.'

That did not stop him wanting to get near the action and, on 15 August, he flew on to Corsica, birthplace of his great hero

Napoleon, from where, on the following day, he boarded a destroyer to watch the American landings on the French south coast. He was trying to do exactly what he had not been allowed to do on D-Day, though in the event it proved an anti-climax. The landings went in fairly easily and, much to his frustration, he

PERSONAL

10, Downing Street,
Whitehall.

Italy.

17 August, 1944

My darling.

We have had a busy but delightful time since we arrived here. A very comfortable guest-house, formerly the villa of a wealthy Fascist, now in a concentration camp, was got ready for us. I have here been able to see or entertain all the principal officers of the Army, also Kathleen Harriman and Dorothy Macmillan. The few days we spent in Naples were relieved by a lovely expedition to the Island of Ischia on the first day, and the second to Capri. I thought the Blue Grotto wonderful. We have had altogether four bathes which have done me all the good in the world. I feel greatly refreshed and am much less tired than when I left England.

On the 14th I flew with two of my party to Ajaccio. (Do you remember when we went to see Napoleon's house there in 1910 ?). General Wilson and

-1-

*First page of letter from Winston to Clementine
Churchill, 17 August 1944*

289

was kept out at sea and away from the beaches; reduced to reading the novel *Berlin Hotel* in the captain's cabin (a work by the Austrian-born writer Vicki Baum about wartime life in a German hotel). He described it all in a letter back to Clementine.

While conceding that the operation had gone like clockwork, he confirmed his fears 'that Eisenhower's operations have been a diversion to this landing instead of the other way round', expressed his view that these armies 'now cast on shore 400 miles from Paris' should 'have come in at St Nazaire [on the Atlantic coast] in about a week and greatly widened the front of our advance with corresponding security against German movement east of Paris', and ultimately complained that

> We have three armies in the field. The first is fighting under American Command in France, the second under General Alexander is relegated to a secondary and frustrated situation by the United States' insistence on this landing on the Riviera. The third on the Burmese frontier is fighting in the most unhealthy country in the world under the worst possible conditions to guard the American air line over the Himalayas into their very over-rated China. Thus two thirds of our forces are being mis-employed for American convenience, and the other third is under American Command.

He also mentioned his ongoing frustrations with de Gaulle, who had refused to meet him, and his fear that a Gaullist France would be very hostile to Britain.

It was just before setting off for Corsica that Churchill revealed to his doctor that he had suffered from a period of depression during his early parliamentary career and that even now he did not like standing near the edge of a railway platform or the side of a ship, where 'A second's action would end everything. A few drops of desperation. And yet I don't want to go out of the world at all in such moments.' It was perhaps another indication of the stress he was under; another rare admission of his own mortality. Like all such moments, it passed quickly. He was soon set on visiting General Alexander, seeing the frontline in Italy, and then travelling to North America to take up the big political and military issues with the President. But the very fact that his focus had switched to Italy is telling. He knew he would be received with full honours and warm hospitality by Alexander (while Montgomery did not drink or smoke) and believed that his voice and his presence could still count for something in the Mediterranean, where British support was vital to Yugoslavia and Greece. It was a recognition that control of the battle for France had passed into other hands.

In Normandy, the final throw of the dice by the German Army was to mount a counter-attack with most of its remaining Panzer units. Operation Lüttich was to be a last-throw counter-attack from Mortain into the flanks of the US 30th Infantry Division. The aim was to disrupt the US advance and buy time for the Germans to withdraw to the Loire, a move that Hitler had sanctioned. The main attack began early in the morning of 7 August and caught many of the Americans by surprise. Just the day before, the US 4th Infantry Division had recorded in its operational log that 'The war looks practically over.' But once again it was Allied air superiority that turned the battle. Reconnaissance aircraft had spotted German armour moving in the open to attack the 30th Division. Eighteen squadrons of RAF Typhoon rocket- and cannon-equipped fighters were ordered into a relentless cycle of attack. Piloted by aircrew from a dozen nations, including from France, Australia and New Zealand, the Germans were pounded from the air and by increasing batteries of artillery firing in support of 30th Division. Worse was to follow for von Kluge as, just before midnight on 7 August, Montgomery launched the 1st Canadian Army on Operation Totalise south towards Falaise. With Patton's 3rd US Army now threatening the German 7th Army's supply base, 'It was clear,' a senior German officer reported, 'that this was to be the knockout blow and the end of the army and the whole of the western front.'

Although many German units still offered stiff resistance, morale was fragile and ammunition stocks very low. On 14 August, von Kluge ordered his troops to break out in a north-easterly direction. On 15 August, some 150,000 Allied troops landed largely unopposed in southern France as part of Operation Dragoon, which, at a stroke, changed the strategic landscape. The German occupation of France was nearing its end, but the army was still in the field fighting. In a rather undignified set of exchanges, Montgomery and Bradley failed to coordinate closing the encirclement of the withdrawing Germans as soon as they might have done. Montgomery was initially keen to plan an encirclement of the Germans on the River Seine. He then changed his mind and belatedly ordered the closing of the Falaise Gap, which ensured the near destruction of the German 7th Army; however, many units had escaped east before the encirclement was complete. On 21 August, von Kluge having been sacked by Hitler and committed suicide, and with Field Marshal Model now in command of what was left of German forces in France, Montgomery issued a declaration to the 21st Army Group: 'The victory has been definite, complete and decisive. "The Lord mighty in battle" has given us the victory.' Not all shared that view. Between twenty to thirty thousand German soldiers, albeit with only about twenty-five tanks, had escaped the encirclement and managed to cross the Seine. Monty's harshest critics were RAF Air Chief Marshals Tedder and Coningham, who believed that Monty had let too many Germans get away.

The final act of the Normandy campaign was the advance towards the River Seine and the liberation of Paris. Hitler had ordered the new military commander of the city, Major General von Choltitz, to raze Paris to the ground and defend it from the ruins. Choltitz soon decided that this would serve no military purpose. The issue began to turn more political than military. Patton's 3rd Army was poised to push towards Paris, with General Philippe Leclerc urging his army commander to allow the French 2nd Armoured Division to be the first into the city. Within Paris, tension was mounting between the communists and the Gaullists, while the remaining Germans streamed out of the city. On 25 August, von Choltitz, after a final lunch with his senior staff, signed the surrender of Paris in a document presented to him by Leclerc, whose troops, along with various US units, had begun to occupy the city earlier that day. De Gaulle arrived in Paris shortly after the surrender. Later, he made his famous speech: 'Paris. Paris outraged, Paris broken, Paris martyred, but Paris liberated!' And then in the style that would mark his subsequent leadership of France, he continued: 'Liberated by herself, liberated by her people, with the help of the whole of France, that is to say of the France which fights, the true France, eternal France.' No doubt when Winston Churchill read those words, he must have reflected on his final conversations with Prime Minister Paul Reynaud in Tours on 13 June 1940, shortly before France capitulated. The wheel had come full circle.

On Monday, May 15, three weeks before
D-Day, e held a final conference in London at
Montgomery's Headquarters in St. Paul's School.
The King, Field-Marshal Smuts, the British
Chiefs of Staff, the commanders of the expedition,
and many of their principal staff officers were
present. On the stage was a map of the
Normandy beaches and the immediate hinterland,
set at a slope so that the audience could see it
clearly, and so constructed that the high
officers explaining the plan could walk about on
it and point out the landmarks. His Majesty
opened proceedings, with a short speech, and I
followed. In the course of my remarks I said,
"I am hardening on this enterprise." General
Eisenhower in his book has taken this to mean
that I was always against the cross-Channel
operation, but this is not what I meant. Ismay
reminds me that I had often used this expression
to signify that the more I thought about it the
more certain I was of its success. Eisenhower
spoke next, and then Montgomery took the stage
and made an impressive speech. His theme was,
"We have a sufficiency of troops, we have all the
necessary tackle. We have an excellent plan.
This is a perfectly normal operation which is
certain of success. If anyone has any doubts
in his mind, let him stay behind." Perhaps he
had been reading Henry V before Agincourt:

He that hath no stomach for this fight
Let him depart.
His passport shall be made
And crowns for convoys put into his purse.

[Note on plan to follow]

Montgomery was followed by the
administrative staff officers, some of whom
dwelt upon the elaborate preparations that had

Draft of Churchill's text for his war memoirs, c. 1951

12

Legacies

'. . . if we open a quarrel between the past and the present, we shall find that we have lost the future'.

THE SUCCESSFUL BREAKOUT in Normandy, when coupled with the Soviet advances against Germany in the east, led inexorably towards the Allied victory in Europe. The British and American commanders took private bets among themselves on how quickly the war would be over, now a matter of when, not if. But there were plenty of signs that the Germans were not going to give up easily. At the Casablanca Conference in January 1943, Churchill and Roosevelt had very publicly announced that they would only accept unconditional surrender from Germany. Then, it had been a way of signalling to Stalin that they would make no separate peace. But now – as the war in Europe entered its final phase – the policy was arguably helping to prop up the Nazi regime, removing any incentive for the German political and military elites to remove Hitler in the hope of negotiating better terms. Coupled with the failure of the Stauffenberg plot, which had resulted in a purge of the German Army, it had led to an intensification of the Nazi grip on power, even as the Allied net closed in.

In Britain the V1 flying bombs continued to fall. As the Allies swept through northern France, many of the initial launch sites were overrun, but, after a short break, attacks resumed from Holland. The self-propelled V1 flying bombs were also launched from German aircraft. Counter-measures were deployed; launch sites and suspected production centres were bombed and incoming flying bombs were shot down, but a steady drip stream of casualties continued, especially in the London area.

Then, on 8 September 1944, four years after the start of the Blitz, the first two V2 rocket bombs fell on London, one of them in Churchill's own constituency of Epping (just to the north-east of the capital). These terrifying new weapons, carrying 1,600 pounds of high explosive, were fast enough to hit without warning, adding a terrifying new dimension to this final, desperate German bombing offensive. Casualties from individual blasts could be high. On 25 November, at twenty-six minutes past twelve in the afternoon, a rocket hit a crowded Woolworth's store in Deptford, south-east London, killing 168 and injuring nearly as many.

It was only in November, in response to German announcements, that Churchill publicly acknowledged the existence of the new rockets in Parliament, admitting that 'Because of its high speed, no reliable or sufficient public warning can, in present circumstances be given.' The government was worried about increasing levels of civilian anxiety. Churchill could take comfort from the intelligence that the Germans were unable to deliver these weapons in sufficient quantities to cause real terror and dislocation, but he could not be sure that there would not be some last terrible chemical or nuclear surprise.

It was not until March 1945 that the threat to Britain was finally eradicated, with most launch sites captured and any remaining weapons now out of range. Between June 1944 and March 1945, nearly two and a half thousand V1 flying bombs fell on London, and almost three and a half thousand on other areas of the country. About six thousand people were killed and over seventeen thousand injured. Then came the rocket attacks. The British Home Front was the other frontline in the aftermath of D-Day. Servicemen abroad like Tony Hugill were naturally worried about their families, while the continued attacks only intensified the growing war weariness and desire for peace and reconstruction among the civilian population.

It is a sentiment that can be seen in this moving letter of February 1945, written from a concerned Chingford family to Churchill, as their constituency MP, about the menace from the German V2 rockets:

> Do please tell us that some effective steps are being taken to put a stop to these murderous German rockets which are daily and nightly descending upon us Londoners, killing us and destroying our homes.
>
> So far we have had no assurance from any responsible Minister that anything is being done about it.
>
> We Londoners can still "take it," but after what we have already endured, why should we have to continue to "take it" at this stage of the War?

Joan Bright, still working in London as she had done through the Blitz in 1940, confirmed that 'real fear' accompanied the sudden arrival of the V1s, as they came at a time when people were unprepared for dangerous interruptions to their daily life. She found herself 'always listening; in the street I wished the traffic would stop, among my friends that they would not talk, because there might be one approaching'. Then if one was heard, listening for that terrible moment as the engine cut out, followed by a 'sickening moment of suspense, then "CRRRRMP" and silence again'.

For Churchill, the last year of the war was not a time for celebration. He was able to enjoy some great set-piece moments that followed in the wake of the advance of the Allied armies. In a day laden with symbolism, he walked down the Champs-Élysées and placed a wreath at the Arc de Triomphe with General de Gaulle on 11 November (Armistice Day, from the war of 1914–18), their political differences temporarily put aside in favour of a mutual celebration of victory. His daughter Mary described the enormous crowds that had gathered in the cold, clear air – 'people had clambered into the trees – and were clinging to the chimney pots'. And later, on 25 March 1945, he triumphantly crossed the Rhine and strode purposefully onto occupied enemy soil.

But most of his time was now taken up with planning for the aftermath. A second Quebec Conference with Roosevelt in September 1944 was followed by a bilateral meeting with Stalin in Moscow in October and the second 'Big Three' conference with the President and Stalin at Yalta in February 1945. His focus in all of them was on the impending European settlement. Britain had gone to war for the defence of Poland in 1939, but now the Soviet Red Army dominated the country. To Churchill's disgust, Stalin had refused to come to the aid of the Polish uprising against the Germans in Warsaw in August 1944. It was increasingly clear that the Russian leader favoured establishing his own government, rather than allowing back the country's exiled leaders who had based themselves in Britain. Would Poland be lost to the Soviet sphere? What would a future Germany look like and how would it be governed by the victorious Allies? Would Greece and the Balkans be dominated from Moscow?

In April 1945, just before the final collapse of Nazi Germany and Hitler's suicide, came the news of President Roosevelt's death. What should have been a moment of jubilation was marred by uncertainty over the new direction in Washington DC and fear of the existing direction in Moscow. Even before the German surrender Churchill was using terms like 'iron curtain' and 'third world war' to refer to the declining international situation with Russia in his private telegrams. In May 1945, as most of the country celebrated the end of five and a half long years of conflict, he asked the British Chiefs of Staff to draw up plans for a limited military campaign against the Soviet Union. Code-named Operation Unthinkable, the plan considered the possibility of using British, American, Polish and even some German divisions to overturn the Soviet position in Poland. Unsurprisingly, the conclusion was that it was truly unthinkable and would only have led to a further protracted total war. Brooke described the whole idea as 'fantastic and the chances of success quite impossible'.

The plan was based on flawed assumptions. Such an operation would never have enjoyed the support of an American government that still wanted Stalin's help in the war in the Pacific. Nor would it have been supported at home. Public opinion in Britain and America still saw the Soviet Union as an ally, and one that had sacrificed much in defeating Germany. Churchill's plan was a non-starter and remained secret until the end of the twentieth century, but it is revealing of the extent of his fears about the Soviet Union.

Change was in the air. Joan Bright took charge of the British administrative arrangements for the Washington, Quebec, Moscow, Yalta and Potsdam summits, attending them all. In 1940, it would have been very rare for a woman to travel outside the country as part of an official delegation, and almost inconceivable that she would find herself in such a position of authority. At Yalta, Joan even pretended to be a major general in order to be taken seriously by the rank-conscious Russians (for contrast, the highest military rank achieved by Churchill was lieutenant colonel in 1916!).

Early 1945 was a period of rising international tension within the alliance, combined with war weariness and a growing desire for change at home. There had not been a General Election in Britain since 1935 and the existence of the national coalition government had meant that there had been few outlets for real political opposition to Churchill's administration. The success of D-Day led to victory in Europe in May 1945, but it also led just as inexorably to the end of the wartime coalition and to the resumption of normal party-political strife. In the final months of the war in Europe, clear differences were emerging between the Conservative and Labour Parties. Churchill, his own health weakened, was finding it harder to manage the domestic political landscape. Condemned by the Labour Party for his policy of supporting the nationalists in Greece and attacked by his own Conservative backbenchers for not doing more for Poland, he remained determined to see the job through to completion and to finish the war in the Pacific, but – like all British Prime Ministers – he had to think about the optimum timing for a General Election. Was it better to move quickly and hold an election in the immediate aftermath of victory in Europe, hoping to benefit from a victory bounce in the polls, or should he try and continue the coalition until after the defeat of Japan? In the case of Japan, the Allies were not yet certain of the atom bomb, and final victory might be a costly and protracted affair. In the end, his hand was forced. Both the rank and file of the opposition Labour Party and many of his senior Conservative political colleagues favoured a quick election. It was clear that his coalition would not last.

Churchill tendered his resignation to the King on 23 May, only a fortnight after VE Day, and was tasked with forming a caretaker government while the election campaign was conducted and the votes counted. Polling took place on 5 July, but the additional difficulty of counting the large number of overseas service votes meant that the result of the ballot was not declared until 26 July. The result was a Labour landslide, a majority of 146. Churchill was out.

To Mary Churchill, who was with her father in his map room as the results came in, this was a terrible humiliation and betrayal: 'Hot tears came & had to be hidden. Everyone looked grave and dazed. We lunched in Stygian gloom.' General Brooke, not always Churchill's greatest admirer, thought it a 'ghastly mistake to start elections at this period in the World's history!' and the next day, when meeting with Churchill and the Chiefs of Staff, he almost broke down at 'a very sad and very moving little meeting'. To Joan Bright, 'They had not rejected Winston Churchill, they had rejected war and its leadership. He would remain for all time one of their greatest Englishmen; they would always be in his debt.' Clementine Churchill had a slightly different take. For her, this was a 'blessing in disguise'. She feared that if her husband continued in office, the continued burden might have killed him. It elicited the characteristically blunt reply from Churchill that it was 'certainly very well disguised'. Yet he put a brave face on the defeat, when Michael Parish, a friend of Mary's, told him he had won the race, he replied with a suitable horse-racing analogy, 'And in consequence I've been warned off the turf.'

There are of course many complex reasons why Churchill lost the 1945 election, but there are a few that relate directly to the themes of this book.

The first is the impact of events on his own health. By the beginning of 1944, Churchill had already served as Prime Minister for three and a half years. The physical toll of holding high office for so long was inevitable and by the end of the war he did have recurring heart and respiratory problems. His sense of frustration and anxiety was at its highest during the enforced period of preparation immediately prior to D-Day. He chafed against being able to influence the military strategy, worried about the likely levels of Allied military and French civilian casualties, and wrestled with the difficulties of putting a country into virtual lockdown to facilitate and protect the Overlord operation. His energy levels never seem to have fully recovered and this surely contributed to a lacklustre and ill-judged performance in the election campaign. His decision to attack the Labour Party, rather than sitting above the political fray, allowed his opponents to exploit a distinction between Churchill the war leader and Churchill the party politician.

A second factor was the contribution of Overlord to the already-changing mood of the British electorate. In the build-up to 6 June 1944, they had endured unprecedented levels of restriction to their daily lives – forbidden from visiting certain areas of the country, their internal travel restricted, their homes blacked out, food rationed, their mail censored, and the countryside turned over to barracks, bases and airfields. The assault on Europe brought with it further separation and loss; it also brought direct retaliation through the onslaught of the V-weapons and the return of terror from the skies. All of this reinforced a natural tendency to want to rebuild a better post-war world; one that would make such sacrifices worthwhile. Both Mary and Sarah Churchill, Winston's daughters, were serving in uniform. They sensed this mood in the young people surrounding them. Churchill apparently did not. Lord Moran recalled a conversation.

'There are two opposing ideas in the country,' I said to him. 'There's pretty universal gratitude to you, and there's a notion about that you aren't very keen on this brave-new-world business.'

Winston answered: 'The desire for a new world is nothing like universal; the gratitude is.'

Churchill was wrong. He was too focused on his new fight against the Soviet Union to realise that not everyone shared his single-minded focus on the international scene.

But D-Day also weakened Churchill because it took the focus away from him. In 1940, Britain was on the defensive and under attack. Then, Churchill had harnessed the wider government information machine and used a series of set-piece broadcasts to rally morale, establishing himself as a visual representation of the people's resistance. In 1944, it was not possible to do this. To broadcast in advance of D-Day risked giving away that the invasion was imminent; to do so immediately afterwards risked compromising the deception plans that hinted that the Allies were yet to do more. Besides, this was now a multi-national operation, and one that was increasingly dominated by the Americans. He lacked the freedom to speak about the military operation without coordinating his words through Roosevelt, the Combined Chiefs of Staff and Eisenhower.

Churchill was not the contemporary voice of D-Day. Moreover, by the time he came to write about it, in Volumes V and VI of his multi-volume history *The Second World War*, published respectively in 1952 and 1954, he was on the back foot – having to respond to suggestions already in print that he had never been a wholehearted supporter of the operation. The race to publish had started as soon as the war had ended. Harry Butcher, Ike's naval aide, had published *Three Years with Eisenhower* in 1946. Read in full, the book is generally admiring of Churchill, but it included some very unflattering vignettes. An entry for 26 August 1942 recounts a report from General Clark regarding a meeting with the Prime Minister at which Churchill smashed a glass, changed his socks in front of guests and later 'walked to the open door, put his back to its edge, vigorously rubbed his shoulderblades [*sic*] against it, and said: "Guess I picked 'em up in Egypt."'

More damaging, perhaps, were the allegations in Eisenhower's own book, *Crusade in Europe*, published in 1948, that Churchill feared the seas would run red with blood and that the British leader was a late convert to Overlord, having announced as late as 15 May that he was '*hardening*' toward this operation, suggesting of course that he had been soft on it up to that date. Then there was Alan Moorehead's biography of Montgomery, also published in 1946, which annoyed Churchill by recounting details of the Prime Minister's visit to Montgomery's headquarters on 19 May, broadcasting their disagreement over Churchill's attempt to interrogate the staff and the General's threat to resign. As Moorehead had been given access to Montgomery's own papers, this led to a somewhat awkward post-war exchange between Churchill and Monty.

The fact that Churchill chose to respond to these issues in his own history showed how much these attacks had wounded him. But he also had to be careful how he responded. By the time he published, he was back in 10 Downing Street, Eisenhower was President of the United States, and Montgomery was NATO's Deputy Supreme Commander in Europe. He needed to work with both men and did not want a public row about the past. In his 'Finest Hour' speech of 18 June 1940 he had warned that 'if we open a quarrel between the past and the present, we shall find that we have lost the future'. So, he was diplomatic in what he wrote, downplaying the disagreements. By 'hardening on this operation' he had meant 'wishing to strike if humanly possible'; and at no time did Montgomery threaten to resign and 'nothing in the nature of a confrontation with his staff took place'.

Churchill's protestations probably only fuelled stories of his wobbling over D-Day. Over time, more information was released about the debates at the top. The memoirs of Lord Alanbrooke, General de Gaulle, Lord Moran and Sir Alexander Cadogan added to a growing publication list, while the release of more official records revealed the extent and complexity of many of the key wartime discussions.

This book has not set out to exonerate all Churchill did. It is impossible to know with certainty whether better or worse results could have been achieved if the British and American Allies had followed a different strategy. What we have aimed to do is to put Churchill's decisions and actions in context and to show the many factors and individuals that coloured his approach to this critical operation.

He was undoubtedly influenced by the First World War and a desire to avoid a repeat of the huge bloodshed of the trench stalemate in France, which would have been catastrophic for the country and almost certainly fatal to his own administration.

He was determined to preserve the British Empire. Any British Prime Minister in 1940 would have been forced to think about the defence of Egypt, Malta and Palestine, and of routes to Canada, India, South Africa, Australia and New Zealand, but Churchill was particularly driven by a desire not to preside over the Empire's liquidation, and his Mediterranean and Balkan policies had both a clear imperial and anti-Soviet dimension. This was certainly a factor in Churchill's desire to keep fighting in these theatres, even after the final decision had been taken to attack in north-west France, and explains why he resented the 'tyranny of Overlord'.

Yet, for all this, as he told his friend Smuts, he regarded the relationship with the United States and the commitment to Overlord as the 'keystone of arch of Anglo-American co-operation'. The major decisions were discussed with Roosevelt and the Combined Chiefs of Staff and taken for sound strategic reasons. Operations in North Africa and Sicily took on their own momentum and further delayed D-Day, but they were launched because the preconditions for an assault on Normandy had not yet been met, because the risks of a frontal assault in France were deemed too high, and because to do nothing while preparing to attack France was politically and militarily unacceptable. The Battle of the Atlantic had to be won, mastery of the skies obtained and the enemy isolated and weakened.

On D-Day itself, Churchill – in spite of his best efforts to get himself a front-row seat on board a British ship – had to wait for news of the battle in London. There is no doubt that the build-up to the launch had been a particularly stressful time. He did not have the same reserves of energy as in 1940, but neither was he a nervous wreck. The weeks leading up to Overlord saw him taking an active interest in all aspects of the operation and using his convening power to ensure that production targets were met and security was maintained. Though often portrayed as a warmonger, one of Winston's consistent concerns had been to minimise military and French civilian casualties. Yes, he drove the War Cabinet and the Chiefs of Staff to distraction, challenging them on the number of vehicles, railing against de Gaulle, and refused to back down on his opposition to the bombing of the marshalling yards, but he did so out of a concern to reduce losses and ensure success. Surely that was his job?

Nowadays, Churchill is rarely talked about in connection with D-Day. The focus tends to be on his role in the events of 1940. Sometimes, he is mentioned in connection with his role in developing the Mulberry harbours; more often he is criticised for trying to delay or obstruct the operation. What we hope we have shown is that he played a key role in the timing and nature of Overlord. He was certainly not standing alone, he was working with others (not always harmoniously), and his moods and motivations shifted with events, but he played a vital role in creating the alliances and the framework that facilitated the liberation of France.

With hindsight, we can say that D-Day was successful. Churchill, Eisenhower and the other commanders could not be so sure at the time. This was an enormous operation upon which so much depended. Surely, Churchill can be forgiven for hedging slightly and for not wanting to put all his eggs in one basket. Ultimately, Overlord can only be judged by its success and Churchill was one of its architects.

And what of some of the others? Hughes-Hallett finished his career in 1954 as a vice admiral. Tony Hugill went on to marry one of Admiral Ramsay's Wrens, using the advance from his wartime memoirs to fund the engagement ring. Both Christian Oldham and Joan Bright gave up their jobs after marriage in accordance with the conventions of the time. Geoffrey Pyke continued to think outside the box but enjoyed little success. His suicide in 1948 prompted *The Times* newspaper to describe him as 'one of the most original if unrecognised figures of the present century'. Percy Hobart retired from the army and Churchill wrote an unsuccessful letter of reference for him to become the Chichele Professor of War at Oxford University. Basil Liddell Hart continued to enjoy a successful career as a historian and military commentator. The Liddell Hart Centre for Military Archives at King's College, London, is named after him and houses his papers alongside those of Alanbrooke, Ironside and others. Jock Colville became Private Secretary to Princess Elizabeth, the future Elizabeth II, before returning to Downing Street to serve Churchill again as his Joint Principal Private Secretary from 1951 to 1955. Roland MacKenzie went home to Canada, resumed his career in banking and rarely talked about his war. Stan Hollis became a publican. T. L. Rodgers was temporarily buried in a cemetery in France. His remains were eventually returned to Covington County, Alabama, where he was laid to rest in the family plot at the Carolina Baptist Church Cemetery. Their stories, like Churchill's, are all threads in the bigger tapestry.

Which brings us back to Churchill College in Cambridge. And to another work of art hanging on the wall, this time in the main library. In 1961, General de Gaulle presented the College with a large, magnificent and colourful tapestry by the artist Jean Lurçat called *Etoile de Paris* (Star of Paris). Rich in imagery, the work celebrates the liberation of the French capital from the Germans in 1944. Sewn into the fabric, in a top corner, is the phrase '*Paris, soi-meme liberé* [Paris liberated itself]'. While recognising the role of de Gaulle and the French Resistance, as well as the literal truth of French troops being allowed to enter the city first, Churchill would surely have disagreed. There were many threads that led to the successful liberation of France. He had played a key role in pulling them together.

If all Winston Churchill's worries and fears about launching a land invasion of Europe from southern England could be summed up in one short sentence, it was the remark he made to his beloved Clemmie on the evening of 5 June 1944: 'Do you realize that by the time you wake in the morning 20,000 men may have been killed?'

These were the 'Black Dog' anxieties born of the scars and memories of Gallipoli in 1915/16, of the ineptitude of the 1940 Norway campaign and of the 1942 disaster at Dieppe. Responsibility, not just for the security of the nation, but for other men's lives, weighed very heavily on Churchill's shoulders. In the event, of the 133,000 men and women who landed on 6 June 1944, there were around 11,000 casualties, of which some 3,800 were killed in the first twenty-four hours. Among the fatalities there were just under a thousand British soldiers, sailors, airmen and marine commandos. But as this narrative has described, 6 June 1944 was but the first of the ninety days of the Normandy campaign. By the time the River Seine had been crossed and Paris liberated, there had been around a quarter of a million Allied casualties, with nearly forty-five thousand British, US, Canadian and Polish soldiers killed among the ground forces and a further sixteen thousand deaths among the Allied air and naval forces. The French civil population suffered about twelve thousand dead or injured. The German Army reported around three hundred and twenty thousand casualties, of which about a hundred and fifty thousand became prisoners. The price in both blood and treasure for all sides was very high. Eighty years on, to younger generations, that figure looks extraordinary, totally unbelievable.

D-Day has become a major landmark not just in the accounts of the Second World War, but as a turning point in global history. Until the Western Allies were able to return to France and pose the dilemma to the Germans of a war on two fronts in Europe, it is conceivable that Nazi Germany could have held its Eastern Front and prevented further Soviet expansion westwards. In those circumstances the Europe of today would have looked very different – a communist East and a national socialist West. It was the steadfast determination of the Western Allies, led by Britain, that Germany must be defeated first and then Japan second that brought about the successful conclusion of the Second World War. From standing isolated and alone in June 1940 and facing defeat, Churchill had orchestrated a successful alliance with the democratic United States and an accommodation with Stalin's communist Soviet Union such that the tyranny of German national socialism and Italian fascism could be expunged from Europe. Normandy was the turning point.

To the dismay of the British veterans who had fought in Normandy and to the disappointment of the families of those who had fought and fallen in the campaign to begin the liberation of Europe, until 2021 Britain had no memorial in Normandy to mark the service and sacrifice of those who fought from the landing beaches to the River Seine. Very belatedly, this national omission has been corrected. The British Memorial in Normandy now stands on the coast by the village of Ver-sur-Mer on a site overlooking Gold beach where Stan Hollis stormed ashore with his Green Howards comrades, near Arromanches, through whose Mulberry harbour so much of the vital logistics flowed to sustain the campaign. The memorial includes the names of the 22,442 service men and women, from over twenty different nations, who died during the Normandy campaign under British command. And there is also a memorial to the French civilians who died in the fighting so that their country and Europe could be free. '*Liberté, égalité, fraternité*' – the national motto of the French. The memorial provides a quiet space to reflect on the sacrifice of those who died to bring peace and freedom to Europe. And it also tells the story of the British leadership of the Normandy campaign – the strategic and political leadership of Winston Churchill, the operational leadership of Bernard Montgomery, and the determined tactical leadership on the battlefield of thousands of fighters like Stan Hollis.

Codenames

Anvil   Initial codename for Allied liberation of south of France

Arcadia   Washington DC Conference, 22 December 1941 – 14 January 1942

Bagration   Soviet offensive on the Eastern Front, June–August 1944

Barbarossa   German invasion of the Soviet Union, June 1941

Bluecoat   British offensive around Caen, July–August 1944

Bodyguard   Overarching codename for all deception plans to protect Allied liberation of Normandy in 1944

Bolero   Build-up of American forces in the United Kingdom

Bombardon   Interlocking steel crosses used to construct artificial harbours

Boniface   Cover name used to protect intelligence obtained from the breaking of the German codes

Chariot   British raid against docks at St Nazaire, March 1942

Cobra   American offensive in Normandy, July 1944

Cockade   Overarching codename for a series of Allied deception operations in 1943

Dragoon   Final codename for Allied liberation of south of France, August 1944

Dynamo   Evacuation of British and French forces from Dunkirk, May–June 1940

Epsom   British offensive in Normandy, June 1944

Eureka   Tehran Conference, 28 November – 1 December 1943

Fortitude North Deception designed to suggest an Allied attack in Scandinavia, 1944. Part of Bodyguard

Fortitude South Deception designed to suggest a second Allied

	landing in the Pas-de-Calais region of France, 1944. Part of Bodyguard
Gold	Beach between Arromanches-les-Bains and La Rivière, taken by the British in June 1944
Goodwood	British attempt to break out of Normandy, July 1944
Gooseberry	An artificial breakwater
Gymnast	Initial British codename for operation against French North Africa, 1942
Habbakuk	Proposal to construct aircraft carriers from a floating ice/wood-pulp mix known as Pykrete. Not implemented
Hillman	German strongpoint defending Caen
Husky	Allied operation against Sicily, July 1943
Jubilee	Unsuccessful British and Canadian raid on Dieppe, 19 August 1942
Juno	Beach between La Rivière and St Aubin-sur-Mer, taken by the British and Canadians, June 1944
Jupiter	British codename for proposed operation against northern Norway. Not undertaken
Lilo	Proposal for artificial breakwater created by piped air. Not implemented
Lüttich	German counter-attack near Mortain, August 1944
Mincemeat	Deception plan involving documents planted on a dead body used to protect Allied landings in Sicily, April 1943
Morris	German strongpoint defending Caen
Mulberry	An artificial harbour
Neptune	The naval operation to bring forces across the Channel, June 1944
Omaha	Beach between Vierville-sur-Mer and Colleville-sur-Mer, taken by the Americans, June 1944
Overlord	The overarching codename for the Allied liberation of France via Normandy, June 1944
Phoenix	Large, hollow concrete units sunk to form artificial harbours and breakwaters
Pointblank	Allied campaign for the strategic bombing of German military, industrial and economic targets, 1943–4
Quadrant	Quebec Conference, 17–24 August 1943

Roundup	Initial codename for large-scale Allied operation in France, 1942-3
Rutter	Superseded plan for operation against Dieppe, 1942
Sledgehammer	Codename for proposed limited Allied operation in France, 1942–3
Starkey	Deception involving a large-scale feigned attack against Boulogne, August–September 1943. Part of Cockade
Sword	Beach between St Aubin-sur-Mer and the River Orne, taken by the British, June 1944
Symbol	Casablanca Conference, 14–24 January 1943
Tentacle	Proposed artificial floating runway. Not implemented
Tiger	Large-scale rehearsal exercise for D-Day, April 1944
Tindall	Deception suggesting sailing of five divisions from Scotland against Stavanger in Norway, 1943
Torch	Final codename for Allied landings in French North Africa, November 1942
Totalise	Canadian attempt to break out in Normandy, August 1944
Trident	Washington DC Conference, 12–25 May 1943
Ultra	Signals intelligence obtained by breaking German codes
Unthinkable	Plan for proposed military operation against the Soviet Union, May 1945. Not undertaken
Utah	Beach between St Martin de Varreville and Pouppeville, taken by the Americans, June 1944
Wadham	Deception suggesting assault by two American divisions on Brittany, 1943
Weserübung	German invasion of Denmark and Norway, April 1940
Whale	Steel pierheads and floating roadways used in artificial harbours

Acronyms and terms requiring explanation

ADC	Aide de Camp, a term for a personal assistant to a senior officer
BEF	British Expeditionary Force
CAC	Churchill Archives Centre, Churchill College, Cambridge
CIGS	Chief of the Imperial General Staff (head of the British Army)
COHQ	Combined Operations Headquarters
COS	Chiefs of Staff
COSSAC	Chief of Staff to Supreme Allied Commander
CSM	Company Sergeant Major
D-Day	The day on which an operation commences. The D stands for day.
DD tanks	Amphibious duplex-drive tanks used by the Allies on D-Day
DUKW	A six-wheel-drive amphibious vehicle
E-boat	Small, fast armed German attack ships
FUSAG	First United States Army Group
H-Hour	The hour an operation commences. The H stands for hour.
LCS	London Controlling Section (unit planning deception operations)
LSTs	Landing Ship Tanks
MI	Military Intelligence
MI (R)	Military Intelligence (Research)
MI5	Security service of the United Kingdom, concerned with counter-terrorism and home security
MI6	Special Intelligence Service of the United Kingdom, concerned with foreign intelligence
MP	Member of Parliament
Pluto	Pipeline under the ocean
PWE	Political Warfare Executive, responsible for British propaganda and damaging enemy morale

SHAEF	Supreme Headquarters Allied Expeditionary Force
SOE	Special Operations Executive, responsible for guerilla operations behind enemy lines
TNA	The National Archives, Kew
U-boat	German submarine
V1	A German pilotless flying bomb. The V stands for *Vergeltungswaffe* (vengeance weapon)
V2	A German rocket-powered missile. The V stands for *Vergeltungswaffe* (as above)
Wren	Member of Women's Royal Naval Service

Allied Army Units

Battalion   Up to a thousand men, divided into companies and normally commanded by a lieutenant colonel.

Regiment   A permanent organisational unit within the army, normally divided into battalions and commanded by a colonel. Regiments will be combined for operational purposes to form brigades and divisions as circumstances require. In the British Army, the term regiment has two meanings. The peacetime organisation of the infantry is within regiments, which can have many battalions. These battalions fight within brigades (see below). The second meaning applies to artillery, engineer, signal and some logistic units, which are called 'regiments' in the same way that the infantry refers to battalions.

Brigade   Composed of two or more battalions or regiments and normally commanded by a brigadier or brigadier general.

Division   Composed of several regiments or brigades and normally commanded by a major general.

Corps   Composed of two or more divisions and normally commanded by a lieutenant general.

Acknowledgements

The letters and diary of King George VI are reproduced with permission from His Majesty King Charles III. Quotes from the speeches, works and writings of Sir Winston Churchill are reproduced with permission of Curtis Brown, London, on behalf of The Estate of Winston S. Churchill, © The Estate of Winston S. Churchill. The work contains public sector information licensed under the Open Government Licence v3.0 and parliamentary copyright materials also licensed under the Open Parliament Licence v3.0. Images of documents from the Churchill Papers collection are reproduced with the permission of the Sir Winston Churchill Archive Trust. Images and quotations from other collections at the Churchill Archives Centre are reproduced with the permission of Churchill College, Cambridge, and the relevant copyright holders where known. Extracts from the diaries of Sir Alan Lascelles are reproduced here with grateful acknowledgement to and permission of the Estate of Sir Alan Lascelles. Substantial quotations from secondary sources are reproduced with the permission of the relevant copyright holders, where known. In particular, thanks are due to the Trustees of the Alanbrooke Estate, David Eisenhower, Christian Lamb, the daughters of Hugh Lunghi, Roddy MacKenzie, the grandchildren of Admiral Sir Bertram Ramsay, Charles Tilbury, The Wavell Estate and James Wilson. Quotes from *The Deception Planners: My Secret War* by Dennis Wheatley reprinted by permission of Peters Fraser & Dunlop (www.petersfraserdunlop.com) on behalf of the Estate of Dennis Wheatley.

The authors would like to thank Rupert Lancaster of Hodder

& Stoughton, Charlie Viney of the Viney Agency, and Gordon Wise of Curtis Brown. David Boler and Amanda Jones were kind enough to read the manuscript. Christopher Knowles at Churchill Archives Centre copied many of the images, Christian Lamb was kind enough to talk about her wartime experiences and Russell Riley suggested the inclusion of his relative T. L. Rodgers.

Notes

Chapter 1: Hindsight Is a Wonderful Thing

pp. 5, 6 'Are you going to lay there and get killed, or get up and do
          something about it?', United States Army, Center of Military
          History; https://history.army.mil/books/wwii/100-11/ch4.htm.

p. 7   'I have also to announce to the House . . .' Churchill's statement
          to the House of Commons, 6 June 1944, *Hansard*, series 5, Vol.
          400, cc1207–11.

p.9   'The immense cross-Channel enterprise for the liberation of
          France had begun . . .' Churchill, W. S., *The Second World War*,
          Vol. 5, p. 558.

p. 15   'Without the title deeds of positive achievement no one had
          the power . . .' Churchill, W. S., *The World Crisis*, Vol. 2, p.
          498.

p. 15   'The landing under cover of the guns of the Fleet . . .' A copy of
          the original paper can be found in the Churchill Acquired Papers
          at Churchill Archives Centre, CAC, Churchill Acquired Papers,
          CHAQ 1/5/3. An edited version is published in Churchill, W. S.,
          The Second World War, Vol. 2, p. 215.

p. 16   'the fearful price we had had to pay in human life and blood for
          the great offensives of the First World War was graven in my
          mind'. Churchill, W. S., *The Second World War*, Vol. 5, p. 514.

p. 17   'essentially a government of committees . . .' Hastings, M., *Finest
          Years: Churchill as Warlord*, p. xx.

p. 18   'In view of the many accounts which are extant and multiplying
          of my supposed aversion from any kind of large-scale opposed-
          landing . . .' Churchill, W. S., *The Second World War*, Vol. 2, p.
          224.

Chapter 2: Dealing with Defeat

pp. 21, 33 'He spoke in English, and evidently under stress.' Churchill, W. S., *The Second World War*, Vol. 2, p. 38.

p. 22 'After this Norway breakdown there is of course a lot of criticism . . .' Unpublished diary of Leo Kennedy, 4 May 1940. CAC, Leo Kennedy Papers, LKEN 1/23.

p. 23 'Churchill was so much larger in every way than his colleagues . . .' Wheeler-Bennett, J. (ed.), *Action This Day: Working with Churchill*, p. 161.

p. 27 'Amphibious operations are a very specialised form of warfare . . .' Ismay, H., *The Memoirs of General the Lord Ismay*, p. 120.

p. 29 'almost impossible task . . . with absolute loyalty and apparent sincerity . . .' Nicolson, H., *Harold Nicolson: Diaries and Letters 1930–1964*, p. 181.

p. 34 'The reader of these pages in future years should realise . . .' Churchill, W. S., *The Second World War*, Vol. II, p. 143.

p. 35 'not to assign to this deliverance the attributes of a victory. Wars are not won by evacuations.' Churchill, W. S. (ed.), *Never Give In*, p. 214.

p. 37 'his confidence that Hitlerism would be smashed . . .' CAC, Churchill Papers, CHAR 23/2.

p. 38 'However matters may go in France or with the French Government . . .' CAC, Churchill Papers, CHAR 9/140A, also reproduced in Churchill, W. S. (ed.), *Never Give In*, pp. 228–9.

p. 40 'Today came the announcement that following Reynaud's resignation . . .' Soames, E. (ed.), *Mary Churchill's War*, p. 37.

p. 42 'The completely defensive habit of mind which has ruined the French . . .' Churchill, W. S., *The Second World War*, Vol. 2, p. 214.

p. 42 'With a shorthand pad and typewriter I could be a valuable . . .' Bright Astley, J., *The Inner Circle*, p. 13.

Chapter 3: Arguments with Allies

pp. 47, 50 'No lover ever studied every whim of his mistress as I did those of President Roosevelt.' Colville, J., *The Fringes of Power*, p. 624.

p. 47 'Never in the field of human conflict was so much owed by so many to so few.' CAC, Churchill Papers, CHAR 9/141A, also published in Churchill, W. S. (ed.), *Never Give In*, p. 245.

p. 48   'If Hitler invaded Hell, I would at least make a favourable reference to the Devil in the House of Commons.' Churchill, W. S., *The Second World War*, Vol. 3, p. 331.

p. 49   'So we had won after all!' Churchill, W. S., *The Second World War*, Vol. 3, p. 539.

p. 53   'What Harry and Geo. Marshall will tell you about has my heart & mind in it.' CAC, Churchill Papers, CHAR 20/52/29.

p. 54   'his lips are blanched as if he had been bleeding internally . . .' Moran, Lord., *Winston Churchill: The Struggle for Survival 1940–1965*, p. 12.

p. 54   'very upright man . . .' From unpublished transcript of interview with Joan Bright Astley. CAC, Brendon Papers, BREN 1/12.

p. 56   'Western Europe is favored as the theater . . .' CAC, Churchill Papers, CHAR 20/52/33.

p. 57   'our soldiers seem very incapable . . .' Dilks, D. (ed.), *The Diaries of Sir Alexander Cadogan*, pp. 432–3.

p. 58   'Well I think 1942 was a horrible year . . .' From unpublished transcript of interview with Joan Bright Astley. CAC, Brendon Papers, BREN 1/12.

p. 59   he had 'no hesitation in cordially accepting the plan'. TNA, Cabinet Office, Defence Committee (Operations) minutes, CAB 69/4.

p. 60   'Unless we are prepared to commit the immense forces . . .' TNA, Prime Minister's Office, PREM 3/333/2.

p. 62   'The Red Army is carrying the brunt of the battle.' Butcher, H., *Three Years with Eisenhower*, p. 7.

p. 63   'he [Churchill] was the man to see first . . .' Butcher, H., *Three Years with Eisenhower*, p. 20.

p. 65   'owing to a recent re-estimate of the number of landing craft . . .' TNA, Prime Minister's Office, PREM 3/333/1.

p. 67   'Mr. Churchill suddenly turned to me . . .' Memoir of Vice-Admiral John Hughes-Hallett. CAC, HHLT. Published as *From Dieppe to D-Day*, p. 45.

p. 68   '. . . the very last thing they'd (the Germans) ever imagine is that we would be so stupid as to lay on the same operation again'. Ziegler, P., *Mountbatten*, p. 346.

p. 71   'they were going to have to be very, very good'. Kennedy, P., *Engineers of Victory*, p. 234.

p. 72   'I do not like the job I have to do . . .' 'Ballade of the Second

Front' by General Wavell. Humphrys, O., *Wavell in Russia*, p. 83.

p. 72   'Stalin appeared quite at home . . .' CAC, Jacob Papers, JACB 1/16.

p. 77   'preparing forces and assembling landing craft in England for a thrust across the Channel'. TNA, Cabinet Office, Record of conference held at Casablanca, CAB 99/24.

p. 79   'as the codeword implies, a landing to "round up" any German units . . .' Wheatley, D., *The Deception Planners*, p. 122.

Chapter 4: It Won't Work, But You Must Bloody Well Make It

pp. 83, 111   '. . . all right if you won't play with us in the Mediterranean . . .' Danchev, A., and Todman, D. (eds), *War Diaries 1939–1945: Field Marshal Lord Alanbrooke*, p. 472.

p. 84   'There followed months of toil in an atmosphere of persisting doubt and uncertainty . . .' Morgan, F., *Peace and War*, p. 155.

p. 84   'A German collapse being extremely unlikely and not to be counted upon this year . . .' TNA, Prime Minister's Office, PREM 3/333/4.

p. 84   'the creation of this vast complicated staff . . .' TNA, Prime Minister's Office, PREM 3/333/15.

p. 85   'To this end the Combined Chiefs of Staff will endeavour to assemble . . .' Morgan, F., *Peace and War*, p. 156.

p. 88   'earned for himself the reputation in his own service of being "sold out to the British" . . .' Morgan, F., *Peace and War*, pp. 158–9.

p. 90   'whole basis of our higher organization was new . . .' Eisenhower, D., *Crusade in Europe*, p. 99.

p. 91   'I was even more anxious about this battle . . .' Churchill, W. S., *The Second World War*, Vol. 2, p. 529.

p. 92   'I had a feeling once about Mathematics, that I saw it all . . .' Churchill, W. S., *My Early Life*, p. 27.

p. 93   'How willingly would I have exchanged a full-scale attempt at invasion . . .' Churchill, W. S., *The Second World War*, Vol. 3, pp. 100–01.

p. 94   'We had to win the Battle of the Atlantic. Losing it would mean losing the war altogether.' Lamb, C., *Beyond the Sea: A Wren at War*, p. 119.

p. 94   '. . . measures to be taken to combat the submarine menace are a first charge . . .' TNA, Cabinet Office, Record of conference held at Casablanca, CAB 99/24.

p. 95 'Signal after signal came in and the teleprinter buzzed on relent-lessly.' Lamb, C., *Beyond the Sea: A Wren at War*, p. 184.

p. 96 'That there must be a substantial reduction in the strength of the German fighter aircraft . . .' Churchill, W. S., *The Second World War*, Vol. 5, p. 69.

p. 98 'By February 1944, the Allies' own analysis was that . . .' Figures taken from a paper of 1 March 1944. CAC, Bufton Papers, BUFT 3/44.

p. 98 '29 years old, 5 foot ten, 145 lbs, confident . . .' MacKenzie, R., *Bomber Command: Churchill's Greatest Triumph*, p. 28.

p. 99 'Through Adversity to the Stars . . .' MacKenzie, R., *Bomber Command: Churchill's Greatest Triumph*, p. 135.

p. 101 'I deem it my duty to warn you in the strongest possible manner . . .' TNA, Prime Minister's Office, PREM 3/333/3.

p. 101 'so very conscious of the poor contribution . . .' TNA, Prime Minister's Office, PREM 3/333/3.

p. 101 'That there should not be more than twelve mobile German divi-sions . . .' Churchill, W. S., *The Second World War*, Vol. 5, p. 69.

pp. 103-4 Figures for landing craft taken from Roskill, S. W., *The War at Sea*, Vol. 3, part 2, p. 19, and Barnett, C., *Engage the Enemy More Closely*, pp. 813–14.

p. 104 'We have victory – a remarkable and definite victory . . .' Churchill, W. S. (ed.), *Never Give In*, p. 341.

p. 108 'Sicily, Salerno, Shrapnel Pass, the Plains of Naples . . .' Carter, R. S., *Those Devils in Baggy Pants*, p. 159.

p. 108 '. . . this operation could be fitted in to our plan without detri-ment . . .' CAC, Churchill Papers, CHAR 20/120/45–46.

p. 109 'Strategically, if we get the Aegean Islands . . .' CAC, Churchill Papers, CHAR 20/120/59–60.

p. 111 'We have now been . . .' Letter from Winston to Clementine Churchill, November 26, 1943. CAC, Baroness Spencer-Churchill Papers, CSCT 2/32. Published in Soames, M., *Speaking for Themselves*, pp. 487–8.

p. 114 'I hope you will realize that British loyalty to OVERLORD is keystone . . .' Churchill, W. S., *The Second World War*, Vol. 5, p. 116.

p. 114 'There I sat with the great Russian bear on one side of me . . .' Wheeler-Bennett, J. (ed.), *Action This Day*, p. 96.

Chapter 5: Bodyguard of Lies

pp. 121, 122 'In wartime . . . truth is so precious that she should always be
attended by a bodyguard of lies.' Churchill, W. S., *The Second
World War*, Vol. 5, p. 338.

p. 127 'I was given a carpet, a long polished table, wall maps, an easy
chair . . .' Bright Astley, J., *The Inner Circle*, p. 66.

p. 129 'but with a strange quietness about his movements . . .' Wheatley,
D., *The Deception Planners*, p. 20.

p. 131 '. . . nearly everyone we approached scarcely bothered to
conceal the fact that he thought this new-fangled deception
racket a lot of nonsense'. Wheatley, D., *The Deception Planners*,
p. 84.

p. 138 '. . . in order to deceive and baffle the enemy . . .' CAC,
Churchill Papers, CHAR 9/204A/79.

Chapter 6: Mulberries and Gooseberries

p. 141 'Gentlemen, I am hardening on this operation.' Churchill, W. S.,
The Second World War, Vol. 5, pp. 542–3.

p. 143 'He was very breathless and anxious-looking . . .' Moran, C.,
Winston Churchill: The Struggle for Survival 1940–1965, p. 151.

p. 143 'Don't worry, it doesn't matter if I die now . . .' Churchill, S., *A
Thread in the Tapestry*, p. 77.

p. 144 'When he [Montgomery] arrived at Marrakesh . . .' Churchill,
W. S., *The Second World War*, Vol. 5, p. 393.

p. 145 'very serious criticism that the proposal to move so many divisions . . .' CAC, Churchill Papers, CHAR 20/179/15–17.

p. 149 'A sufficient number of flat-bottomed barges or caissons . . .' A
copy of the original paper can be found in the Churchill
Acquired Papers at Churchill Archives Centre, CAC, Churchill
Acquired Papers, CHAQ 1/5/3. An edited version is published
in Churchill, W. S., *The Second World War*, Vol. 2, p. 216.

p. 150 'They must float up & down on the tide . . .' CAC, Churchill
Additional Papers, WCHL 13/4. Also published in Churchill, W.
S., *The Second World War*, Vol. 5, p. 66, with original document
reproduced as an excerpt.

p. 150 '. . . we ought to have three or four miles of this pier tackle'.
TNA, Prime Minister's Office, PREM 3/216/1.

p. 151 'This matter is being much neglected . . .' TNA, Prime Minister's
Office, PREM 3/216/1.

p. 151   'On Sunday, June 20, I went with Brian Egerton and Richard Fenning . . .' Memoir of Vice-Admiral John Hughes-Hallett. CAC, HHLT. Published as *From Dieppe to D-Day*, p. 107.

p. 152   'Our Army boys . . . are determined to have a port of their own . . .' Memoir of Vice-Admiral John Hughes-Hallett. CAC, HHLT. Published as *From Dieppe to D-Day*, p. 118.

p. 157   'to fit up a number of steam tractors with small, armoured shelters . . .' CAC, Churchill Papers, CHAR 2/103/53–56.

p. 159   'A man of quite exceptional mental attainments . . .' CAC, Churchill Papers, CHAR 20/67/7.

p. 163   'I do not agree with the loose talk which has been going on . . .' CAC, Churchill Papers, CHAR 20/161/113–14.

p. 164   '. . . the Prime Minister let go with a slow-starting but fast-ending stemwinder . . .' Butcher, H., *Three Years with Eisenhower*, p. 463.

p. 164   'one of his typical fighting speeches . . .' Eisenhower, D., *Crusade in Europe*, p. 269.

p. 165   'I may add however that I still consider that the proportion . . .' Churchill, W. S., *The Second World War*, Vol. 5, p. 544.

Chapter 7: Lockdown

pp. 173, 174 'We must beware of handing out irksome for irksome's sake . . .' Telegram from Churchill to Ismay, 4 January 1944. CAC, CHAR 20/179/34.

p. 174   'telling them that there must be no attempt to forecast dates . . .' CAC, Churchill Papers, CHAR 20/137A/18–20.

p. 177   'In particular I deprecate the wholesale character of these orders.' TNA, Prime Minister's Office, PREM 3/345/4.

p. 178   'the large number of Irishmen who are fighting so bravely in our armed forces . . .' *Hansard*, 14 March 1944, series 5, Vol. 398, cc36–8.

p. 182   'our interests because it would leave us in the dark . . .' TNA, Prime Minister's Office, PREM 3/345/7.

p. 184   'In the course of a general conversation about military matters . . .' TNA, Prime Minister's Office, PREM 3/345/8.

p. 185   'that it was pretty clear that we would not undertake operations . . .' TNA, Prime Minister's Office, PREM 3/345/8.

p. 186   'I think he should be frightened out of his wits . . .' TNA, Prime Minister's Office, PREM 3/345/8.

p. 186 'from the time the Normandy landing was achieved . . .' Liddell
Hart, B., 'The Military Strategist' in Taylor A. J. P. *et al.* (eds),
Churchill: Four Faces and the Man, p. 196.

p. 187 'You probably have no idea of the enormous inconvenience . . .'
TNA, Prime Minister's Office, PREM 3/345/2.

p. 188 'The first scene was 1938 – back to Munich.' Soames, E. (ed.),
Mary Churchill's War, p. 259.

p. 188 'Mon 20 March – P.M. looked flushed and was very woolly.'
Dilks, D. (ed.), *The Diaries of Sir Alexander Cadogan*, pp. 611 and
621.

p. 189 'He said he could still always sleep well, eat well . . .' Danchev, A.
and Todman, D. (eds), *War Diaries 1939–1945: Field Marshal Lord
Alanbrooke*, p. 544.

p. 189 'he said it was inhuman to talk of soldiers in such cold-blooded
fashion . . .' Eisenhower, D., *Crusade in Europe*, p. 266.

p. 190 'So there was a pregnant silence . . .' From unpublished transcript
of interview with Joan Bright Astley. CAC, Brendon Papers,
BREN 1/12.

Chapter 8: The Last Ounce of Available Force
p. 197, 205 'There was a limit to the slaughter and the resulting anger . . .'
TNA, Prime Minister's Office, PREM 3/334/2.

p. 198 'the only efficient support which Bomber Command can give to
OVERLORD . . .' CAC, Bufton Papers, BUFT 3/44.

p. 200 'but we must never forget that all the time, night after night . . .'
CAC, Churchill Papers, CHAR 9/141A/57. Also published in
Churchill, W. S. (ed.), *Never Give In*, pp. 244–5.

p. 202 'The Cabinet today took rather a grave and on the whole an
adverse view . . .' TNA, Prime Minister's Office, PREM
3/334/2.

p. 203 'the effect which would be achieved by bombing attacks on
railway centres . . .' TNA, Prime Minister's Office, PREM
3/334/2.

p. 205 'This slaughter was likely to put the French against us . . .' TNA,
Prime Minister's Office, PREM 3/334/2.

p. 205 'by continuing the attacks over a long period . . .' TNA, Prime
Minister's Office, PREM 3/334/2.

p. 206 'the raids in the Paris area have not been satisfactory . . .' TNA,
Prime Minister's Office, PREM 3/334/1.

p. 206 'casualties to civilian personnel are inherent in any plan for the full use of Air power . . .' TNA, Prime Minister's Office, PREM 3/334/2.

p. 206 'we are shouldering a grim responsibility . . .' TNA, Prime Minister's Office, PREM 3/334/2.

p. 207 'fully realized that our use of air power before OVERLORD would assume . . .' TNA, Cabinet Office, War Cabinet Minutes, CAB 65/16.

p. 209 'It must be remembered on the one hand that this slaughter . . .' TNA, Prime Minister's Office, PREM 3/334/3.

p. 209 'However regrettable the attendant loss of civilian lives is . . .' CAC, Churchill Papers, CHAR 20/164/77.

p. 213 'It would seem right as we urged to give a high priority to operations of this sort . . .' TNA, Prime Minister's Office, PREM 3/334/4.

p. 213 'I don't believe the figure of 10,000 which you gave was greatly exceeded.' TNA, Prime Minister's Office, PREM 3/334/4.

p. 216 'where he would be on D-day or rather the night before . . .' Royal Archives, PS/PSO/GVI/C/069.

p. 217 'I think I shook the King by asking him whether he thought the project . . .' Hart-Davis, D. (ed.), *King's Counsellor*, p. 224.

p. 219 'same smell of grass trodden down, same toughness in the meat . . .' CAC, Hugill Papers, HUGL 1.

Chapter 9: This Agonising Moment

pp. 223, 238 'Do you realize that by the time you wake up in the morning 20,000 men may have been killed?' Pawle, G., *The War and Colonel Warden*, p. 302.

p. 224 'one more appeal to you not to go to sea on D-Day . . .' CAC, Churchill Papers, CHAR 20/136/4.

p. 224 '. . . as Prime Minister and Minister of Defence, I ought to be allowed to go . . .' CAC, Churchill Papers, CHAR 20/136/6–8.

p. 225 'It's hell here – impossible to get a moment to oneself . . .' Bright Astley, J., *The Inner Circle: A View of War at the Top*, p. 144.

p. 226 'a final familiar sight – an early 19th century house . . .' CAC, Hugill Papers, HUGL 1.

p. 230 'Their features were young and plebeian . . .' CAC, Lawford Papers, LWFD 1.

p. 231   'Luncheon was long and not genial . . .' CAC, Lawford Papers, LWFD 1.

p. 232   'We are going to liberate Europe . . .' De Gaulle, C., *War Memoirs: Unity 1942–1944* (translated by R. Howard), p. 227.

p. 232   'quite content with the battle, which he felt showed that the United States, Great Britain and France were all together . . .' TNA, Prime Minister's Office, PREM 3/345/1.

p. 236   'There must be a lot of people in the Whitehall area walking around with their fingers crossed.' CAC, Hugill Papers, HUGL 1.

p. 237   'The PRIME MINISTER said that if General de Gaulle . . .' TNA, Cabinet Office, War Cabinet Minutes, CAB 65/46.

p. 237   'tried very hard on many occasions during four years . . .' TNA, Prime Minister's Office, PREM 3/339/6.

p. 240   'the critical period around H-Hour . . .' Love, R. and Major, J. (eds), *The Year of D-day: The 1944 Diary of Admiral Sir Bertram Ramsay*, p. 83.

p. 240   'General Brooke wished "to God it were safely over" . . .' Danchev, A. and Todman, D. (eds), *War Diaries 1939–1945: Field Marshal Lord Alanbrooke*, p. 554.

p. 240   'Our landings in the Cherbourg-Havre area have failed to gain a satisfactory foothold . . .' Eisenhower Presidential Library, Online documents, accessed October 2023.

Chapter 10: We'll Start the War from Here
pp. 243, 266 'As it was in the beginning so may it continue to the end.' Montgomery, B., *Memoirs*, p. 253.

p. 252   'Though they [the King and Churchill] had lunched together . . .' Hart-Davis, D. (ed.), *King's Counsellor*, p. 231.

p. 252   'The past 5 months have not been an easy time . . .' TNA, Prime Minister's Office, PREM 3/339/13.

p. 253   'I promised to report to the House later on in the Sitting.' Churchill's second statement to the House of Commons, 6 June 1944. *Hansard*, series 5, Vol. 400, cc1323–4.

p. 255   'By speaking immediately after Eisenhower . . .' De Gaulle, C., *War Memoirs: Unity 1942–1944* (translated by R. Howard), p. 230.

p. 255   'He [Churchill] said that nothing would induce him to give way . . .' Eden, E., *The Reckoning*, p. 456.

p. 257   'to send for the commissioners . . .' CAC, Churchill Papers, CHAR 20/166/19–21.

p. 258   'If for any reason the supplementary currency is not acceptable to the French Public . . .' CAC, Churchill Papers, CHAR 20/166/82–3.

p. 258   'be well for you to warn the press that there are two sides to this story . . .' CAC, Churchill Papers, CHAR 20/152/6.

p. 260   'My colleagues and I cannot but admit that the history of warfare . . .' CAC, Churchill Papers, CHAR 20/166/79.

p. 261   ' "When this war is over," he growled . . .' Cowles, V., *Winston Churchill: The Era and the Man*, Hamish Hamilton, 1953, p. 344.

p. 261   'This was a fine feat . . .' CAC, Churchill Papers, CHAR 20/152/6.

p. 263   'I earnestly hope that when Members go to their constituencies . . .' *Hansard*, series 5, Vol. 400, cc1522.

p. 263   'We do not wish in any way to be a burden on you or your headquarters . . .' CAC, Churchill Papers, CHAR 20/152/6.

p. 264   'Will meet you and give you full picture . . .' TNA, Prime Minister's Office, PREM 3/339/11.

p. 265   'We drove through our limited but fertile domain in Normandy . . .' Churchill, W. S., *The Second World War*, Vol. 6, p. 11.

p p. 265   'did not seem in any way pleased to see us arrive . . .' Danchev, A. and Todman, D. (eds), *War Diaries 1939–1945: Field Marshal Lord Alanbrooke*, p. 557.

p. 265   'Standing bare-headed in the sunshine . . .' Pawle, G., *The War and Colonel Warden*, p. 303.

p. 267   'Ever since 1907, I have in good times and bad times . . .' CAC, Churchill Papers, CHAR 20/137C/288.

Chapter 11: Tyranny of Overlord

pp. 271, 279   'All right, if you insist on being damned fools . . .' Danchev, A. and Todman, D. (eds), *War Diaries 1939–1945: Field Marshal Lord Alanbrooke*, p. 565.

p. 272   'On the first day, we suffered about ninety casualties, a comparatively low figure . . .' Hastings, R., *An Undergraduate's War*, p. 126.

p. 275   'Winston was in very good form, quite 10 years younger . . .' Danchev, A. and Todman, D. (eds), *War Diaries 1939–1945: Field Marshal Lord Alanbrooke*, p. 560.

p. 276   '. . . realize that if we took the season of the year and the topography of the country . . .' Danchev, A. and Todman, D. (eds), *War Diaries 1939–1945: Field Marshal Lord Alanbrooke*, p. 562.

p. 277 'was too far removed from General Eisenhower's battle-front for an Allied landing . . .' TNA, Cabinet Office Papers, Chiefs of Staff Meetings, CAB 79/76. Published in Gilbert, M. and Arnn, L. (eds), *The Churchill Documents*, Vol. 20, pp. 572–5.

p. 278 'for continued use of practically all the Mediterranean resources . . .' CAC, Churchill Papers, CHAR 20/167/89.

p. 280 'he [Churchill] was in a maudlin, bad tempered, drunken mood . . .' Danchev, A. and Todman, D. (eds), *War Diaries 1939– 1945: Field Marshal Lord Alanbrooke*, p. 566.

p. 283 'I do not believe myself that this vast enterprise could have been executed earlier . . .' CAC, Churchill Papers, CHAR 9/200A/20–21 for an early draft of the speech. Published in Rhodes James, R., *Winston Churchill: His Complete Speeches*, Vol. 6, p. 6972.

p. 284 '. . . all my life I have been grateful for the contribution France has made . . .' CAC, Churchill Papers, CHAR 9/200A/47–48 for an early draft of the speech. Published in Rhodes James, R., *Winston Churchill: His Complete Speeches*, Vol. 6, p. 6980.

p. 285 'once we joined battle in Normandy "Anvil's" value was much reduced . . .' Churchill, W. S., *The Second World War*, Vol. 6, p. 51.

p. 288 'It is worth noting that we had now passed the day in July . . .' Churchill, W. S., *The Second World War*, Vol. 6, p. 62.

p. 290 'We have three armies in the field.' CAC, Baroness Spencer-Churchill Papers, CSCT 2/33.

p. 292 'The victory has been definite, complete and decisive . . .' Cited in Beevor, A., *D-Day*, p. 478.

p. 293 'Paris. Paris outraged, Paris broken, Paris martyred . . .' Cited in Beevor, A., *D-Day*, p. 512.

Chapter 12: Legacies

p. 295, 303 'if we open a quarrel between the past and the present, we shall find that we have lost the future'. Taken from Churchill's 'Finest Hour' speech, 18 June 1940, see Churchill, W. S. (ed.), *Never Give In*, p. 221.

p. 297 'Do please tell us that some effective steps are being taken . . .' CAC, Churchill Papers, CHAR 7/74B.

p. 297 'always listening; in the street I wished the traffic would stop . . .' Bright Astley, J., *The Inner Circle: A View of War at the Top*, p. 147.

p. 300   'Hot tears came & had to be hidden . . .' Soames, E. (ed.), *Mary Churchill's War*, p. 349.

p. 301   ' "There are two opposing ideas in the country," I said to him . . .' Moran, C., *Winston Churchill: The Struggle for Survival 1940–1965*, p. 251.

p. 302   'walked to the open door, put his back to its edge . . .' Butcher, H., *Three Years with Eisenhower*, p. 64.

Picture Acknowledgements

Images within the text

p. 120: Letter from Eisenhower to Churchill, 25 March 1944. CAC, Churchill Papers, CHAR 9/204B/175. Public domain US.

p. 126: Letter from Churchill to Postmaster-General, 16 October 1943. CAC, Churchill Papers, CHAR 20/94B/201. Crown Copyright.

p. 128: Telegram from Churchill to Montgomery, 28 March 1943. CAC, Churchill Papers, CHAR 20/108/121. Crown Copyright.

p. 130: Telegram from General Wavell to Churchill, 21 May 1942. CAC, Churchill Papers, CHAR 20/75/68. Crown Copyright.

p. 140: Minute on 'Piers for Use on Beaches', annotated by Churchill, 26 May 1942. CAC, Churchill Additional Papers, WCHL 13/4. Crown Copyright.

p. 154: Paper prepared for Chiefs of Staff, outlining requirements for constructing artificial harbours, 20 January 1944. CAC, Churchill Acquired Papers, CHAQ 2/3/62/13. Crown Copyright.

p. 164: Seating plan for OVERLORD conference at St Paul's School, 15 May 1944. CAC, Churchill Papers, CHUR 4/335/42. Curtis Brown.

p. 172: Telegram from Churchill to Ismay, 4 January 1944. CAC, Churchill Papers, CHAR 20/179/34. Crown Copyright.

p. 183: Telegram from Churchill to Roosevelt, 15 April 1944. CAC, Churchill Papers, CHAR 20/162/35. Crown Copyright.

p. 196: Diagram from papers of Air Vice-Marshal Bufton illustrating the type of damage to railway lines needed to disrupt the enemy, c.1944. CAC, Bufton Papers, BUFT 3/44, part 3. Crown Copyright.

p. 215: Letter from Admiral Ramsay to Churchill, 16 May 1944. CAC, Churchill Papers, CHAR 20/136/11. Crown Copyright.

p. 218: Letter from King George VI to Churchill, 31 May 1944. CAC, Churchill Papers, CHAR 20/136/10. King Charles III, with permission.

p. 222: Clementine to Winston Churchill, 5 June 1944. CAC Baroness Spencer-Churchill Papers, CSCT 1/28/2. Churchill College.

p. 242: Telegram from Churchill to Stalin, 6 June 1944. CAC, CHAR 20/166/4. Crown Copyright.

p. 262: Handwritten telegram from General Montgomery to Chief of Staff, 7 June 1944. CAC, Selwyn Lloyd Papers, SELO 3/39. Crown Copyright.

p. 270: Draft for Churchill's speech to House of Commons, 2 August 1944. CAC, Churchill Papers, CHAR 9/200A/18. Curtis Brown.

p. 286: Material on casualties compiled for Prime Minister's speech, 1 August 1944. CAC, Churchill Papers, CHAR 9/200A/11. Crown Copyright.

p. 289: Letter from Winston Churchill to Clementine, 15 August 1944. CAC, Baroness Spencer-Churchill Papers, CSCT 2/33/1. Curtis Brown.

p. 294: Draft of Churchill's text for his war memoirs, c.1951. CAC, Churchill Papers, CHUR 4/335/57. Curtis Brown.

8-page inset

p. 1 above: Churchill with Allied commanders,1943. CAC, Churchill Press Photographs Collection, CHPH 1A/F3/11. Crown Copyright.

p. 1 below: Churchill's map room. CAC, Broadwater Collection, BRDW V 3/5/50. Curtis Brown.

p. 2 above: Churchill inspects U.S. Paratroops,1944. Alamy Stock Photo/ Keystone Press.

p. 2 below: Invasion training, Kirkham Priory, Yorkshire, 1944, CAC, Broadwater Collection, BRDW V 3/5/52. Curtis Brown.

p. 3 above: With Monty, France, 1944. CAC, Broadwater Collection, BRDW V 3/5/48. Curtis Brown.

p. 3 below: Supreme Commanders, Churchill and Eisenhower, c. 1945. CAC, Kinna Papers, KNNA 1/5. Unknown believed Crown Copyright - official wartime image.

p. 4 above: Mastery of the seas. CAC, Davis Papers, WDVS 10/5/ Image 23925. Crown Copyright.

p. 4 centre: Mastery of the skies. CAC, Davis Papers, WDVS 10/5/ Image 23096. Crown Copyright.

p. 4 below: Breaking Hitler's Atlantic Wall, 1944. CAC, Davis Papers, WDVS 10/5/ Image 23995. Crown Copyright.

p. 5 above: Ready to go ashore, 1944. CAC, Davis Papers, WDVS 10 5/ Image 23997. Crown Copyright.

p. 5 centre: Flack and obstacles on beaches, 1944. CAC, Davis Papers, WDVS 10/5/Image 23993. Crown Copyright.

p. 5 below: Storming ashore, 1944. CAC, Davis Papers, WDVS 10/5. Crown Copyright.

p. 6 above left: Commandos on the beach, 1944. CAC, Davis Papers, WDVS 10/5/ Image 23944. Crown Copyright.

p. 6 centre right: Gen. O'Connor, Churchill, Smuts, Montgomery and Brooke, 12 June 1944. CAC, Churchill Press

Photographs Collection CHPH 1A/F3/28. Crown Copyright.

p. 6 below: Churchill talking to troops, Normandy, 1944. CAC, Churchill Press Photographs Collection CHPH 1A/F3/29. Crown Copyright.

p. 7 above right: Gen. De Gaulle, France, 1944. CAC, Davis Papers, WDVS 10/5. Crown Copyright.

p. 7 centre left: Joan Bright Astley, Yalta, 1945. CAC, Lunghi Papers, LUNG 1/5. Courtesy of the daughters of Hugh Lunghi.

p. 7 below right: Roland MacKenzie DFC. Courtesy of Roddy MacKenzie.

p. 8 above left: Christian Oldham (later Lamb) as a young Wren. Courtesy of Christian Oldham.

p. 8 centre right: Company Sergeant Major Stanley Hollis. The Green Howards Museum, PH-6-1944-2b. The Green Howards Trust.

p. 8 below: T. L. Rodgers with Pathfinders. Public domain, photographer unknown.

Select Bibliography

1: Primary Sources

Churchill Archives Centre (CAC)

AMEL	Papers of Leopold Amery
BREN	Papers of Dr Piers Brendon (for interview with Joan Bright Astley)
BUFT	Papers of Air Vice-Marshal Sydney Osborne Bufton
CHAQ, CHAR and CHUR	Papers of Sir Winston Churchill
CLVL	Papers of Sir John Colville
CSCT	Papers of Baroness (Clementine) Spencer-Churchill
HHLT	Papers of Vice-Admiral John Hughes-Hallett
HUGL	Papers of John Antony Crawford Hugill
JACB	Papers of Sir Ian Jacob
LKEN	Papers of Leo Kennedy
LWFD	Papers of Valentine Lawford
MART	Papers of Sir John Martin
MISC 68	Copy of Operational Intelligence Centre Special Intelligence Summary: 'The Use of Special Intelligence in connection with Operation Neptune January 1944–September 1944', 1945
PYKE	Papers of Geoffrey Pyke
SELO	Papers of Lord Selwyn Lloyd
WCHL	Churchill Additional Material
WDVS	Papers of Admiral Sir William Davis

The National Archives
CAB 65   Minutes of the War Cabinet
CAB 69   Minutes of Defence Committee (Operations)
CAB 99/24   Record of conference held at Casablanca, January 1943
PREM 3   Prime Minister's Office operational correspondence and
            papers

Other
Hansard   Record of Parliamentary Debates
Royal Archives   King George VI wartime diary and correspondence
                 with Churchill

2: *Published Diaries, Memoirs and Primary Sources*

Bright Astley, J., *The Inner Circle: A View of War at the Top* (Hutchinson, 1971)

Butcher, H., *Three Years with Eisenhower: The Personal Diary of Captain Harry C. Butcher, USNR, Naval Aide to General Eisenhower, 1942 to 1945* (Heinemann, 1946)

Carter, R. S., *Those Devils in Baggy Pants* (revised edition, Jan-Carol Publishing, 2021)

Churchill, S., *A Thread in the Tapestry* (Deutsch, 1967)

Churchill, S., *Keep on Dancing* (Weidenfeld & Nicolson, 1981)

Churchill, W. S., *The World Crisis*, 6 vols (Thornton Butterworth, 1923–31)

Churchill, W. S., *The Second World War*, 6 vols (Cassell, 1948–54)

Churchill, W. S., *Never Give In! The Best of Winston Churchill's Speeches* (Easton Press, 2003) – edited by his grandson

Colville, J., *The Fringes of Power: Downing Street Diaries 1939–1955* (Hodder & Stoughton, 1985)

Danchev, A. and Todman D. (eds), *War Diaries 1939–1945: Field Marshal Lord Alanbrooke* (Weidenfeld & Nicolson, 2001)

De Gaulle, C., *War Memoirs*, Vol. II, *Unity*, Richard Harwood (trans.) (Weidenfeld & Nicolson, 1959)

Dilks, D. (ed.), *The Diaries of Sir Alexander Cadogan* (Cassell, 1971)

Eden, A., *The Eden Memoirs: The Reckoning* (Cassell, 1965)

Eisenhower, D., *Crusade in Europe* (Heinemann, 1948)

Gilbert, M. and Arnn, L. (eds), *The Churchill Documents*, Vol. 20 (Hillsdale, 2018)

Grehan, J. (ed.), *Hitler's V-Weapons: The Battle Against the V-1 & V-2* (Frontline, 2020) – a published version of the official history

Hart-Davis, D. (ed.), *King's Counsellor: Abdication and War – The Diaries of Sir Alan Lascelles* (Weidenfeld & Nicolson, 2006)

Harvey, J. (ed.), *The Diplomatic Diaries of Oliver Harvey, 1937–1940* (Collins, 1970)

Hastings, R., *An Undergraduate's War* (Bellhouse Publishing, 1997)

Hickman, T., *Churchill's Bodyguard* (Headline, 2006) – based on memoirs of Inspector Walter Thompson

Hughes-Hallett, J., *From Dieppe to D-Day: The Memoirs of Vice Admiral Jock Hughes-Hallett* (Frontline, 2023)

Ismay, H., *The Memoirs of General the Lord Ismay* (Heinemann, 1960)

Lamb, C., *Beyond the Sea: A Wren at War* (Mardle, 2021)

Love, R. and Major, J. (eds), *The Year of D-day: The 1944 Diary of Admiral Sir Bertram Ramsay* (Hull University Press, 1994)

Macleod, R. and Kelly, D. (eds), *The Ironside Diaries, 1937–1940* (Constable, 1962)

Macmillan, M., *War Diaries: Politics and War in the Mediterranean 1943–1945* (Macmillan, 1984)

Montgomery of El Alamein, *The Memoirs of Field-Marshal the Viscount Montgomery of El Alamein* (Collins, 1958)

Moran, Lord., *Winston Churchill: The Struggle for Survival 1940–1965* (Constable, 1966)

Morgan, F., *Peace and War: A Soldier's Life* (Hodder & Stoughton, 1961)

Nel, E., *Mr Churchill's Secretary* (Hodder & Stoughton, 1958)

Nicolson, H., *Diaries & Letters 1930–1964* (Penguin, 1984)

Norwich, J. J. (ed.), *The Duff Cooper Diaries* (Weidenfeld & Nicolson, 2005)

Pawle, G., *The War and Colonel Warden* (Harrap, 1963) – based on memoirs of Commander Thompson

Rhodes James, R. (ed.), *Winston Churchill: His Complete Speeches*, 8 vols (Chelsea House, 1974)

Soames, E. (ed.), *Mary Churchill's War: The Wartime Diaries of Churchill's Youngest Daughter* (Two Roads, 2021)

Soames, M., *Speaking for Themselves: The Personal Letters of Winston and Clementine Churchill* (Doubleday, 1998)

Spears, E., *Assignment to Catastrophe*, 2 vols (Heinemann, 1954)

Wheatley, D., *The Deception Planners: My Secret War* (Hutchinson, 1980)

Wheeler-Bennett, J. (ed.), *Action This Day* (Macmillan, 1968) – memoirs of Churchill's Downing Street team

3: Published Secondary Sources

Barnett, C., *Engage the Enemy More Closely: The Royal Navy in the Second World War* (Hodder & Stoughton, 1991)

Beevor, A., *D-Day: 75th Anniversary Edition* (Penguin, 2014)

Bishop, P., *Operation Jubilee – Dieppe 1942: The Folly and the Sacrifice* (Penguin Books, 2021)

Bowman, G., *Empire First: Churchill's War against D-Day* (self-published, 2020)

Cowles, V., *Churchill: The Era and the Man* (Hamish Hamilton, 1953)

D'Este, C., *Eisenhower: Allies Supreme Commander* (Weidenfeld & Nicolson, 2003)

Gilbert, M., *Winston S. Churchill*, Vol. VI, *Finest Hour* (Heinemann, 1983)

Gilbert, M., *Winston S. Churchill*, Vol. VII, *Road to Victory* (Heinemann, 1986)

Hamilton, N., *Monty: Master of the Battlefield, 1942–1944* (Hamish Hamilton, 1983)

Hastings, M., *Finest Years: Churchill as Warlord 1944–1945* (Harper Press, 2009)

Hinsley, F. H., *British Intelligence in the Second World War*, Vol. 3, Part 2 (HMSO, 1988)

Holt, T., *The Deceivers: Allied Military Deception in the Second World War* (Folio Society, 2008)

Humphrys, O., *Wavell in Russia* (privately published, 2017)

Kennedy, P., *Engineers of Victory: The Problem Solvers Who Turned the Tide in the Second World War* (Allen Lane, 2013)

Kiszely, J., *Anatomy of a Campaign: The British Fiasco in Norway, 1940* (Cambridge University Press, 2017)

Knight, N., *Churchill: The Greatest Briton Unmasked* (David & Charles, 2008)

Lampe, D., *Pyke: The Unknown Genius* (Evans Brothers, 1959)

MacKenzie, R., *Bomber Command: Churchill's Greatest Triumph* (Air World, 2022)

Macksey, K. J., *Armoured Crusader: A Biography of Major-General Sir Percy Hobart* (Hutchinson, 1967)

Macrae, S., *Winston Churchill's Toyshop* (2nd edition, Amberley, 2010)

Milton, G., *The Ministry of Ungentlemanly Warfare* (John Murray, 2016)

Morgan, M., *D-Day Hero, CSM Stanley Hollis VC* (Sutton Publishing, 2004)

Olusoga, D., *Black and British* (Macmillan, 2016)

Overy, R., *The Air War 1939–1945* (Europa, 1980)

Overy, R., *The Bombing War: Europe 1939–1945* (Penguin, 2014)

Packwood, A., *How Churchill Waged War* (Frontline, 2018)

Packwood, A. (ed.), *The Cambridge Companion to Winston Churchill* (Cambridge University Press, 2023)

Prior, R., *Conquer We Must* (Yale University Press, 2022)

Reynolds, D., *In Command of History* (Allen Lane, 2004)

Roberts, A., *Masters and Commanders* (Allen Lane, 2008)

Roberts, A., *Churchill: Walking with Destiny* (Allen Lane, 2018)

Roskill, S., *The Navy at War* (Collins, 1960)

Roskill, S., *The War at Sea, 1939–1945*, Vol. 3: *The Offensive, Part 1: 1 June 1943–* (HMSO, 1960)

Roskill, S., *The War at Sea, 1939–1945*, Vol. 3: *The Offensive, Part 2: 1 June 1944 –* (HMSO, 1961)

Ryan, C., *The Longest Day* (Victor Gollancz, 1960)

Soames, M., *Clementine Churchill* (revised edition, Doubleday, 2002)

Stafford, D., *Churchill and Secret Service* (John Murray, 1997)

Taylor, A. J. P. *et al.*, *Churchill: Four Faces and the Man* (Allen Lane, 1969)

Thorpe, D. R., *Selwyn Lloyd* (Jonathan Cape, 1989)

Vale, A. and Scadding, J., *Winston Churchill's Illnesses 1886–1965* (Frontline, 2020)

Ziegler, P., *Mountbatten* (Guild, 1985)

Index

Entries in italics denote documents, illustrations, maps, portraits etc.

**BRITISH
NORMANDY
MEMORIAL**

The British Normandy Memorial stands above 'Gold Beach'. It is Britain's national memorial commemorating the names of the more than 22,000 men and women in British units who lost their lives on D-Day and during the Battle of Normandy.

For decades after the Second World War, the United Kingdom was the only principal Allied nation which did not have a national memorial in Normandy. In 2015 the Normandy Memorial Trust was set up to fulfil the hopes of Normandy Veterans to establish a British memorial in Normandy. The completed memorial was opened by the then Prince Charles, Prince of Wales on 6 June 2021.

Close to the memorial is 'The Winston Churchill Centre', an exhibition and education centre developed to ensure that future generations remember the events of 1944 and understand their significance.

There are more details at www.britishnormandymemorial.org where you can find information about the *Guardian* scheme to support the memorial's care and maintenance.

INTERNATIONAL CHURCHILL SOCIETY

Since 1968 the International Churchill Society (ICS) has been the world's preeminent organisation educating and inspiring present and future generations to be outstanding leaders in their fields through the example of Sir Winston Churchill. By celebrating the timeless values of Sir Winston Churchill, ICS emboldens all generations to understand the historical context of Churchill's life and defend, enhance and promote the values he embodied: freedom, democracy and human rights.

ICS is a non-profit organisation in the United States and a registered charity in the United Kingdom with over 3,000 global members on seven continents. It publishes a quarterly magazine, *Finest Hour*, provides research funds to students and authors and hosts an international conference, among many other activities and efforts. It has formal partnerships with the Royal United Services Institute, George Washington University and America's National Churchill Museum. You can learn more and become a member by visiting winstonchurchill.org.